JOHN CARTER BROWN TRAVEL DIARIES, 1823–1824

THE YOUNG
JOHN CARTER BROWN
IN EUROPE

Travel Diaries, 1823–1824

Edited by Donald G. Rohr

With an Epilogue by J. Carter Brown

Published with the Cooperation of
the John Nicholas Brown Center
for the Study of American Civilization

JOHN CARTER BROWN LIBRARY

Providence, Rhode Island

2005

Correspondence should be directed to: The John Carter Brown Library,
Box 1894, Providence, Rhode Island 02912. Additional information may
be found at www.JCBL.org.

The John Carter Brown Library is an independently funded and adminis-
tered institution for advanced research in history and the humanities,
founded in 1846 and located at Brown University since 1901.

ISBN 0-916617-65-3

In memory of

J. Carter Brown

1934–2002

Contents

List of Illustrations

Foreword

T HE HISTORICAL PAPERS preserved by the Brown family of Rhode Island, stretching over more than 300 years, from the late seventeenth century to the early twenty-first, is a single continuous documentary record of one family that is almost unique in scope among such annals in the United States. The collection at present is concentrated in three locations in Providence, all in close proximity to each other: the John Carter Brown Library, the Rhode Island Historical Society Library, and the John Nicholas Brown Center for the Study of American Civilization. The last is a comparatively new institution, established at the Brown family home at 357 Benefit Street in 1979, and deeded to Brown University in 1994.

From the oldest documents in the collection, ca. 1700, through the early twentieth century, the family papers record primarily the business affairs of a series of companies and the public activities of the individuals involved. But occasionally in the nineteenth-century collection, and predominantly for the period after 1914, one finds material more related to the personal lives and the cultural interests of the family.

About the early years of John Carter Brown (1797–1874), among the most distinguished members of a distinguished family, relatively little has been written, and the sources are thin. One can imagine, then, our surprise and delight in 1993 when Robert Emlen, at the time Director of the John Nicholas Brown Center, informed us that the staff had found amidst the thousands of family manuscripts in the house on Benefit Street five small notebooks recording impressions and details of John Carter Brown's first sojourn in Europe, when he was in his mid-twenties.

Although the present book has taken us twelve years to produce, it was the intention of the John Carter Brown Library from the beginning to publish these youthful diaries. We assume, in the first place, a responsibility to make known in print almost anything of significance we can find out about the founder of this estimable institution. Moreover, the diaries seemed to us to have general or independent historical value, even if the author of them had not been John Carter Brown. Impressions of Europe recorded by Americans in the 1820s are not abundant, and such works inform us first-hand about the character of the American elite in the early nineteenth century. In this rare case, the perceptions are of a still very young, albeit precocious, American responding to the wonders of Europe at every level.

Here is John Carter Brown, at age twenty-six, talking about Leonardo da Vinci's Bella Feronia, mistress of Francis I, who, he notes, "by some is thought to be most lovely of mortals." She "did not seem to me to be in point of beauty any thing so very extraordinary," Brown wrote. "Perhaps, however, my taste in these matters is not sufficiently improved to allow me to be a judge."

Consistently, his reactions to the sights of the Continent are well articulated. Of the splendor of the Basilica of St. Peter in Rome, he wrote: "I had heard & read so much that my expectations were raised to the highest pitch, & in truth I cannot say they were disappointed.... Such an impression it made upon my mind can never be lost." Continuing on a second visit a day or two later, he wrote, "no description can give a just idea of this astonishing masterpiece of human art," especially to an American, he observed, "who has never yet seen any of the Catholick Cathedrals of Europe." He wondered "how mortal man could conceive, much less execute so stupendous a structure."

The John Carter Brown Library is situated on the Brown University campus in a handsome Beaux Arts building completed in 1904. The building houses the collection of books about the Americas, North and South, that was begun by John Carter Brown in ca. 1846 and that has been added to continuously since that day, initially by John Carter Brown himself until his death in 1874 and then by his widow, Sophia Augusta Brown, and his two sons, Harold and John Nicholas Brown.

John Nicholas Brown (b. 1861) was given full legal ownership of the collection in 1897 by his mother, and immediately began to draw up plans, both architectural and financial, for establishing the Bibliotheca Americana, as the library was then known, as an independent research center in its own building. When he died prematurely in 1900, barely forty years old, leaving a four-month-old son, also named John Nicholas Brown (II), these plans for development had to be realized posthumously.

In the history of the John Carter Brown Library, we think of John Carter Brown (d. 1874) as the "Founder" and John Nicholas Brown (I) (d. 1900) as the "Benefactor." It was John Nicholas Brown who expressed his devotion to his father by making of the collection a memorial to him and leaving a fortune in endowment to effectuate this dream.

In the vestibule of the John Carter Brown Library there is a handsome bronze plaque, produced by Tiffany & Co., that gives us a glimpse into the character of John Carter Brown, the Founder: "In memory of John Nicholas Brown of the Class of 1885 who gave this Library with its building and endowment to commemorate the name and work of his father, John Carter Brown of the Class of 1816, from whom he inherited with the Library Love of Knowledge, Devotion to Historical Research and Appreciation of Beautiful Things. Speak to the Past and It Shall Teach Thee."

The plaque was installed in 1907, as one of the last touches added to the new building. The qualities attributed to John Carter Brown on this plaque are quite evident in these youthful diaries, and they have been transmitted through the generations, continuing to inspire those responsible for the advancement of the John Carter Brown Library.

———

To prepare this book, we needed first to transcribe the diaries. To that end we secured the permission of the Brown family and of the archivist at the John Nicholas Brown Center, Joyce Botelho, to lend the five little pocket "volumes" to the JCB for "a while." We are grateful to the Center for tolerating a loan that lasted about a decade! The transcriptions were ably made by a succession of Brown University graduate students, each working only part-time—Barbara A. Matthews, Edward G. Gray, and Sarah Purcell—who were also J. M. Stuart Research Fellows at the JCB Library in the process of completing doctoral dissertations.

In 1994, a professor emeritus of history at Brown University, Donald G. Rohr, agreed to edit the volume for publication, which entailed his fastidious review of all of the transcriptions for accuracy; the establishment of an editorial method that would preserve the original text while yet allowing for some modifications for the sake of readability; annotation of the work to elucidate references and to bring out meaning; and the writing of a substantive introduction.

The outstanding qualifications that Professor Rohr brought to this project cannot be overstated. Dogged in research, meticulous as an editor, learned in both European and American history, elegant as a writer, Professor Rohr had every trait we needed. The merits of this book are entirely due to his devoted and careful work.

Inputting of Professor Rohr's notes was undertaken by Heather Jespersen, who also assisted Professor Rohr with the final changes in the electronic file. Valerie Krasko input Professor Rohr's Introduction to the volume.

A major portion of the cost of the design and manufacture of this book has been covered by grants and gifts from members of the Brown family, including Angela Brown Fischer, Nicholas Brown, and the late J. Carter Brown, all great-grandchildren of John Carter Brown. Friends of J. Carter Brown also contributed, in particular Vincent J. Buonanno, Anne Hawley, and Clinton I. Smullyan, Jr., and the Library drew funds as well from its Maurice L. Clemence Publications Fund.

In October and November 1996, the John Carter Brown Library celebrated the 150th anniversary of its founding. Among the featured events of this celebration was a Brown University Convocation, called in honor of the Library's sesquicentennial, at which J. Carter Brown was invited to speak. Mr. Brown chose "Voyaging" as the topic of his address, wherein he reflected on the inveterate traveling urge of his remarkable family. He had hoped that this talk could somehow be connected to the publication of the youthful travel diaries of his great-grandfather, and we are including it here as an epilogue, in a volume that is dedicated to his memory.

Preface

THESE DIARIES RECORD the itinerary and impressions of John Carter Brown (1797–1874), a young merchant from Providence, Rhode Island, who in April 1822 crossed the Atlantic on business errands for his father's firm, Brown and Ives. Fascinated by what he found in Europe and bored by his commercial duties, he managed to convert his business trip into a grand tour and to stretch it out over two and one-half years. During that time he spent several weeks in Amsterdam overseeing the sale or warehousing of cargoes shipped there by Brown and Ives, but his diaries are silent on those command performances. Instead they recount his sight-seeing travels through the British Isles, France, Italy, northern Germany, and the Netherlands, travels that took him to visit historic sites and allowed him, while observing European society on different levels, to measure his tastes and manners, his education, against those of a world more sophisticated than his own.

Although John Carter Brown's diaries and letters showed little enthusiasm for gathering "practical" information by visiting mills, mines, and port facilities, as his father urged him to do, he made no effort before, during, or after his travels to explore careers other than the business career that his father had in mind for him. He showed no signs of envying the many members of his generation who, as heirs of the American revolution, declared their personal independence by choosing their own careers and inventing their own lives.[1] But, while he cheerfully bore the commercial responsibilities he had inherited, he never let them crush out or even overshadow his interests in history, art, and literature —interests which he had begun to develop as an adolescent. His travels in Europe during the early 1820s served to deepen and sharpen those interests which, in time, distinguished him as a prototypal merchant prince devoted to book-collecting and the advancement of scholarship.

All five of the travel diaries were recorded in pocket-size booklets, the smallest measuring four by six inches, the others measuring four and one-half by seven and one-half inches. Two of them were bound in imitation calf, the other three in cardboard, covered with marbled paper. The second diary (August to September 1823) was designed by a London stationer as a "Tourist's Pocket Journal" and, in addition to eighty blank pages, offered three pages of vertical columns for entering daily expenses as well as several pages of advertisements and helpful hints for the wayfarer. John Carter Brown ignored vertical columns and horizontal lines in this and other diaries to write his observations across the page as he wished, leaving very narrow margins. He probably meant to conserve space but, in retrospect, need not have bothered: he left blank pages in all five booklets. He wrote with black ink, now faded to rust but still legible, on paper that yellowed but did not crumble. The bindings, however, are all in fragile condition.

---

1. Joyce Appleby, *Inheriting the Revolution* (Cambridge, Mass., 2000), p. 25.

FIG. 1. The five travel diaries.

Although they were shelved with other family papers for some 170 years, the five diaries did not suffer the neglect of dead storage. There is mute evidence that they were occasionally consulted by the diarist himself before he set out on trips to Europe in later life and by family members who were planning to travel abroad. Scraps of paper, left between the diaries' pages, included skeleton itineraries, some mid-nineteenth-century notes on railway connections, and the calling card of John Carter Brown Wood. At some point, probably in the early twentieth century, someone, probably a secretary or a custodian of family papers, pasted typewritten, identifying labels on the covers and spines of the diaries, such as "John Carter Brown/diary, Europe. Mar. 17 – Apr. 18, 1823." Several of the labels have peeled off.

Readers might think of John Carter Brown at the end of a strenuous day on the road, sitting at a makeshift desk, or standing at a convenient shelf, writing in his diary by lantern or candlelight in a country inn or a noisy city lodging. His entries inevitably show signs of fatigue, haste, distraction, and an understandable nonchalance about the niceties of spelling, punctuation, and grammar. With respect to editorial method I have tried to preserve the rough texture of his original except where it obscured his meaning. Erroneous, obsolete, and inconsistent spellings have been left unchanged and usually unaccompanied by bracketed "[sic]"s that would have made every page a bramble patch. His punctuation has been left unchanged except that occasionally the small hook or squiggle that JCB sometimes used for a comma or a period has been converted into a definite comma or period. Capitalization too has been left unchanged no matter how unconventional it might sometimes appear to be. I have, however, consistently capitalized the first word in a new sentence.

With respect to other editorial decisions, I have tampered with the original only where clarity demanded. Easily recognizable contractions have been left as is and I have not added apostrophes to "dont" and "wont" when they are not in the manuscript. I have expanded idiosyncratic contractions ("Prov^e^" to "Providence") and the contraction of present and past participles ("rec^g^" and "rec^d^" to "receiving" and "received"). Common abbreviations (such as A.M.) have been left as is. Those that are unfamiliar have been expanded (for example, "B.&I." is changed to "Brown and Ives"). I have left most signs and symbols as they are with the exception of "a/o" which has been changed to "account."

Here and there I have introduced a new paragraph. The manuscript, in any case, does not always make clear when JCB intended to do so. I have systematically begun a new paragraph with every new "day" of the journal, a practice that JCB himself usually followed. Blank spaces in the text are indicated by [*blank*]. Illegible words have been indicated [*illeg.*]. Italics always indicate an editorial intervention. Where JCB underlined a word I have also underlined it rather than converting it into italics.

In his foreword, Norman Fiering has already thanked many of those who helped to prepare this text. I want to add my thanks to his and, most emphatically, acknowledge his initiatives, encouragement, and direct involvement in the work of emending transcripts and reading drafts. The number of those who helped me individually with particular information and advice included departmental colleagues: Tim Harris, Karl Jacoby, Tony Molho; and faculty colleagues: Anthony Oldcorn, Juergen Schulz, Pat Malone, Don Wilmeth. Other scholars who were generous with their time were John B. Hattendorf (Naval War College, Newport, R.I.) and Silvia Marzagalli (University of Bordeaux).

At the Brown University Archives, Martha Mitchell and Gayle Lynch offered both expert direction and heavy lifting. At the John Nicholas Brown Center, Joyce Botelho and, in her absence, Denise J. Bastien graciously opened document collections. In the Circulation Department of the Rockefeller Library, Charles Flynn not only exercised his mastery of new technology to make fresh sources readily available, but conducted me through the underworld of books in storage to resurrect early nineteenth-century material. In the Reference Department, S. Duane Davies and Peggy Mutter made my work easier as did Andy Moul in Special Collections. Gordon Blaker in Georgia and Alex Wood in Connecticut helped with particular lines of inquiry. Finally, I want to thank a friend and neighbor, Vanna Cahill, for help with the Italian sections of the fourth diary.

Introduction

As the Spanish proverb says, "He, who would bring
home the wealth of the Indies, must carry the wealth
of the Indies with him." So it is in traveling, a man
must carry knowledge with him, if he would bring
home knowledge.

—James Boswell, *The Life of Samuel Johnson*,
17 April, 1778

R EADERS MAY want to know what knowledge John Carter
Brown carried with him on his European travels. What had
he inherited or learned from his upbringing? From his formal
education? From his early business travels? What had he read
that whetted his curiosity, or focused his attention, or biased his
outlook on foreigners and foreign scenes? This introduction
attempts to answer some of those questions.

FAMILY AND EDUCATION

The first of John Carter Brown's ancestors to arrive in North
America, Chad Browne, landed in Massachusetts, but chose to
move south to a new colony, later to be known as Providence
Plantations. He, his wife, and son settled there in 1638. Three
generations of Chad's descendants helped to develop the colony
as surveyors, retailers, shippers, manufacturers, and bankers,

often in joint ventures with other businessmen.[1] Their fortunes rose and fell, but for the most part rose, with those of Providence. During John Carter Brown's boyhood in the first decade of the nineteenth century, the town's population nearly doubled to reach some 12,000. An itinerant Yankee businessman who moved to Providence in 1804 to open a cotton mill remarked in his memoirs that the community was noteworthy for its concentration of energetic and cultivated citizens. Referring specifically to the Browns, he said: "What is very unusual in the United States, this family has increased in wealth through three generations—a circumstance which I do not recollect to have occurred before, as it has been almost a universal practice for the children to squander what the father has accumulated."[2]

One reason for the Brown family's continued prosperity was that it did not fall into a common pattern of changing generational aspirations, a pattern identified as the "Buddenbrooks syndrome" by the economic historian, W. W. Rostow.[3] According to this pattern, the first generation concentrates single-mindedly on getting rich; the next generation, accustomed to wealth, seeks

---

1. James B. Hedges, *The Browns of Providence Plantations*, Vol. I: *The Colonial Years* (Providence, 1952), *passim*.

2. Ebenezer Thomas, *Reminiscences of the Last Sixty-five Years*, 2 vols. (Hartford, Conn., 1840), II, p. 45. Thomas could speak to this point with some authority. By the time he wrote his memoirs he had left business to become a newspaper editor in a career which took him from Boston as far south as Charleston and as far west as Cincinnati.

3. W. W. Rostow, *Stages of Economic Growth* (Cambridge, Eng., 1960). Rostow refers to Thomas Mann's novel *Buddenbrooks* which traces the rise and dissolution of a north German mercantile family. Cf. John Adams: "I must

political and social status; the third generation, having money, power, and prestige, turns to cultivating the arts. Successive generations of the Brown family, by contrast, divided their energies between business enterprises, politics, and cultural activities in highly individual ways, but without loss of family solidarity. The most striking example of this strength through diversity may be found in the mid-eighteenth-century generation of four brothers born between 1729 and 1738.[4] Nicholas, the first-born, described as "plodding," built systematically on the foundations laid by his father. His younger brother, John, was more venturesome and innovative. Joseph, the second-born, turned away from business to interest himself in architecture, science, and technology. The youngest brother, Moses, had the broadest range of interests and sympathies among the four and pioneered in developing textile mills as well as in organizing a society for the abolition of slavery.[5]

The Brown family also drew strength from its ability to recruit and absorb talented outsiders. A notable example was

study Politicks and War that my sons may have liberty to study Mathematicks and Philosophy. My sons ought to study Mathematicks and Philosophy, Geography, natural History, Naval Architecture, navigation, Commerce and Agriculture, in order to give their Children a right to study Painting, Poetry, Musick, Architecture, Statuary, Tapestry and Porcelaine." JA to Abigail, written in France, April – May 1780 and posted on May 12.

4. Hedges, *The Browns*, I, pp. 1–21.

5. Mack Thompson, *Moses Brown, Reluctant Reformer* (Chapel Hill, 1962). The Brown brothers' involvement in the African slave trade is mentioned in James A. Rawley, *The Transatlantic Slave Trade: A History* (New York, 1981), p. 380. A running account may be found in Hedges, *The Browns*, I, *passim*. See also the Rhode Island Historical Society pamphlet, *Rhode Island and the Slave Trade: John Brown and the Colonial Economy of Slavery* (Providence, 2002).

Thomas Poynton Ives (1769–1835), an orphan who began his career clerking for Nicholas [1] Brown.[6] In 1792 Ives married Nicholas's daughter, Hope, and in 1796 formed a business partnership with Nicholas's son, Nicholas [2]. Ives's sons, born in 1794 and 1798, would in turn become partners and mainstays of the firm Brown and Ives which has survived into the twenty-first century.[7]

Early in 1791, five years before forming his partnership with Ives, Nicholas [2] Brown married Ann Carter, daughter of a local newspaper publisher, John Carter (1745-1814). A Pennsylvanian who had trained as an apprentice in Benjamin Franklin's print shop in Philadelphia before moving to Rhode Island, Carter set up his own press in Providence and eventually became proprietor of the *Providence Gazette* and the town's postmaster. His daughter, Ann, bore Nicholas [2] three surviving children— Nicholas [3] in 1792, Ann Carter in 1795, and John Carter in 1797. Within a year of John Carter Brown's birth his mother died and, although Nicholas [2] remarried in 1801, he fathered no more children. John Carter Brown grew up then as the youngest member of a family presided over by a step-mother. As a boy and as a young man, he was able to stay on good terms with all of his immediate family despite a running quarrel between his father and his brother. That estrangement became complete when Nicholas

---

6. The Brown family recycled given names without the formal addition of Roman numerals or Latin adjectives to distinguish one generation from another. To avoid confusion here the first Nicholas (1729-1791) will be Nicholas [1], his son (1769-1841), Nicholas [2], and his grandson (1792-1859), Nicholas [3].

7. See James B. Hedges, *The Browns of Providence Plantations*, Vol. II: *The Nineteenth Century* (Providence, 1968), *passim*.

[3] moved his young family away from Providence leaving John Carter Brown the sole heir presumptive to his father's business.

Nicholas [2] Brown's most immediate legacy to his son John was a family tradition of public leadership and philanthropy. He had helped to organize a private elementary school, a subscription library, and a hospital for the insane. Unwilling to surrender his conscience to any organized group, he refused formal membership in a church, but he contributed to several religious congregations and worshipped regularly at the First Baptist Church of Providence. He also gave liberally to Baptist missions and tract societies. Shortly after graduating from Rhode Island College in 1786, he became its most generous patron. A Baptist institution, chartered in 1764, the College was inspired by the example of "New Light" Presbyterians who had founded the College of New Jersey (now Princeton) some twenty years earlier. Nicholas [2] Brown's father and uncles had open-handedly supported its foundation and had aggressively campaigned for its location in Providence. When, in 1804, Nicholas [2] capped a decade of gifts to his alma mater by endowing a chair of oratory and belles lettres, Rhode Island College changed its name to Brown University.[8]

John Carter Brown spent roughly ten years of his boyhood in schools founded or endowed by his grandfather, his father, and his uncles. He got his primary schooling at the Providence Academy, once known as the George Street Academy, which had

---

8. A brief account of the four Brown brothers' support for Rhode Island College may be found in J. David Hoeveler, *Creating the American Mind: Intellect and Politics in the Colonial Colleges* (Lanham, Md., 2002), pp. 193–195.

been organized by his father and his uncle Ives.[9] The Academy, it is worth noting, was not an example of the "privatism" which may have characterized elite behavior in other American cities on the Atlantic seaboard.[10] It was founded only after the Browns and the Iveses had tried and failed to persuade the freemen of Providence to vote taxes for a public school. The Academy opened in 1799 to admit boys and girls at the age of five or six to classes in the traditional three R's with "oratory" as an extra. Instruction was non-denominational but hardly secular. Samples of the pupils' work, which were mounted for display, show that JCB learned penmanship by copying homiletic passages from the Rev. Edward Young (*Night Thoughts*) and the Rev. Jonathan Maxcy, president of Brown University. Reading lessons were similarly alive with religious and moral sentiment.[11]

Boys left the Providence Academy at the age of eleven or twelve to prepare for college. When his time came, JCB did not follow his brother and Ives cousins to the local preparatory school maintained by Brown University. Instead, he followed his sister to a flourishing co-educational school in Hartford, Connecticut, presided over by George Jeffrey Patten, a graduate of

---

9. Brown Papers, JCBL, Box 1196, file 1.

10. Sam Bass Warner, *The Private City* (Philadelphia, rev. ed., 1987), pp. 4, 111–117.

11. "JCB" was commonly used by family and friends for quick reference to John Carter Brown and will be used frequently hereafter. Similarly, "MBI" and "RHI" will be used to refer to Moses Brown Ives and Robert Hale Ives, respectively.

Rhode Island College, class of 1792.[12] Patten had taken on the management of a dame-school opened by his widowed mother in the 1780s and had expanded it until by 1810 it enrolled up to 300 pupils. Patten "prepared" the boys by drilling them in Greek and Latin. His sisters taught the girls while his mother looked after the fifty or so boarders. She called them her "family." Discipline was relaxed; the atmosphere was one of piety and benevolence. Mrs. Patten was addressed as "Grandma."[13]

In 1812, at the age of fifteen, John Carter Brown left the warm bosom of the Pattens' school and entered a more spartan course of studies at Brown University. The curriculum there was very much the same as it had been during his father's student days.[14] All undergraduates at all levels did required exercises in writing and public speaking. All members of the same class took the same courses. All freshmen and sophomores translated Greek and Latin texts and recited them in class; all juniors and seniors memorized and recited assignments from eighteenth-century textbooks in theology, philosophy, literature, science ("natural philosophy"), and political philosophy. There was some brief, bookish instruction in applied subjects such as sur-

---

12. Brown Family Papers, JCBL, Box 295, file 1.

13. William Patten, *Memoirs of Mrs. Ruth Patten of Hartford, Conn.* (Hartford, 1834), *passim*. Mrs. Patten was the widow of a prominent clergyman and the daughter of the Rev. Eleazer Wheelock, first president of Dartmouth College.

14. Walter C. Bronson, *The History of Brown University, 1764–1914* (Providence, 1914), pp. 102–107; 146. Brown University Archives, Asa Messer's Letterbook, ltr. of August 25, 1815, to Col. Thos. Reed.

veying, navigation, and "practical astronomy"—subjects which an older generation of shippers and landowners had been forced to pick up on their own. The entire curriculum was as shallow as it was broad but was well designed for boys in their late teens who might go on to professional studies in divinity, law, or medicine, or might get vocational training on the farm or in the counting house.

Some New England educators considered Brown University "narrowly sectarian" or even "bigoted" because its charter stipulated that its president and a majority of the corporation be Baptists.[15] But such critics were much too quick to find fault. The charter also stipulated that faculty appointments "shall be free and open to all denominations of Protestants and that Youths of all Religious Denominations shall and may be freely admitted." Further, according to the charter, "sectarian differences" were to be no part the college's "Public and Classical Instruction."[16] The Greek texts of the New Testament evangelists were translated in class—along with Homer and Lucian—as a language exercise. Otherwise, scripture reading was left to chapel devotions. The theology texts assigned to juniors and seniors in 1815 and 1816 were the work of Anglican prelates who were concerned to prove the rationality of religious belief in general and the irrationality of Enlightenment skeptics in particular. Bishop Joseph Butler's *The*

---

15. William G. McLoughlin, *New England Dissent, 1630–1839* (Cambridge, Mass., 1971), Vol. I, pp. 494–498.

16. Brown University Charter of 1764, Appendix A in Bronson, *History of Brown University, op. cit.*

Analogy of Religion was meant to refute David Hume and to confirm undergraduates at Brown, as it did those at Oxford University, in the faith of their fathers.[17] Archdeacon William Paley's *Evidences of Christianity* defended all Christian beliefs against the mockery of Edward Gibbon's history. Paley's *Principles of Moral and Political Philosophy*, a set text at Cambridge University as well as at Brown, called for "complete toleration of all dissenters from the established church."[18]

During JCB's years as a student, the University drew criticism not because it wrapped students in a sectarian cocoon but because it was too settled in outmoded teaching methods and course offerings. In 1815 this criticism became a clamor for reform with the publication of a letter to the corporation signed by "Alumnus Brunensis."[19] The letter was a particularly severe attack on Brown's medical program (opened in 1811, closed in 1833), but it also had positive proposals for overhauling undergraduate instruction. It called for: more lectures by professors with special competence in fields such as literature or law; less teaching by rote or recitation; the introduction of new courses in the sciences and the planting of a botanical garden and the collection of mineral specimens to support such courses. "Alumnus Brunensis" also wanted changes in financial planning with an

17. On Butler and Paley, see Roy Porter, *The Creation of the Modern World: The Untold Story of the British Enlightenment* (New York, 2000), pp. 97–98, 180, 261–262, 422–423.

18. William Paley, *Principles of Moral and Political Philosophy* (1785), Book VI, ch. 10.

19. Bronson, *History of Brown University*, pp. 160–166.

acquisition budget for the library and more scholarship aid to needy students. Many of these changes had been mooted well before 1815; "Alumnus Brunensis" gave them new urgency. In the controversy that followed publication of this letter, Nicholas [2] Brown, the wealthiest and most influential member of the corporation, was necessarily involved. So too was his son who, soon after the letter's publication, joined in organizing an undergraduate society—the Philendean Society—to provide books to students who could not afford to buy them.

Extracurricular life at the University in the early nineteenth century revolved around independent student clubs. The value of athletics as an outlet for adolescent energy had yet to be discovered. Good-natured but disruptive pranks were common; outbreaks of vandalism, some of them serious, were annual events. A Praying Society, founded in 1802, may have sublimated some animal spirits, but the groups that sparked the most enthusiasm among students and absorbed most of their spare time were the literary societies.[20] They had no faculty supervisors or advisors. They bought and kept their own libraries, arranged their own schedules of events, and, in effect, educated themselves in modern history, modern literature, domestic politics, and international affairs. The first of these at Brown, the Philermenian Society, organized in the 1790s, had a *numerus clausus* of forty-five and was broadly Federalist in political outlook.[21] Its rival, the

20. Frederick Rudolph, *The American College and University: A History* (New York, 1968), ch. 7, "The Extracurriculum."

21. Bronson, *History of Brown University*, pp. 173, 180–181.

United Brothers Society, was founded in 1806 in reaction to the Philermenians' elitism and was generally Jeffersonian-Republican in its views. In March 1814, JCB joined the United Brothers, perhaps at the urging of his cousin and classmate, Robert Hale Ives, who had already been initiated.[22]

During his junior and senior years, JCB used the United Brothers library, opened his room in college for committee meetings, helped plan their commencement festivities, and took part in their debates, which were a running critique of the University's course of studies. In April 1814, they debated the utility of Latin and Greek and voted that studying dead languages was not worth the effort. A few months later they answered yes to the question: "Has the reading of the best English authors a tendency to improve the style and spirit of our composition?" Other discussions in which JCB participated took up modern history (the Inquisition; the beheading of Mary Queen of Scots) and current events (the War of 1812; Allied meddling in post-Napoleonic France; military conscription). They also speculated on the future: should Congress encourage manufactures? should the Republic welcome immigrants?[23]

When JCB graduated in September 1816, he was one of twenty-eight commencement orators and the only one to address a historical subject. The text of his oration, if there was one, has

---

22. Brown University Archives, United Brothers Society, Constitution and Records, 1811–1865.

23. Brown University Archives, United Brothers Society, Constitution and Records, 1811–1865, and Box A.

not survived, but his title, "The Revolution of Empires," suggests that he was thinking of the dramatic events of that time—the collapse of Bonaparte's empire and the revolt of South American colonies against imperial Spain. The oration following JCB's was entitled "South American Revolutions."[24] JCB's grander theme had a long historical pedigree. Since the rise of Roman power in the first century B.C., Greek and Roman historians who aspired to write "universal history" had traced the successive rise and fall of three empires, Assyrian, Persian, and Greek, as prologue to the ascendancy of Rome. Patristic and medieval scholars fused this classical-cyclical view of political history with an Old Testament passage which prophesied a sequence of "four kingdoms" as serial manifestations of God's will.[25] Centuries later, that mystical interpretation of history was fossilized in Bishop George Berkeley's verses "On the Project of Planting Arts and Learning in America" (1752). His sixth stanza seemed to forecast the rise of America and came to have an incantory attraction for some public speakers in the young Republic.

> Westward the course of Empire takes its way
> The first four acts already past,
> A fifth shall close the drama of the day:
> Time's noblest offspring is the last.[26]

---

24. Reuben A. Guild, *History of Brown University* (Providence, 1867), p. 384.

25. *The Book of Daniel*, VII, pp. 17–23; J. W. Swain, "The Theory of the 'Four Monarchies'," *Classical Philology* xxxv (1940), pp. 1–21.

26. E. S. Gaustad, *George Berkeley in America* (New Haven, 1979), pp. 71–75; Conrad Cherry, *God's New Israel*, rev. ed. (Chapel Hill, 1998), p. 120.

Whether the inspiration for JCB's oration came from his classical-Christian schooling or from his reading of current events, his choice of subject indicates an early interest in great historical themes. By contrast, his father at his commencement thirty years earlier had delivered an oration on "The Advantages of Commerce."[27]

COMMERCIAL TRAVELER

A short downhill walk would take John Carter Brown from his father's house on Benefit Street to his family's place of business near the Providence waterfront. There in 1816 he and his cousin Robert Hale Ives joined Moses Brown Ives as full-time apprentices. The offices of Brown and Ives, occupying a plain, three-storied brick building, were headquarters for a complex enterprise whose interests ranged from land holdings on the American frontiers to investments in New England textile mills. But in 1816 the company still regarded overseas trade as its primary concern.[28] They had suffered setbacks during the last phase of the Napoleonic wars when trade restrictions and privateering had choked sea-borne commerce. With the coming of peace they set to work to refloat the trade with Asia and Europe which had been so profitable around the turn of the century. Their ships sailed to Jakarta and Canton as they had first done in the 1790s. They carried both Asian and American staples—tea, coffee, rice,

---

27. Bronson, *History of Brown University*, p. 85.

28. Hedges, *The Browns*, II, p. 183.

tobacco, and cotton—to ports on the North Atlantic, Mediterranean, and Baltic seacoasts. Not until the mid-1820s did their maritime trade fall into the decline that led them to abandon it altogether in 1838.[29]

Brown and Ives conducted their overseas business in English through a network of merchant bankers and commission agents, most of them Englishmen or Scots who had established firms in the world's busiest markets. Ties between Brown and Ives and their agents were personal rather than contractual and were cemented over time by trust, rising from experience, or by habit, rising from convenience. For example, in 1801 they began to clear shipments to Amsterdam through the Scottish traders Daniel Crommelin and Sons, and continued to do so until 1838, despite occasional reports that the Crommelins seemed to connive with Dutch brokers against the best interests of Brown and Ives.[30]

By going abroad, young merchants such as John Carter Brown and his cousins could begin to learn the intricacies and risks of long-distance trade. Face-to-face meetings with their agents and correspondents would allow them to judge their business acumen and integrity. They wanted also to observe foreign markets in operation to discover how deals were brokered in different countries. More generally, they needed to get away from ledgers and copy-books to inspect the sources of the products

---

29. *Ibid.*, pp. 135–158.

30. Brown Papers, JCBL, Brown and Ives, Correspondence, Miscellaneous Letters, Series II, Box 40. Letter, September 20, 1823. See Hedges, *The Browns*, II, p. 79.

they traded, to bargain at first-hand with their buyers, and to seek out opportunities to improve their trade patterns as well as to open new fields for investment. Travel, while they were still young enough to learn from it and hardy enough to survive its rigors, was an invaluable preparation for a commercial career. Perhaps the fact that neither Nicholas [2] Brown nor Thomas Poynton Ives had had opportunities to travel in their youth reinforced their decision to provide those advantages to their sons.

All three cousins, while they were still undergraduates, had traveled, singly or in pairs, to major centers in the Northeast—to meet with a Brown and Ives lawyer in Washington, D.C., to visit theaters and tailors in Philadelphia, and, once, to escort Charlotte Rhoda Ives to a female seminary in New Jersey. Moses Brown Ives, however, was the first of the rising generation to be sent out on extended business trips, and his exemplary concentration on his duties set a high level of expectation for those who were sent out later. In 1815 he was dispatched to the northwestern frontier to look into land purchases in Ohio and the tobacco trade in Kentucky. Three years later he was sent to Europe, where he worked most closely with Daniel Crommelin and Sons in Amsterdam, but also paid calls on mercantile houses in Antwerp, Le Havre, Paris, and London before returning to Providence in 1819. What Moses Brown Ives learned from his *Wanderjahre* was summed up by his friend and associate, Francis Wayland, president of Brown University, in a eulogy delivered in 1857. "While abroad," said Wayland, "his object seems to have been, not so much to see sights, and walk through galleries, as to observe men, and acquaint himself with the habits and manners of merchants of distinction. I have heard him frequently refer to this period of his life, but I think never for any other purpose than to illustrate the modes of doing business in the several capitals which he had occasion to visit."[31]

Soon after Moses had returned safely from Europe, Robert Hale Ives and John Carter Brown were dispatched to the Ohio valley on what JCB called a "tour of observation."[32] They left Providence on November 2, 1819, for New London, Connecticut, where they boarded a steamboat for New York and then transferred to a mail coach for Philadelphia. They spent several days enjoying life in the metropolis until their letter of instructions arrived from the home office.[33] According to that letter, they were to travel west across Pennsylvania to Ohio, Kentucky, and Indiana, then to go southeast through Kentucky, a corner of Tennessee, and across northern Georgia to Augusta. They were to study the land market in Ohio, the tobacco market in Kentucky, and the cotton market in Georgia. They were also charged with one important business deal: to buy bulk tobacco in Kentucky and to arrange its shipment by riverboat to New Orleans. Little was left to their discretion. They were told to make the deal through Brown and Ives's commission agent in Lexington, Kentucky,

31. Francis Wayland, *A Discourse in Commemoration of the Life and Character of Moses Brown Ives* (Providence, 1867), p. 10.

32. See "Diary of a trip to the western country, Nov. 2, 1819 to Dec. 28, 1819," MS, Codex 102. John Carter Brown Library.

33. The letter, dated November 8, 1819, is in Brown Papers, JCBL, Miscellaneous Letters, Box 398.

John Corlis, a former resident of Providence.[34] They were told how much tobacco to buy (200–250 hogsheads), how much to pay ($3.00 to $5.00 each), and what bank would clear payments. They were warned about the weakness of Kentucky and Ohio dollars, and, as if to ensure that they would follow orders, they were to present a letter to Sullivan Dorr, another Providence merchant who was active in Lexington at that time, a letter which in effect asked Dorr to monitor their transaction.[35]

JCB's diary of his western trip is much more laconic, much less discursive, than the diaries he kept later in Europe. Perhaps he saw less to excite his attention; perhaps he was exhausted by days of plodding on horseback along wilderness roads in freezing weather. Few entries stretch into paragraphs. Many are simple notations of stopping places and the distances between them. The diary ends abruptly on December 28 when he had paused for a few days in Lexington. He did take time later, however, to append a list of some forty stops between Philadelphia and Cincinnati and from Cincinnati around south-central Ohio to Columbus and back. By then he estimated that his "tour of observation" had covered more than a thousand miles.[36]

---

34. On Corlis's relations with Brown and Ives, see Hedges, *The Browns*, II, pp. 78–80, 178.

35. A Massachusetts native who, after some experience in the China trade, settled in Providence. Sullivan Dorr's daughter, Anne, would marry MBI in 1833; his son, Thomas, would lead a popular rebellion in Rhode Island in 1842.

36. "Diary...to the western country," *passim*.

The western trip inured John Carter Brown to the hardships of the road. Along the way two saddle horses and one pack horse had to be replaced. After a hard day's ride through the wild mountains of western Pennsylvania he remarked: "...although on the Turnpike, the Roads very bad, muddy, and much cut up. It was a bad day for the horses and they were much beaten out on reaching the Town [Greensburg]."[37] The travelers too were worn down by the primitive roads and the rigors of the season. When the tour had been originally planned in Providence, John Carter Brown and Robert Hale Ives were to be accompanied by a third companion, Thomas Poynton Bancroft, an Ives cousin and a University classmate. Bancroft's health broke down a few days after leaving Philadelphia and, unable to ride horseback, he had to be carried in a wagon over the Alleghenies from Harrisburg to Pittsburgh where the expedition halted. Even after a layover of two weeks Bancroft was too weak to go with JCB and RHI when on a bitterly cold December morning they left Pittsburgh and headed south to Marietta, Ohio, en route westward to Lexington.[38]

A hardy traveler, John Carter Brown was also an openminded observer of life on the frontier. He felt snubbed in Pittsburgh and wrote, on leaving: "I candidly confess I never want to see the place again."[39] He did not himself sniff at the westerners

---

37. *Ibid.*, transcript, p. 5.

38. *Ibid.*, p. 3.

39. *Ibid.*, p. 7. One host in Pittsburgh, a paterfamilias, ceremoniously showed JCB and RHI the door, probably because he suspected that his young guests were flirting with his daughters.

he met. Most of them were, after all, transplanted New Englanders, many of them from Rhode Island, eager to create in their outposts a seaboard way of life. In Paris, Kentucky, he found a wayside inn which was "much before anything we have of the kind in Rhode Island."[40] He admired the brick architecture of Lexington but acknowledged that a log building could be made comfortable. He yawned at a "great Route," or holiday party, given just after Christmas by one of the leading hostesses in Lexington, only because the festivities struck him as "pretty much the same as in Providence."[41]

By the spring of 1822, John Carter Brown was mature enough, in the eyes of the senior partners, to undertake an unaccompanied commercial trip to Europe, as his cousin Moses had done four years before him. JCB's letter of instructions, April 8, 1822, laid out his itinerary but gave him greater responsibilities and many more options than he had been given for his western trip.[42] He was to ship out of Providence on the *General Hamilton* with the commission of supercargo—the ship's officer responsible for its cargo of bulk tobacco. The ship was to sail directly to Gibraltar where he should sell the tobacco if market conditions were favorable. He would then buy 10,000 silver dollars, milled in Spain, take on ballast, and set sail for St. Petersburg where he was to buy naval stores, canvas, and duck cloth for the Brown

---

40. *Ibid.*, p. 10.

41. *Ibid.*, p. 19.

42. Brown Papers, JCBL, *General Hamilton* file, letter, April 8, 1822.

and Ives fleet. For his return voyage JCB was given a choice. He might stay with the *General Hamilton* as far as Copenhagen, debark there, and set out overland for Amsterdam. Alternatively, he might stay with his ship until it reached England, debark there, and spend some time in London before visiting Holland and France. Meanwhile letters of introduction for him were being addressed to Gibraltar, St. Petersburg, Amsterdam, and Paris.

On May 16, 1822, after a voyage of thirty-five days the *General Hamilton* dropped anchor at Gibraltar. Two weeks later JCB took passage for Cadiz. His first impressions of the Old World, then, were of the exotic, British-held entrepot and of the glistening Spanish seaport which had been the official center of Spain's trade with the New World. In 1822 Gibraltar was very much the same as it was when it was described a few years later by the young Benjamin Disraeli in a letter to his father:

> I write to you from a country where the hedges consist of aloes all in blossom, fourteen, sixteen, feet high.... I say nothing of geraniums and myrtles, bowers of oranges, and woods of olives, tho' the occasional palm should not be forgotten for its great novelty and uncommon grace.... This rock is a wonderful place with a population infinitely diversified—Moors with costumes radiant as a rainbow or as an Easter melodrame, Jews with gabardines and scull caps, Genoese, Highlanders, and Spaniards, whose dress is as picturesque as that of the sons of Ivor.[43]

---

43. J. A. W. Gunn, ed., *Benjamin Disraeli, Letters: 1815–1834* (Toronto, 1982), pp. 128–129. An "Easter melodrame" was a spectacular variety show commonly staged by London theaters at Eastertime. JCB attended one such. See below, diary entry for April 4, 1823.

As for Cadiz, Disraeli exclaimed: "...charming! Brilliant beyond description. 'Fair Florence' is a very dingy affair compared with it. The white houses and green jalousies sparkle in the Sun. Figaro is in every street and Rosina in every balcony."[44]

John Carter Brown's letters from Gibraltar were less effusive. He was sobered to find that market conditions were unfavorable and was irritated to meet one obstacle after another in the discharge of his business. He had little difficulty in arranging the purchase of 10,000 silver dollars, having them packed in five boxes and taken on board. But he could find no one to buy his tobacco which, he was told, was green and uncured.[45] His excursion to Cadiz in late May was a vain search for a better market there. Meanwhile, bulletins from tobacco wholesalers in Antwerp and Hamburg promised nothing better. He decided, then, in early June after his return from Cadiz to warehouse the tobacco in Gibraltar and trust agents there to sell it when the market improved. Even then he could not leave port because manpower shortages delayed the loading of sand ballast to replace the cargo. Two of the *General Hamilton*'s crew had jumped ship in Gibraltar, leaving her captain, James Tefft, ominously short-handed. Local workers were slack and undependable. JCB reported on June 5: "...the numerous holidays among Catholics and Jews at this time of year render it impossible to conduct business."[46]

---

44. *Ibid.*, p. 137.

45. Brown Papers, JCBL, *General Hamilton* file, letter, May 16, 1822.

46. *Ibid.*, letter, June 5, 1822.

Finally, in mid-July, the *General Hamilton* set sail for St. Petersburg, only to be becalmed or to fight strong headwinds in the Atlantic. In the English Channel on the night of July 21–22, Captain Tefft tried to make up for lost time by running before the wind. Suddenly he thought he saw shore lights to the northeast. Afraid that he was off course he decided to haul in sail and lay by until daybreak. John Carter Brown, who had kept the deck until after midnight, described what happened next:

> The light sails with the spanker were already taken in and Captain Tefft had just gone below to consult his charts when the watch on deck cried: 'Breakers ahead!' The helm was immediately put hard about but before the ship could answer her helm she struck. The waves washed over us and the ship continued to beat and thump in a most violent manner and, as self-preservation is always the first impulse, we began to get out the longboat for... there was every appearance of capsizing. But as day began to break we could perceive that instead of being upon a reef as at first supposed, we had run against the shore.... As the tide ebbed, the ship lay over easy until finally she was left high and dry. We soon found out that we were unhappily cast upon the French Coast, nine miles south of Boulogne.[47]

The wreck of the *General Hamilton* could have been worse: no hands were lost; no large cargo had to be salvaged. But officers and crew were stranded on a foreign shore and instead of the "protection and assistance" which JCB expected, they were greeted with hostility, surrounded by an armed guard and ordered

---

47. Brown Papers, JCBL, *General Hamilton* file, letter, July 25, 1822.

to produce a bill of health from the French consulate in Gibraltar. Unable to do so they were marched to a "filthy hovel a few rods from the beach" and there placed under quarantine.[48] After a cursory inspection, the French Naval Commissariat charged the Americans with attempting to smuggle silver into France. JCB suspected that he and his shipmates were being treated as hostages and that they could win their release only by surrendering their five boxes of silver dollars. This he was determined not to do. Meanwhile, he and Captain Tefft and the thirteen crew members were kept under twenty-four-hour surveillance, crowded into a shed, sweltering under a summer sun by day, chilled by ocean fogs by night, subsisting only on the ship's stores.

French authorities allowed JCB to send word of his detention to the American vice-consul in Boulogne and, later, to the American consul in Calais. But their official protests were slow to get a hearing by local offices in the port cities or by the central bureaucracies in Paris, even after Albert Gallatin, the American minister to the Bourbon court, added his voice.[49] At last the quarantine was lifted in mid-August. The ship's crew collected their pay and dispersed. Captain Tefft, under armed guard as far as Boulogne, took the silver to England where he deposited it with Thomas Dickason and Company, Brown and Ives's principal agent in London. JCB was left behind to deal with the wreckage. After six weeks of haggling, thoroughly disheartened by bureaucratic interference, he reported from Boulogne that all efforts to

---

48. *Ibid.*

49. *Ibid.*, letter, August 2, 1822.

refloat the *General Hamilton* had failed and that he had sold the hulk together with its tackle and stores for a "trifle," barely enough to cover his expenses and the fees imposed by the French government which included import duties on the silver.[50]

The summer of 1822 was an unhappy season for Brown and Ives's European trade. The beaching of the *General Hamilton* came just a few days after their brig *Hector*, carrying a shipment of iron from Sweden, ran aground off the coast of Scotland.[51] News of both disasters was relayed, with appropriate commiseration, from London by Dickason and Company and reached Providence in early September. Relief at Brown and Ives that JCB had survived the shipwreck, mixed with admiration for his management of its aftermath and sympathy for his long ordeal, moved the senior partners to grant him some time away from business at least until spring when they would have new shipments arriving in Europe. JCB was free, then, to spend the fall and winter of 1822–23 in Paris where his way was prepared by French mercantile and banking houses that had dealings with his father.[52] JCB kept no record of his months in Paris but scattered references in his diaries and his letters show that he enjoyed the theater, the sightseeing, and the social rounds there until mid-

---

50. *Ibid.*, letter, September 24, 1822.

51. *Ibid.*, letter, February 14, 1823, from RHI to JCB.

52. One of these was Hottinguer and Company whose founder, Baron Jean-Conrad Hottinguer, in 1793 while an émigré in London, had married Martha Redwood, the heiress of a Rhode Island fortune. See Brown Papers, JCBL, Correspondence, Hottinguer and Company, 1823.

March when he left behind his life of *fainéantisme* to go to England. At that point his diaries begin.[53]

DIVERSION

Cumulatively, the five diaries that John Carter Brown kept at intervals between March 1823 and August 1824 show how he bracketed his commercial duties with the sight-seeing trips that over the months made up his "Grand Tour." The first diary (March–April 1823) records his arrival in London and his first few weeks there. The second diary picks up four months later after he had finished a stint in Amsterdam working with Crommelin and Sons on the unloading and marketing of shipments from Brown and Ives. On returning to England, he had the unexpected pleasure of finding that Robert Hale Ives had been sent out from Providence to assist him and, perhaps, to fix his mind on business. JCB, nevertheless, persuaded his cousin to accompany him on a leisurely tour of south-central England, which is the subject of the second diary (August–September, 1823).

Back in London, John Carter Brown received a letter from his father that gently rebuked him for failing to write home more often and for allowing himself to be distracted from business matters. More particularly, his father wanted JCB to observe the new machinery and processes which gave English industry its dynamism. Rhode Island textile mills since 1815 had been losing

---

53. Harvey Levenstein, *Seductive Journey: American Tourists in France from Jefferson to the Jazz Age* (Chicago, 1998), p. 23, appears to misread remarks in JCB's diary (entry for March 27, 1823), citing them as reflections on Paris rather than on London where they were written. He certainly misreads another passage cited later, p. 32.

market share to English manufacturers. Nicholas [2] wanted his son to scout out the competition. In reply, JCB wrote at unusual length to apologize for his desultory correspondence, but, more importantly, to prove that he had mastered current trade figures and knew his way around the Exchange. For the most part his reply was a thick serving of market quotations from Gibraltar, Le Havre, Antwerp, and Amsterdam for tea, coffee, tobacco, flour, and rice. He garnished these numbers with some gossip about the House of Rothschild and the dark intimation that Dutch merchants could not always be trusted.[54]

Buried toward the beginning and toward the end of JCB's reply to his father were two revealing personal notes.[55]

Having noticed that you dwell much on manufactures they have not escaped our attention; but when one takes into consideration the abundance and cheapness of labour here, when compared with what it is in the U.S. . . . we must think Mr. Jefferson was correct in saying that 'our work shops should be in Europe.' Far, however, from siding with the anti-manufacturing interest of the U.S., I heartily rejoice to hear that they are going on at the full tide of experiment.

—

Regarding myself, I have to say that I had partially concluded to return to America this Winter. But the unlooked for arrival of Mr. Ives etc. etc. may probably prolong my stay—unless other advices are received—This much on this subject which you in a former letter asked me to elucidate.

---

54. Brown Papers, JCBL, Brown and Ives, Miscellaneous Letters, Series II, Box 400, letter, September 10, 1823.

55. *Ibid.*

Hoping that this letter would allay concerns in Providence, JCB lost no time in planning wide-ranging tours that would occupy him for the next eight months, one of them a solitary journey to the romantic north, the other a joint trip with his cousin to the classical south. In mid-September 1823, he arranged for RHI to go to France and deal with a cargo of coffee that had recently arrived at Le Havre. He then set out by himself on a strenuous tour of northern England, Scotland, Ireland, and Wales, the subject of his third diary (September–December, 1823). Just before Christmas he joined forces with RHI for what would be their longest and richest adventure, touring the Rhone Valley, sailing from Marseilles to Naples, and traveling up the Italian peninsula from Naples to Venice and Milan with stopovers in Rome and Florence. The fourth diary (December 1823–March 1824) gives an account of this journey as far as Milan. From there the cousins went through Switzerland to France and spent most of the month of May in Paris.

During the winter of 1823–24 the senior partners at Brown and Ives made no effort to rein in their itinerant sons. Transatlantic communication was slowest and riskiest at that time of year. Letters which JCB and RHI sent from Rome in February did not reach Providence until May. Then, at last, Thomas Poynton Ives and Nicholas [2] Brown recalled their sons to business in Europe and set an approximate date for their return to America.[56] The letter announced that shipments were scheduled to arrive at Le

---

56. Brown Papers, JCBL, Brown and Ives, Miscellaneous Correspondence, Box 401, letter, May 10, 1824.

Havre in the late spring and that the *Ann and Hope* was due at Texil with a cargo of tea to be sold in Amsterdam. The letter included a request that JCB and RHI inquire through the United States minister in Paris about Brown and Ives's claims for indemnities from France for "unjust searches and seizures under the reign of Bonaparte."[57] Finally, the parents stated that they would expect their sons to leave Europe sometime in summer but no later than October.

These instructions from Providence reached Paris in late June but John Carter Brown did not see them until late July. Shortly before they arrived he had gone off on another trip, this time to northern Germany. He probably wanted to demonstrate to Brown and Ives his seriousness of purpose by going to visit important trading partners in Hamburg and Bremen, making calls which he might have been advised to consider in 1822 when the *General Hamilton* was scheduled to sail the North Sea and the Baltic. The first part of the fifth diary (June–July 1824) is JCB's account of his German trip and his return to London by way of Amsterdam. When in late July he found a copy of his father's instructions awaiting him in London, he wrote an immediate reply to confirm his homecoming.[58] He promised that in

---

57. Brown and Ives had been pressing these claims since June 1813. In 1824 they hoped that a recently concluded Franco-American trade convention would loosen French fists. See Brown Papers, JCBL, Brown and Ives, Miscellaneous Correspondence, Box 401, letter, June 29. The claims were settled in 1836. See Hedges, *The Browns*, II, p. 158.

58. Brown Papers, JCBL, Brown and Ives, Miscellaneous Correspondence, Box 402, letter, July 20, 1824.

the fall he would take ship for Providence from Liverpool and hinted that en route to Liverpool he would take time to view the manufacturing centers in the English Midlands. He did not, however, mention that he planned beforehand to take a late-summer excursion to the English West Country—Cornwall and Devon—a sight-seeing tour that is recorded in the second half of the fifth diary (August 1824).

John Carter Brown concluded his letter of July 20, 1824, with a plaintive note to his father about the steady but uncertain advice he had been given regarding his business career. Perhaps Nicholas [2] Brown's counsel was deliberately vague because he was following a family tradition of allowing sons to act on their own inclinations. Perhaps he was reluctant to play the dictatorial parent or hard taskmaster because he was already estranged from his older son and was determined to deal amicably with the younger. Whatever the explanation, it is remarkable that John Carter Brown, who would turn twenty-seven in September, 1824, had as yet no settled plans for his future.

> In all your letters to me you have mentioned the subjects of trades, manufactures, etc. etc. without stating anything specific or definite on either of these points. I could have wished that you had been more full in these particulars so that I might have reflected at my leisure on any plans you may have in view. Commission business seems to me by far better than anything else and in Europe it is customary for young men to purchase (or their parents for them) a share in an established house and to partake in proportion of the loss or gain.

> I don't know that this thing is yet understood with us.

Historically and strictly defined (and generally capitalized), the "Grand Tour" was a form of graduate education, or a finishing school without walls, for the English upper classes of the seventeenth and eighteenth centuries.[59] In its earliest phase it was a secularized pilgrimage. "Evolving out of and, in Protestant northern Europe, reacting against the medieval practice of pilgrimage in response to a demand for a non-superstitious justification for travel, the Grand Tour began as an exclusively educational phenomenon."[60] Central to this leisured learning experience was the opportunity it gave the English elite to meet and form connections with their counterparts on the Continent. By the 1820s it was receding into history. A quarter-century of political upheaval and warfare that began in 1789 had thrown up barriers to the free movement of travelers across national boundaries while profound social and economic changes were hastening the *embourgeoisement* of travel, a process which gathered momentum with the coming of steam transportation.

John Carter Brown's travels in the British Isles and on the European continent in 1823–24 qualified as a Grand Tour in their scope and intention. He was a young man of means and position who had completed his university studies and wanted,

---

59. The term is often used loosely in the United States as referring to any extended foreign travel or even to any carefully planned visit no matter how brief. So a corporate executive or a general may be given in one day a "grand tour" of a new plant or installation.

60. Edward Chaney, *The Evolution of the Grand Tour* (London, 1998), p. 203.

as his diaries show, to observe foreign customs, manners, and institutions and to compare them with those of his upbringing. He wanted to see what was unique to Europe—cultivated landscapes as well as scenic wonders such as waterfalls and volcanic craters. He wanted most of all to explore Europe's rich cultural life, to visit historical monuments, examine architectural landmarks, attend concerts, operas, and plays and view great collections of art, opportunities which were not at hand on the American seaboard or its western frontier.

"Travaille in the younger Set, is a Part of Education," said Sir Francis Bacon in his essay on travel which included a packet of advice to young men on how they could make the most of their time abroad.[61] He told them to learn the language of a country before going there and he prescribed shortcuts that would sharpen their understanding of whatever they learned. They should hire knowledgeable tutors as companions. They should carry with them and consult descriptive literature. They should get letters of introduction and frequent public places where they could have casual meetings with the locals. Bacon insisted that they keep diaries. Otherwise the rush of new information and new impressions would overwhelm their powers of recall.

Whether or not he had read Bacon's essay, John Carter Brown acted on many of its precepts. His diaries were a series of rather terse memoranda written for himself, never intended for publication. He knew no Spanish, Italian, German, or Dutch but

---

61. Francis Bacon, *The Essayes or Counsels Civill and Morall*, ed. Michael Kiernan (Cambridge, Mass., 1985), p. 56.

he had at least an elementary command of French. He never hired a tutor as a companion but, as need or opportunity arose, he employed local guides—a *valet de place* in Lyons, cicerones in Rome and Florence. Having little success with letters of introduction, he relied most heavily on the descriptive books he took with him for help in selecting major destinations and planning side trips.[62] Comprehensive, compact guidebooks such as John Murray's or Karl Baedeker's, with their lists, ratings, and timetables, were a mid-nineteenth-century innovation.[63] For John Carter Brown, discursive travel writers and contemporary litterateurs, notably Sir Walter Scott and Lord Byron, were the guides who whetted his appetite, directed his steps and shaped his perceptions. Some attention to their influence will help to explain where he chose to go and what he chose to see.

Leading the list of books that guided JCB on his Grand Tour was *A Journal of Travels in England, Holland and Scotland* by Benjamin Silliman which was published in 1810 and given a second edition in 1812.[64] At the age of seventeen, as a student at Brown University, JCB borrowed a copy from his fraternity

---

62. JCB frequently complained about the uselessness of his letters of introduction. Many of them were addressed to Baptist clergymen in England who evidently had neither the inclination nor the connections to open doors for him.

63. On the origin of travelers' handbooks, see Samuel Smiles, *A Publisher and His Friends: Memoir and Correspondence of the Late John Murray* (London, 1891), II, pp. 459 ff.

64. Benjamin Silliman (1779–1864) is honored as a pioneer organizer of scientific studies in the United States. He was appointed professor at Yale College in 1802 and in 1805 sent to Europe to meet men of science and to buy books

library and, later, bought a copy of the third edition which had appeared in 1820. Four of JCB's travel diaries refer directly to Silliman's *Journal*. There is evidence in his first diary that he had the book with him in London in the spring of 1823.[65] There is stronger evidence that, in the following summer, he took the book, or it took him, on his trip to the Isle of Wight and subsequent swing through England's south-central counties. The third diary shows how he traced Silliman's route north to Edinburgh by way of York and Newcastle, and the fifth shows how his final excursion, a tour of the West Country, was inspired by Silliman's account of his sight-seeing there in 1805. For example, Silliman said this of his visit to Land's End: "I tied my horse to a rock and hastened to place my foot on the last cliffs of this proud island." Nineteen years later JCB followed Silliman's path on foot and quoted him (inexactly): "From Senan we walked nearly a mile and [*a*] half to the very Land's End & 'I hastened to set my foot on the last rock of this proud Isle.'"[66]

There were many reasons why Silliman's *Journal* cast a spell over the adolescent John Carter Brown as it did over the reading public at large. Silliman had a good eye for detail and sometimes

---

and equipment for courses in natural history. His private account of his travels was revised for publication in 1809. See Chandos Michael Brown, *Benjamin Silliman: A Life in the Young Republic* (Princeton, 1989).

65. See Diary entry for March 27, 1823.

66. Benjamin Silliman, *Journal of Travels in England, Holland, and Scotland*, 3rd ed. (New Haven, 1820), II, p. 187. JCB's citation appears in the diary entry for August 14, 1824.

"attempted painterly effects in prose."[67] Further, Silliman had studied law and English history before he took up natural science. So, he could comment knowingly on English institutions and enliven his descriptive passages by evoking literary and historical associations. Another strong attraction of the *Journal* was that it helped Americans, at least those of English descent, adjust their thoughts and sentiments about the "Mother Country." Silliman, whose father had held the rank of general in the American revolutionary forces, could not be accused of toadying to the English. Indeed he registered shock at the corruption in public services, the insolence of city mobs, the vulgarity of popular entertainment, and most particularly condemned the frivolous behavior of the upper classes assembled at Bath. But when, as in his account of his visit to Land's End, he referred to England as "this proud island," he evidently shared the pride. He was proud of the cultural heritage, the traditions, which the English and Americans still held in common a generation after the War of Independence.

John Carter Brown's observations on what he saw in Britain were his own, but he reflected many of Silliman's views. He cited Silliman's ridicule of the house of Percy's genealogical tree as displayed at Alnwick Castle but noted the Percys' reputation for philanthropy.[68] English foppery offended Silliman but amused JCB; the preening of "bucks and fashionables" on promenade in

---

67. Brown, *Silliman*, p. 169.

68. Silliman, *Journal*, III, pp. 166 ff.; JCB diary entries for September 30 and October 1, 1823.

St. James Park and the hideous joy of box-holders at the opera made him smile with disbelief. While Silliman shuddered at the crudity and bad breath of popular entertainment, JCB seemed ready to join the fun. On the other hand, Silliman was only a little troubled by the laxity of Anglican clergymen while JCB criticized ill-prepared sermons and registered disgust at what he considered the parodic conduct of an afternoon service in Canterbury Cathedral.[69]

For his continental tours John Carter Brown relied on two very different travel writers: John Chetwode Eustace and William Berrian. Eustace's *A Classical Tour Through Italy* was a detailed and magisterial text, grounded on the author's classical scholarship but growing directly from his experience as a tutor and tour guide to English Catholic families.[70] Eustace recommended that those who planned a winter trip to Italy should begin at Naples and head north by slow stages with the advance of warm weather. JCB followed that advice; he also consulted Eustace in charting side trips around Naples and Rome and in selecting churches and art collections to be visited in those and other major cities. William Berrian's *Travels in France and Italy in 1817 and 1818* is a personal, sometimes jaundiced account that gave JCB information on what to see in the Rhone Valley and provided him with a

69. Diary entries for March 18 and 28, and April 5, 1823.

70. John Chetwode Eustace (1761–1815) was an Anglo-Irish Roman Catholic priest and classical scholar whose ecumenical theological views disqualified him for a teaching position in Catholic seminaries. As tutor to the sons of the "old Catholic" aristocracy, he shepherded one of them on his Grand Tour in 1802.

narrative example of an outsider, an American Protestant, coming to terms with the baroque religious art and the often bizarre religious devotions of the Italian faithful.[71]

The difference between Eustace and Berrian as guides to Italy was not just the difference between a generally sympathetic Roman Catholic and a generally disapproving Episcopalian. It was far more a difference in sensibility. Eustace's enthusiasm for what he saw launched him on flights of fancy such as that in Pompeii where he was seized by "a secret power that captivates, I had almost said melts, the soul."[72] He quoted lines from Book II of the *Aeneid* where Virgil describes the destruction of Troy in a rain of fire. Then in his mind's eye he repopulated the streets of Pompeii and remarked that in turning a corner he took care not to jostle the ancient citizens. Berrian would have none of these fantasies. Referring specifically to Eustace (and analogous vaporings of Mme. De Stael), he said "I confess...that these daydreams of travelers...only lead to disappointment on the spot; and I could no more imagine this collection of ruins to be an inhabited, or even a deserted city, than I could expect to find the living among the dark and mouldering monuments of the dead."[73]

---

71. William Berrian (1787–1862), a native of New York City, graduated from Columbia in 1808 and became assistant rector of Trinity Church in Manhattan in 1811. Taking leave because of ill health in 1817, he sailed to Bordeaux and traveled through southern France and Italy. He published his *Travels* in 1821 and was named rector of Trinity in 1830, a position he held until his death.

72. John Chetwode Eustace, *A Classical Tour Through Italy, 1802*, 4 vols. (London, 1815), III, pp. 55–57. References hereinafter are to the sixth edition (London, 1821).

73. Berrian, *Travels*, pp. 176–177.

After visiting Pompeii and Herculaneum, John Carter Brown noted in his diary that he felt "neither the ardour of Eustace nor the indifference of Berrian."[74] He was eager to see the excavations but not to indulge in an imaginative recreation of the cities' life and death under the volcanic ash and lava thrown up by Mount Vesuvius in 79 A.D. He wanted rather to grasp the exact dimensions of the tragedy by seeing the site at first-hand. It is highly probable that, as a schoolboy, he had read the account of the eruption given in letters of Pliny the Younger to Tacitus, an account which is high in drama but short in circumstantial detail.[75] JCB admitted: "I had a very confused and indifferent idea of Pompeii before visiting it."[76] He therefore "examined attentively" the streets, shops, and private dwellings as well as the law court, the temples, barracks, and theaters, and he noted the measurements of the city walls. In Pompeii, as elsewhere, he wanted to substantiate his knowledge of historic events by surveying their actual settings. Samuel Johnson remarked: "The use of travelling is to regulate imagination by reality, and instead of thinking how things may be, to see them as they are."[77] JCB regulated his imaginings of the past by trying to see things as they had been.

---

74. Diary entry for January 31, 1824.

75. Pliny the Younger, *Letters*, VI. 16, 20.

76. Diary entry for January 31, 1824.

77. Bruce Redford, ed., *The Letters of Samuel Johnson*, 5 vols. (Princeton, 1992–1994), II, p. 78, letter to Hester Thrale, dated September 21, 1773. T. M. Curley in *Samuel Johnson and the Age of Travel* (Athens, Ga., 1976) argues at length that Johnson drew on John Locke's philosophy to reach the conclusion that travel is a process of discovery and verification and, more broadly, that all

Many of John Carter Brown's excursions were literary pilgrimages. He joined hundreds of other votaries at the shrines in Stratford-upon-Avon and went out of his way to see Glamis Castle in Angusshire where Macbeth had murdered sleep.[78] He was well-read in English writers of the eighteenth century and, acting on their recommendations, sought out particular sights which they had found impressive. So it was with Samuel Johnson's comments on the Fall of Foyers in Scotland or Joseph Addison's praise for the Giusti Gardens in Verona.[79] Sometimes he just happened on places that evoked memories from his reading, as when a coach ride from London to Cambridge recalled a popular road song by William Cowper.[80] But JCB was most deeply influenced not by those voices from the past but by two contemporaries—Lord Byron and Sir Walter Scott.

With *Childe Harold's Pilgrimage* (1812–1818) Lord Byron caught a mood and set a tone for a generation of English-speaking tourists who thronged continental Europe after Napoleon had been sent into exile.[81] JCB was no exception. As did many other journal-keepers and letter-writers, he quoted the opening lines of

---

human life is a journey on which everyone is duty-bound to find truth through direct experience rather than at second-hand.

78. Diary entries for September 4 and October 9, 1823.

79. Diary entries for October 18, 1823, and March 29, 1824.

80. Diary entry for August 2, 1824.

81. On Byron as a travel guide, see Mona Wilson, "The Decline of the Grand Tour" in R. S. Lambert, ed., *Grand Tour: A Journey in the Tracks of the Age of Aristocracy* (New York, 1937), pp. 153–160.

Canto IV: "I stood in Venice on the Bridge of Sighs;/A palace and a prison on each hand."[82] He followed Childe Harold around the canals to see outdoor sculpture and an indoor art collection. He reflected the anger of Lord Byron and other *bien-pensants* over the extinction of the Venetian Republic and shared their resentment of the "iron yoke of Austria" in northern Italy at large. While he almost never commented on political conditions in the countries he visited, he remembered to quote the sneer at the Habsburg regime in Parma which he had found in Byron's *The Age of Bronze* (1823).[83]

Byron's poetry was one of John Carter Brown's guides to contemporary Italy; Sir Walter Scott's poetry and prose fed his interest in British history. In the fall of 1823 JCB toured the western highlands of Perthshire to explore the setting of Scott's *The Lady of the Lake* (1810). He scouted the adventurous path of Scott's sixteenth-century hero, James V of Scotland, and was stirred to quote a few lines. But reality, he discovered, failed to match Scott's lavish descriptions. The Trossachs did not offer "the scenery of a fairy dream"; Loch Katrin was not "a burnished sheet of living gold."[84] On the other hand, Scott's descriptive prose in the Waverley novels was too spare to satisfy JCB's curiosity. *The Abbot* (1810), for example, in telling the story of Mary Stuart's captivity and escape from the island stronghold at

---

82. Diary entry for March 22–26, 1824.

83. Diary entries for March 27 and 30, 1824.

84. *The Lady of the Lake*, Canto I, vii–xiv. Diary entry for October 25–26, 1823.

Loch Leven in 1568, merely sketched in the backdrops of the fortress and lake shore. To visualize more fully and distinctly how the queen and her accomplices had escaped the castle walls and crossed over to the mainland, JCB spent an afternoon at Loch Leven examining and measuring the terrain and structures there much as he would examine the ruins at Pompeii a few months later.[85]

This fascination with minutiae may suggest a prosaic or literalist turn of mind. But JCB's fact-finding search for clear and exact historical images went well beyond literalism. It grew out of a respect for the past and an impulse to grasp or intuit the past's reality. Biographers of Sir Walter Scott have commented on his splendid ability to combine serious historical-philosophical interests with the passionate antiquarianism he displayed at Abbotsford, his country house whose walls were hung with legendary relics and whose structural materials had been salvaged from the remains of historical buildings.[86] At a lower level of intensity JCB also fused historical and antiquarian interests. He did not collect old coins, weapons, or other heroic memorabilia, but he did experience a numinous sense of communion with historical figures through contact with their material possessions, by handling, or just seeing, things they had once used or by entering rooms they had once occupied. At Holyrood Palace, for instance, he was

---

85. Diary entry for October 4, 1823.

86. John Sutherland, *The Life of Sir Walter Scott: A Critical Biography* (Cambridge, Mass., 1995), pp. 47–48; Edgar Johnson, *Sir Walter Scott: The Great Unknown* (New York, 1970), pp. 93, 580, 1260–1261.

awe-struck upon seeing the ruined chapel where "the lovely Queen of Scotland used to say her prayers."[87] He noted the tattered furniture of her bedchamber and regretted that he could not open her workbox, as Silliman claimed to have done. JCB found nothing grand or imposing about the Palace but summed up: "Altho. all that is now to be seen at Holyrood is in fact nothing at all, yet I could not but feel satisfied that I had visited the very identical apartments that were once inhabited by so interesting a personage as Mary of Scotland whose misfortunes and sufferings even at this remote period excites the pity of every one who reads her story."[88]

---

87. Diary entry for September 29, 1823.

88. *Ibid.* Cf. JCB's musings at Stonehenge, August 6, 1823.

FIG. 2. Silhouette of John Carter Brown made in Saratoga, New York, August 3, 1843, by August Edouart (1789–1861). Collection of the New-York Historical Society.

FIG. 3. John Carter Brown, ca. 1865. Photograph made by Manchester Bros., 73 Westminster Street, Providence, Rhode Island. John Carter Brown Library.

FIG. 4. Marble bust of John Carter Brown by Franklin Simmons, 1874. This sculpture sits on the fireplace mantel in the Reading Room of the Library.

JOHN CARTER BROWN TRAVEL DIARIES, 1823–1824

Book One

March 17 to April 15, 1823
FRANCE AND ENGLAND

Since my Shipwreck on the Coast of France in July last and my long confinement on the Downs, I have kept no Journal of my proceedings, for most of the time I have been in the City of Paris & so engaged as to make it altogether inconvenient.[1] I however have kept a Memoranda & at some future day shall put my thoughts upon paper. I left Paris about 10 days ago in the "Diligence" for Boulogne S. Mer where I remained 4 days in a very pleasant family of my acquaintance. No Boat about sailing for Dover I left there for Calais & arrived at 11 oclk.AM. where I remained 'til the next day, & took passage in the Steam Boat "Dart"[2] & after a pleasant sail of 3½ hours, we were landed safe at Dover,—the first time I ever set my foot upon English ground. The day was remarkably fine & the French Coast was plainly seen from this side of the Channel.—I went to the "Green Inn"

---

1. For an account of his shipwreck and confinement, see the Introduction. "Downs" refers to a sandy beach (French, *les dunes*) where JCB was held for twenty days in a quarantine hut. This sandy tract, nine miles south of Boulogne, is not to be confused with "the Downs," chalk hills in southeastern England.

2. Paddlewheel steamboats crossing the Strait of Dover were put into service shortly after the end of the Napoleonic wars.

where I had been recommended by friend Farq.[3] After some little refreshment I went to visit the Castle of Dover, situated on the hights near the town. This is a very strong fortress & of great antiquity, but many of the guns are dismounted & the garrison is now very small. A part of this building is the work of the Romans, at the time they first landed in Britain. With the exception of the Castle, there appeared to me to be nothing particularly interesting in this place, the Town well known to be supported principally by the Packets. At the Castle I saw the famous "Pocket peice of Queen Anne," a Brass Cannon 24 ft in length.[4]

The next day, the 18 after the breakfast I took a Seat on the top of one of the Coaches for London. I prefered this place as you then have a very fine view of the Country, tho' are exposed to the rain if there be any. This was the case to day, for we had hardly started before the atmosphere became very thick & rain followed soon after, notwithstanding this I kept my seat 'til we arrived at Canterbury, where I concluded to stop for the day, to avoid the bad weather & also to visit the famous Cathedral. In fact I was anxious to have a pleasant day to make my first entrance into

---

3. A probable reference to Farquhar Jameson, manager of Hottinguer & Cie.'s branch bank in Le Havre. Jameson was married to Anna Hottinguer (1794–1886) whose father, founder of the bank, had been one of JCB's hosts in Paris during the autumn and winter of 1822–1823. See above, p. xliv, n. 52.

4. The long brass cannon at Dover Castle bore several names. Cast in Utrecht early in the sixteenth century, later presented to Elizabeth I by the Dutch States General, it became known as "Queen Elizabeth's Pocket Pistol." Its original name was engraved on the barrel in a verse: (as translated from the Dutch) "O'er hill and dale I throw my ball/Breaker, my name, of mound and wall."

London. This building is perhaps one of the most famous in all England, at least of the Church kind, for it was here Thomas A. Becket was killed in the reign of Henry 2d—the very spot was shewn me, & I also saw the Tomb of Edward the Black Prince with the very armour & shield he wore at the battle of Poictiers. Various other Monuments & Tablets were also pointed out. I will not be silly enough to attempt to describe this building, or any other, for of what use is the best description without engravings—you have just as good an idea when you get through as when you commence. At 3 Oclk P.M. I attended service in a small Chapel, attached to the Cathedral, which I understood was formerly one of the Cloisters of the old Monks; but it was a most ridiculous exhibition indeed—a complete burlesque on religious exercises. A few young, jolly, port wine faced looking fellows rattled thro' the service, laughing & grinning all the while, & they seemed to try to see which could get thro' with his part the quickest. As to audience there was no body present excepting a poor miserable old beggar & myself. I retired from this scene of folly & I might say of iniquity, with disgust; for who can be more depraved than those who professing to teach the gospel, make such a mockery of it.

In this Church are some very fine specimens of painted Glass. One can form some idea of its immense size from its being 560 ft in length. Canterbury all together is a very pleasant inland town, adorned with a fine public walk, & the houses well built. I was comfortably lodged that night, & the next morng. resumed my seat on the Coach. The Country thro' which we passed appeared well cultivated & the roads remarkably fine, & above all, the Coaches & horses. What a contrast between them & the French Diligences! But the weather was not pleasant & my object in stopping at Canterbury was defeated, for as I approached the great City the fog & smoke increased, & the number of Coaches which drove in all directions appeared to me to be almost innumerable. Being entirely alone, or more properly having no companions with me, & knowing none in London, I at first was at a loss where to go, accordingly I continued in the Coach, which drove across London Bridge, to Grace Church St. & then wheeled short into a back yard full of Stable boys, Porters, Coachmen & Coaches from every quarter. I at first thought of the England Coffee House; but also having often heard persons speak of Dicks C.H. I decided upon the latter, had a coach called & drove off.[5] Fortunately I arrived in time to take the last room in the house, & was very glad to get into some good quarters, after riding all day in the cold & wet. I must confess that I felt very lonesome, being in such an immense place, without a single companion, altho' I had been travelling so much, since leaving home & had resided in the great City of Paris. In fact to make travelling agreeable, a pleasant, intelligent, companion having the same views with yourself, is necessary. But to stroll around a large Town entirely alone, without any person to communicate with, is rather disheartening, at least it is so to me.

---

5. Opened in 1680, "Dick's [or Richard's] Coffee House" was located on Fleet Street near Temple Bar. Favored by country gentlemen, it stood there until 1899. There is no record of an "England Coffee House." JCB might have meant the "British Coffee House" in Charing Cross.

I dined to day at 7 & afterwards took a walk out altho' it was dark & rainy, but I was careful not to lose my way. The brilliancy of some of the Shops in the Strand attracted my attention & on my return homeward, I was accosted by some of the numerous prostitutes with which this great City abounds. Altho' I declined their solicitations, I could do no otherwise than give the poor creatures some pence to buy Gin, to keep out the cold. As it is probable that I shall now reside for a few weeks in London, I shall endeavor to note down, as occasion may offer, some of the daily occurrences. As to attempting to give a description of every thing wonderful in this mighty Town, I shall not do it; it would be too laborious, & I do not love labor & toil sufficiently well, to undertake such a herculean task.

March 19th. The weather continued unpleasant to day, but after breakfast I called at Messrs. Dickason's Counting House in West Broad St.[6] Knowing nothing of the City, I to day made use of Coach, so as to save time & not to lose my way.—Mr. D. was not within, but I saw Mr Nevett his partner, who received me very politely. After some conversation, in which he imparted a good deal of advice necessary to a stranger, we walked to my lodgings, where Mr N. introduced me to Mr Dorr, of Boston but who has resided in Europe many years. He is a bachelor & completely a man of the World. At the same time I became acquainted with Mr

6. Dickason and Company was the principal London correspondent of Brown and Ives. From the time of JCB's shipwreck in 1822 to the time of his departure from England in 1824, Dickason's business letters to Providence regularly carried brief reports on his activities.

Ellery & Mr Wyllys, both of Boston.[7] The views & objects of the latter Gentleman being the same as my own, we concluded to go in company to view the various Curiosities. I was much gratified with this circumstance, as Mr W. is a respectable Gentleman, keeps good Society & above all is a very great traveller, having just made the <u>complete</u> <u>tour</u> of the continent

20th. Thursday. It has rained continually to day & I have done almost nothing at all, excepting to eat & to drink—

Friday 21st. To day also it has been very thick & foggy. Mr. W[*yllys*] called but I was out. I saw Mr Nevett a few moments, & afterwards sauntered alone upon the royal Exchange but it not being 'Change hours, the number of people was not very great. The building out side has nothing at all striking, but within has a venerable, appearance. Around the Galleries are ornamented with statues of various Kings & Queens.[8]

22d. The Weather to day was as fine as they often have in London, & I improved the opportunity to visit Westminster Abbey. It is a place for which I have always had the greatest veneration & felt perhaps a greater desire to see that than any of the other Monuments here. The outside presents the most imposing

---

7. I have been unable to identify these three Bostonians, Mr. Dorr, Mr. Ellery, and Mr. Wyllys.

8. In 1823 the Royal Exchange at Threadneedle Street and Cornhill occupied buildings dating from the late seventeenth century that were later destroyed by fire.

appearance, & gives one a fine idea of Gothic Architecture. I spent more than 2 hours there meditating among the Tombs. I was determined to take it leisurely & to pay particular attention to every thing in this burial place of the Great.

It would be useless to name all those Tombs which attracted my attention. The Poets Corner was the most interesting, here are Tablets to most of the principal Bards of England. In this Quarter Handel, the Musician has a splendid Monument, & also one to Garrick, but of all the others in the Abbey I thought that to Lord Chatham the best adapted.[9] The number of Tombs in all is very great, some of which very ancient.

In a small chamber there were a few wax figures, large as life, Queen Elizh. In her State robes, Wm & Mary, & Ann.[10] That of Ann's I think is the finest countenance I almost ever saw, so much sweetness & good nature & that not without dignity. The painted Glass in the Abbey is considered remarkably fine, but I

---

9. George Frideric Handel (1685–1759), German-born, cosmopolitan master of baroque music, lived in England after 1712 and Anglicized the spelling of his name as given above. See below, p. 31, n. 6. David Garrick (1717–1779), the celebrated actor, was a less celebrated playwright. For a sample of his poetry, see below p. 50.

William Pitt (1708–1778), 1st earl of Chatham, pre-eminent British statesman of the mid-eighteenth century, was known as the "Great Commoner" and admired for his vigorous leadership in the Seven Years War (1756–1763). His figure in marble was executed by John Bacon (1740–1799).

10. Wax effigies of deceased sovereigns, wearing court dress, were borne to Westminster Abbey as part of their funeral processions. Many were stored there in the loft of Islip Chapel until removed from public view in 1841. Damaged during World War II, they were later restored and put on display in the Abbey's Norman Undercroft.

have not as yet seen any to please me so well as that at "Notre Dame" at Paris. I however dont pretend to be a judge in these things. I noticed the Tomb Stone of old Parr who died aged about 152 years & who lived during the reign of 8 Sovereigns—[1] I left the Abbey extremely well pleased with my visit & then wandered into St. James Park. Not feeling inclined to return to the City, I extended my walk thro' Hyde Park & Kensington Gardens, the further end of which I saw the palace of the Duke of Sussex—a common plain brick house, nothing at all to be compared to Mr J—on the hill in Providence.[2] As I returned thro' Hyde Park, I saw a good deal of fashionable Company, who had been taking the air. I continued on thro' H. P. place, St James' Street, Pall Mall, &c &c to my lodgings—At ½ past 5, I went to drive with Mr Nevett, where I met Mr Dickason, who I found to be a very pleasant man & who received me very kindly. There was present also a Mr Roach formerly of New Bedford, Mr W[yllys] & a Mr Stewart of Connecticut.[3] The Evening passed very pleasantly & after a

---

1. Thomas Parr (1483?-1635), a Shropshire farm worker, was killed by the kindness of Thomas Howard, earl of Arundel, who brought him to London and put him on exhibit.

2. Kensington Palace, once the residence of sovereigns from William III to George II, was thereafter divided into apartments for royal dukes and princesses. In 1823 one of these was occupied by Augustus, duke of Sussex (1773-1843), fifth son of George III. JCB probably saw only one wing, or one of its outbuildings, and so compared it unfavorably to the John Brown House, a grand but hardly palatial, private residence built in 1786-1789 on College Hill in Providence by his great-uncle.

3. I have been unable to identify Mr. Roach of New Bedford and Mr. Stewart of Connecticut.

game of whist I have come home & shall enjoy a good nights rest after the fatigues of the day—

23d. I have to day taken a long walk with Mr. W[yllys] to the Tower of London our object being merely to walk round its ramparts & view the inside of the Establishment—the tower part I mean for there are a number of houses within its walls & some quite long streets. It being Sunday we could not see the curiosities or Menagerie,[4] accordingly we attended service in the chapel & heard a very good Sermon delivered. The Officers and troops were present, & every thing was conducted with propriety & order. I shall take some other occasion to examine the secrets of this celebrated fortress—it is undoubtedly a formidable place, but I did not see many Cannon mounted, its great strength appears to consist in the deep & wide ditches which entirely surround it. These are filled with water from the Thames, & I should think that a small force could easily defend it from any popular tumult. The remainder of the day was spent in walking about in the City, & in the Evening I dined with Mr Dickason. He lives very fashionably & in a very fashionable part of the Town. Mrs D. is a very pleasant old lady, & he has but one Daughter, Mrs Hay, not handsome, but genteel in person. Mr G. I should suppose was a lawyer from his flippancy of tongue. Mr Wyllys was present & also an Oxford Student.—I forgot to mention that last Friday Evening I attended for the first time Drury Lane

---

4. The Royal Menagerie at the Tower of London was badly run-down in 1823. Its remaining animals were removed to the Zoological Gardens in 1835.

Theatre.[5] It was only a sacred concert, but I had an opportunity of hearing some very fine singing.—The celebrated pieces of the Creation by Hayden & Messiah by Handel were performed with great effect, & I heard the famous Miss Stephens [*sing*] that charming little song of "auld Robin Gray."[6] Miss S. is certainly a first rate singer & altogether a very pretty girl. Her form is small, with an expressive countenance. The other performers were more than good, particularly Mr Nicholson, who I think gave us as great a flute as I almost ever heard.[7] The outside of the old Drury, appears to be immense, but within it did not equal my expectation in point of size.—it has been lately fitted up, with a good deal of gilding work, but it is by no means so splendid as the Opera at Paris, & not much more so, if any than the first "Theatre francaise".[8] The Association of ideas which attend the old Drury fill the mind with very pleasing reflections; but this is the case with every thing I meet with in London, & would be through out all England.

---

5. The "New Theatre Royal, Drury Lane" had been built in 1811–1812, a reconstruction of the "Old Drury" which had burned down in 1809. Its seating capacity was roughly 2,000.

6. Since the mid-eighteenth century London theaters had regularly scheduled Lenten performances of sacred oratorios such as Handel's *Messiah* (1742) and Franz Josef Haydn's *The Creation* (1779). Secular relief was provided in March 1823 by Catherine Stephens (1794–1882), a dramatic soprano. Much admired for her repertory of folk songs, she joined the company at Drury Lane in 1822. See below, p. 33, n. 8.

7. Charles Nicholson (1795–1837), principal flautist of the Philharmonic Society, achieved an unusual tone by widening the lateral holes in his flute.

8. The Paris Opera or Académie royale de musique had moved into new

24th. To day I have been to see the famous Brew House of Barkly, Perkins & Co. in the Boro'.[9] These Establishments from their immense size, are among the greatest curiosities of London, & are visited by all foreigners, who have nothing of the Kind in their own Country. This of Barkelys is said to be the largest, for we were told the buildings of the Establishment cover 10 acres of land, & between 3 & 400 men of every description are employed constantly. As I do not sufficiently understand the process of brewing, I will not presume to give any detailed account of the operations of such an immense piece of machinery.—This has been done over & over again by abler & better hands. I will merely observe, that the whole is moved by the power of Steam. There are about 100 large vats, some of which are capable of containing 7000 barrels of beer. The number of granaries are 28, each of which contain 9000 bushels, & 170 horses are employed in the transportation of the beer, &c &c. What an immense capital it must take to carry on such an establishment but the wealth of England is beyond all calculation, her Merchants, Bankers & even Shopkeepers, rank in point of wealth among the Princes of

---

premises in 1821, shortly before JCB's visit to Paris. The older Théâtre Français was built in 1782–1783.

9. Barclay and Perkins, located in the Borough of Southwark, was named for its partners in 1781 when they bought it from the estate of Henry Thrale for £135,000. In 1815 it became the first brewery in London to reach an annual production of over 300,000 barrels. Its capital on deposit in 1823 was £636,565. It kept the name Barclay and Perkins until 1955 when it merged with Courage Ltd.

the Earth. This is the Brew House which formerly was the property of Thrale, the friend of Dr Johnson.

25th. After having walked thro' St James Park, down Piccadilly, thro' the Burlington Arcade[1] &c &c I parted from Mr W[*yllys*], but about 3 Oclk passing by St. Pauls, I saw the door's open & accordingly entered among a number of other people. I found they were performing Service, but as this was the first time I had ever been in this Splendid Cathedral, my attention was more taken up with viewing its magnificence & the numerous monuments it contained, than with the preaching. Every thing that has been said in praise of St Pauls, it certainly deserves. The dome is of immense hight, but as the day was not perfectly clear I did not ascend. From the Top, you have a complete view of London, better I understand than even from the Monument.[2]

It is not long since the Government first commenced burying in this Church, yet the number of Tombs, or more properly of Monuments are already numerous. That of the Great Nelson,

---

1. An architectural innovation completed in 1816, the Burlington Arcade, forerunner of twentieth-century malls, was a row of shops with a common roof and skylight. It was built on order of Lord George Cavendish to prevent passersby from throwing refuse into his grounds.

2. The inner dome of St. Paul's rose 225 feet above the pavement; the outer dome, some sixty feet higher. The Monument was a fluted Doric column 202 feet high. Designed by Sir Christopher Wren, it was built on order of Charles II in the 1670s to commemorate London's Great Fire of 1666. It stood on Fish Street Hill, a short distance from Pudding Lane where, according to popular belief, the fire started. It was hollow so visitors could climb a marble staircase to the top, which afforded a spectacular view of the city as rebuilt.

first attracted my attention, the only inscription upon it is this, "Copenhagen, Nile, Trafalgar." The hero is as large as life, & on his right is Britannia directing the attention of 2 young sailors to him for their example. I saw that of General Abercrombie, & also of the gallant Sir Jno Moore, who fell at Corrunna.[3] On some other occasion I shall visit St. Paul's again.

26th. As the weather was very disagreeable I only rambled a little in the City. Stopped in at "Lloyds"[4] to see the Ship news & then returned home, but in so doing I lost my way, & continued on from one St. to another, 'till I found myself near the "Monument" not far from London Bridge.—I had before seen this Commemoration of the great fire in 1666, but to day I viewed it attentively & read the inscription, which states that the fire was the work of the papists, be this as it may—it is none of my business.[5] This is considered by the English as a very splendid affair

---

3. Horatio Viscount Nelson (1758–1805) was memorialized here for his crushing defeats of enemy navies at Abukir Bay in the Nile delta (1798), at Copenhagen (1801), and off Cape Trafalgar (1805). His fame and popularity eclipsed those of other heroes of the Napoleonic wars, Ralph Abercromby (1734–1801) and Sir John Moore (1761–1809).

4. Lloyd's, opened as a coffee house in the 1690s, later became a center for the exchange and publication of shipping news as well as a market for marine insurance. In 1823 it was located in the Royal Exchange.

5. An inscription, added to the base of the Monument in 1681 on order of the city government, blamed the Great Fire on "the treachery and malice of the popish faction." This action was part of an anti-Catholic campaign to keep James, the Catholic duke of York, from succeeding his brother Charles II. Once enthroned in 1685, James II ordered the inscription obliterated. After

& no doubt it is considering the time of its erection, but it is nothing in comparison with the Column of Bronze in the place Vêndome at Paris.[6]

In the Evening of to day I went to Spring Gardens to view the Panorama of the coronation. It was well worth 2 s. & gave me a complete idea of that royal pageant. Many of the likenesses are from life. The whole is exhibited <u>in 5</u> separate views & is painted on <u>100 sq. ft.</u> of canvas.[7]

27th. I now begin to be somewhat acquainted with the bearings of this part of the Town, but London as a whole is such a Mamoth, overgrown place that it requires a long residence & much observation to know it well. In fact it is well known, that there are hundreds or thousands living in our part of London, who are no more acquainted with other parts than they are with the Emperor of China's dominions. A year or two's residence at least is requisite to know it thoroughly—It will be my object to <u>see</u> what I can, to <u>hear</u> & gain all the information that will be in my power. It would be much more satisfactory to me if I had some Companion, with the same views & objects as myself. For I find

---

his overthrow three years later, it was re-chiseled. In 1831, two years after Catholic Emancipation, it was again removed.

6. The Vendôme Column, erected in Paris (1805–1810) imitating Trajan's Column in Rome (113), was faced with a spiral of bronze plaques celebrating Napoleon's military victories in 1805. It was 143 feet high.

7. Spring Gardens was the name of several pleasure grounds in London. That in Knightsbridge had an exhibition hall which displayed such panoramas as that described by JCB.

that in these large Cities it is not so easy to make acquaintances as one would imagine, particularly among the English & the Americans too,—for they are both <u>equally</u> reserved.—I find, or rather hear of but few Americans travelling for pleasure. Most of them are young Drs. who come to study Medicine, who spend their time in a hospital, & generally reside in an out of the way part of the town, (this was the case at Paris & probably is so in London, with this difference that here are more "Business men"[)]. Now, unless you meet some one of these persons, on their <u>first arrival</u> their acquaintance is of but very little service to you, for if they have seen "the Lions"[8] of the place before you, they do not wish to spend their time & <u>money</u> to visit them the second time, & you certainly do not wish to ask them to do it. Of all the Curiosities at Paris, how few were there that I visited with an American? I there however, was fortunate in the society of an Englishman of learning & of consequence in his own Country, tho' it was only for a short time. After that I had an agreeable French Society in the family in which I lived.[9]

It unquestionably adds to the pleasure of travelling to be in connection with one of your own standing & as I have observed before, with the same views & objects as yourself—but as this is

---

8. Here as elsewhere in his diaries, JCB uses the word "lions" to refer not to celebrities but to tourist sights. This usage probably derived from the practice of taking visitors in London to see the lions caged at the Tower of London menagerie.

9. During the winter of 1822–1823, JCB was the occasional guest of the Parisian banker, Jean-Conrad Hottinguer (1764–1841), a principal correspondent of Brown and Ives in France. See Introduction and p. 4, n. 3, above.

not the case with me it will be my object in London to do as well as I can without. I find old Mr W[*yllys*] pleasant & intelligent & regret he leaves London so soon, he has travelled all over most of the Continent of Europe, & has seen such Society as all Americans do see,—his letters I know are from the first people in Boston & why should they not be? He is highly respectable & very wealthy.

As I have now got settled in London I shall make use of some of my introductory letters. It is to me a disagreeable office to perform, to impose upon others the necessity of paying me some attention, for in these larger places, oftentimes no notice is taken <u>at all</u> of such letters, & if there is, nine times out of ten, they are answered only by a formal, ceremonious dinner—& there ends your acquaintance, excepting perhaps a passing call, or a Card left at your door,—I however shall try it & wait the result. At any rate there can be no harm done.

I have extended my walk to day as far as the Tower, passing thro' the Jewry & Crutched Fryers.[1] The tower hill where formerly took place all the executions & where the Earl of Stafford[2] was beheaded, appeared to be nearly built over with houses, & the platform opposite the river on which Mr Silliman[3] mentions was a battery of 60 [*illeg.*] of Cannon, is now entirely destitute of

---

1. Jewry Street led to Crutched Friars Street. The first was once the site of tenements occupied by poor Jews. The other was named for a religious house of "Crossed Friars" founded in 1298.

2. Thomas Wentworth, earl of Strafford, was impeached in 1640 and beheaded on Tower Hill in 1641, events in a parliamentary coup that preceded the outbreak of civil war. JCB may have confused Strafford with William, first viscount Stafford who was beheaded on Tower Hill in 1680, a victim of religious hysteria.

3. Benjamin Silliman, *Journal of Travels in England, Holland and Scotland,*

any thing of the Kind.—Returning I passed thro' Lombard St. & stopped to notice the house which was formerly the residence of the celebrated Jane Shore, the beautiful mistress of Edward;[4] the house has the appearance of being very old tho' it has undergone repairs. The shop where her husband kept a Jeweller's shop is now occupied by a Boot Maker but 'tis said that until lately, it has always been kept by some Jeweller.

28. This is Good Friday & I have not been to Church as I intended to do. After breakfast I took a very long walk into the Boro', to call upon Dr Rippon.[5] I did not find him at home, but left the letter & my card.—Towards Evening I went to promenade in St. James' & Hyde Park's. It was rather late before I arrived but as it was a holy day, there were a good many Bucks & fashionables.— For a simple observer like myself, these things are as good as a play.

29th. Having resolved to commence the delivery of my letters of introduction I to day went to the Middle Temple to see Mr Price having a letter from his Brother who is married to a friend of mine in America, he not being at home I left the letter with my

---

3rd ed. (New Haven, 1820) I, pp. 177–178. Silliman noted the battery of sixty-one nine-pounders was fired only on ceremonial occasions. On Silliman's book, see Introduction.

4. Jane Shore (d. 1527?), a native of London and wife of a goldsmith, in 1470 became the mistress of Edward IV (1442–1483) and of several courtiers after Edward's death.

5. John Rippon (1751–1836), a prominent hymnologist and Baptist minister, sympathized with the colonies during the American War of Independence and was awarded (in absentia) an honorary D. D. by Rhode Island College in 1792.

Card, as I understand this is the style in London.[6] After which, went to call on Messrs. Dunlop,—was received. as well as could be expected; then upon Messrs. J & A to whom I had a letter from Mr Bethune of N York.[7] Mr A, the particular friend. of Mr B. was not within. Mr J. was a broad mouthed Scotch man most literally.[8] What the result of these letters will be time will determine.—I do not expect however any thing more than a Dinner; & <u>perhaps</u> I may not get that.

30th. Sunday. To day I went to attend Service in Westminster Abbey, but it was late before I arrived & accordingly lost all the fine music. A Sermon was preached by the Bishop of Exeter, [1] but it appeared to be a cold, heartless discourse, & the "good man" seemed to have more in view the good dinner which he would shortly eat, than of the Sermon he was then preaching— judging from the manner in which he hurried thro' it. At 3 OClk: I called upon Mr D[*ickason*] who took Mr Mason of Boston & myself in his carriage to see our Minister Mr Rush.[2] He resides

---

6. I have been unable to identify Mr. Price and the Messrs. Dunlop as well as Messrs. J & A who are mentioned in this passage.

7. Divie Bethune, a business associate of Brown and Ives, was born in Scotland in 1771. He emigrated in 1792 to New York where he prospered as a merchant.

8. "Broad-mouthed" was a term commonly used to describe Scots who spoke with a particularly thick or broad accent.

1. William Carey (1769–1846) had been attached to Westminster Abbey before he became bishop of Exeter in 1820. In 1830 he was translated to St. Asaph.

2. Richard Rush (1780–1859) was United States minister to the Court of St. James (1817–1825). JCB's companion on this Easter visit was probably Jonathan Mason (1795–1884) of Boston.

some little distance from town, on an eminence commanding a fine view of London, where he has a neat little snug box. We only saw my lady, Mr R. being out.—The fact is, our national representative is obliged to live in the Country, as his salary will not admit of his keeping up a town Establishment, for what is £2000 to a man living in style & fashion in London, & what footing can he keep with the other Ambassadors who have an income perhaps of 10 or 20 times that sum,—besides their own princely fortunes.[3] London seems to be extending itself on all sides, & notwithstanding the great outcry of distress, every part of England, is rapidly improving & the population augments apace. In the Evening: I dined in a sociable way with Mr D[ickason] this Mr M[ason] I find is an artist, or pretends to be one, what little I saw of him pleased me much, & I hope that this acquaintance will prove more useful than some others which I have made in Europe,—unfortunately he is considerably deaf, but perhaps this has been the means of correcting that boldness, & hauteur of manner which is too often prevalent among the Bostonians of fortune.

31.—Easter Monday being a celebrated annual fair at Greenwich, Mr W[yllys] & myself concluded we should like to see how they managed matters of this kind in England.[4] So we took a small

---

3. Minister Rush complained of his straitened finances in correspondence with President Madison. JCB's estimate of an income sufficient for the upper levels of English society is close to that of the earl of Durham: "…£40,000 a year, a moderate income—such a one as a man might jog on with." See *Creevey Papers*, ed. Hebert Maxwell, 2 vols. (London, 1903), letter, September 13, 1821.

4. Greenwich Fair in the 1820s was recalled by Charles Dickens as a "sort of

boat at the Tower Steps & went down by water, which gave me a chance of viewing the immense navigation on the Thames & wonderful it was, for we sailed thro' shipping without number & the river appeared to be one entire field of masts, & yet we saw nothing of the vast numbers of East & West India shipping, for they were all in the Docks.—This it is which supports the great power of England; contributing to her wealth & defence. On our arrival at Greenwich we found there were already collected a great crowd of people of all sorts & sizes. Cooks, Scullions & Chamber Maids, Apprentice boys & Milliners; Soldiers & Sailors (with their girls) & Sharpers & pick-pockets, without number, whose business it is to assemble on like occasions.—This host of Idlers amused themselves with the mountebanks & showmen, who were there in great numbers. Towards the close of the day as the multitudes began to wax warm with fun & liquor the crowd became very great in the Park where they amused them-selves with rolling or running down hill, which is a very ancient pastime & always observed on these occasions. As for ourselves we were in every part of the village—determined to see the whole performance. Sometimes we were in the middle of the crowd, where a general hustle took place,—there it was that every thing & every body were "higgledy piggledy", helter skelter, some here, some there, girls screaming, men swearing, & old women turned over, with all their apples & merchandize rolling about the Sts. But any description would fall far short of the reality of such a

---

spring rash, a three days' fever which cools the blood for six months after-ward." See *Sketches by Boz* (1836), "Scenes, xii."

scene. Many or most of the houses & taverns were crowded with people drinking & dancing & we found a great many of the Londoners of fashion, who were here like us, seeing the sport & having a little bit themselves.—We returned in the evening by land, but the crowd had by no means diminished, & I suppose they will keep it up all night, as is generally usual. Of course I had no time to visit the Hospital, but I shall by no means omit seeing this celebrated Establishment for, some time hence, I shall go down & spend a day in Greenwich to see the various curiosities.[5]

April 1st. Slept rather late this morning being very much fatigued with yesterday's operations. found that Mr Coster a Gentleman I had seen in Paris had arrived[6]—after breakfast walked out with him & took a look in the park—then lounged a little while in Bond St. & returned home—at 2 Called on the Reverend Mr Ivimey with a letter from Dr Carter;[7] unfortunately he was laying ill & I did not see him—left the letter with his wife.—Met Mr Nevett & walked on 'Change with him;[8] he pointed out & explained to me

---

5. The Royal Hospital, Greenwich, had been a royal palace. It was made over as a naval hospital by Sir Christopher Wren by order of Mary II after she had seen the suffering of sailors wounded in a naval battle in 1692.

6. Most likely a member of Coster Brothers and Company, a New York firm which did business with Brown and Ives.

7. Joseph Ivimey (1773–1834), a prominent Baptist minister and historian, was chosen pastor of the Baptist church, Eagle Street, Holborn in 1804. He was active in missionary organizations and the anti-slavery movement. Benjamin Bowen Carter (1771–1831) was JCB's maternal uncle. See Introduction.

8. The phrase "on 'Change" meant "at the Exchange" (see p. 8, n. 8 above). The different areas where business was conducted there were called "walks."

the various walks, & the most considerable merchants then on 'Change—the mode of transacting business; negotiating bills of Exchange &c. &c. Dined & spent the Evening with Mr N.—He keeps house tho' a bachelor & lives in very handsome style. Like most English- men he loves his bottle of Port, & is always very lavish of it to his friends—

2nd. This Evening for the first time, I attended the "Theatre royal Covent Garden"[9] the house itself appeared larger than Drury Lane, tho' not so magnificent,—it was by no means well lighted, & the play that was performed was exceedingly dull & stupid; it was the new Tragedy of Julian.—Mr Mcready was the only Actor above ordinary, & as for the actresses they were nothing more than good middling.[1]—I have often seen plays performed in Providence where every part has been better supported than this Evening—the Salons of Covent Garden were also very inferiour for a house of this size. nothing to be compared with those at the great Theatres in Paris. The Company this evening was not at all brilliant.

3d. To day I attended the Lord mayor's Court in the "Mansion House", where I had the pleasure of seeing his Lordship dis-

---

9. The Royal Opera House, Covent Garden, had been rebuilt after a destructive fire and reopened in 1809. Modeled on a Greek temple, it too had to be rebuilt after a fire in the 1850s.

1. William Charles Macready (1793–1873) acknowledged that the Covent Garden production of *Julian* by Mary Mitford in March 1823, was at best a "moderate success" because of its weak supporting cast. See his *Reminiscences* (London, 1875), I, ch. 17.

pense justice in a pretty summary manner.[2] The object of this Court is only for the <u>first</u> examination of such persons as may be apprehended the night previous; or such as may be summoned by his Lordship to answer to any charges which may be alleged against them. The first case I heard was that of a very dirty fellow, a porter, who was charged by some Shop Keeper, for taking more than the rates allowed; his case was soon finished, by a fine of 5 shillings. The next was a most infamous, wretched looking woman, one of the lowest order of prostitutes. she was charged with making a noise in the Sts. & assaulting the neighbours. Notwithstanding she plead hard that she would never do the like again, she was sent off to Bridewell for a month.[3] The last case that I heard was that of a very genteel looking young fellow. he was brought up on a charge of stealing sundry goods from a Shop. After a good many questions in which he appeared much confused he was sent to New Gate to be tried the next assizes for his life, as theft is a capital crime in this Country.

From the Mansion House, we went to "Guild Hall" this is the famous hall where the great dinner is held on the Lord Mayors day.[4] It is really very large & capable of containing a great many

---

2. The lord mayor of London in 1823 was William Heygate (d. 1844), a banker. Police court sessions were held in Mansion House, the lord mayor's official residence.

3. Bridewell was a prison for those convicted of such minor offenses as prostitution or vagrancy. (See diary entry for August 6, 1824.) It was abolished when the City Prison was built in 1863. Newgate was a prison for major offenders which was abolished in 1902. Until 1868 executions were held outside its walls.

4. Built in the fifteenth century, Guildhall was used as a meeting place by the

persons. The two famous statues of Gog & Magog are here to be seen, & the hall is also ornamented with monuments erected to the memory of the Earl of Chatham & and his son Wm Pitt.[5] There is likewise a splendid monument to Nelson, & one to Mr Beckford, twice Lord Mayor of London, & who is so famous for the speech which he made to Geo: the 3d. The speech is given at length under the monument. We saw after this, the Council Chamber,—here are various portraits of Admirals and Generals & a view of the destruction of the Spanish flotilla before Gibraltar.—Having previously seen this celebrated rock, I took a good deal of satisfaction viewing the painting knowing as I did all its various bearings.

There are no pieces of sculpture worth naming excepting a full length statue of Geo: 3d. by Chantry.[6] To his left hangs a fine

---

Corporation of London and became the center of municipal government. The tall wooden figures of Gog and Magog represented two legendary giants whose struggle preceded the founding of Albion's capital city in 1000 B.C. Those seen by JCB were carved in 1708 and destroyed during the blitz of 1940. They were later replaced by smaller versions.

5. The practice of erecting monuments to national heroes in this center of local government did not begin until the late eighteenth century. The statue of Chatham went up in 1782, that of Nelson in 1810, and that of Pitt the Younger in 1813. They were preceded by the statue of William Beckford (1709–1770) who was twice lord mayor of London in the 1760s. A Jamaica-born tycoon, Beckford was a partisan of John Wilkes's popular reform movement. As lord mayor he outraged George III by a protest against the king's curt dismissal of a remonstrance from the Corporation of London. The statue in his honor was intended as a silent rebuke to the king.

6. Francis Legatt Chantrey (1781–1841), a prominent portrait sculptor whose works include a statue of George Washington in the State House, Boston.

full length painting of the late Princess Charlotte, from all accounts & certainly from the portrait she was a most lovely woman, & no Englishman mentions her name without being full of her praise. On the other side of the old King is the portrait of the late Queen Caroline; she is here made to be a tolerable handsome woman. Alas poor creature, she now like the rest of us all after death, begins to be almost forgotten.[7] The Courts were not sitting in Guildhall at the time I was there, but I shall go some time, to see how they manage business here.

Today I also looked into the "bank" [and] the "Bullion office" there is nothing worth mentioning that I saw connected with these Establishments.[8] The bank comprises a number of different apartments & of course a vast number of clerks must be employed in the transaction of all their business. The building itself is not at all striking from without, it is very low & has no windows being lighted from a skylight. But this remark would perhaps apply to almost all the public buildings in London. They are generally so much confined & so surrounded by other

---

7. Princess Charlotte Augusta (1796–1817), only legitimate child of George, prince of Wales, was his heiress apparent until her untimely death. Her mother, Caroline of Brunswick (1768–1821), married George in 1795. Caroline's misfortunes included her marriage, scandalous divorce proceedings in the House of Lords in 1820, and exclusion from Westminster Abbey when her husband was crowned George IV in 1821. On Charlotte, see below, p. 34, n. 1.

8. A cluster of financial and business offices, located in or near the Bank of England, included the Bullion Office and the Auction Mart. The latter, built in 1808–1810, to house public sales, was razed in 1865. The original Royal Exchange building was destroyed by the Great Fire; the second, opened in 1669, burned down in 1838.

houses, that they do not shew to advantage. I looked in to the Auction mart & Stock Exchange as I was passing to day. The former is only a plain building erected for the better accomodation of the Auctioneers. It was too late for the Exchange but I shall go again, & have something more to say about it hereafter. In the Evening I attended the Olympic Theatre, Wych St. The performance consisted altogether of the acting of a Frenchman, Mr. Alexander. He indeed shew astonishing powers in Ventriloquism & carried on an entire play & amused the Audience, without the least assistance, from any one else.—This is so much the more wonderful, from his being a foreigner.[9]

4th. Another dark & dismal day—did not arise very early.—In the Evening went with Mr. C[*oster*] of New York, to the Theatre at "Sadlers Wells", where we saw "Dr. Syntax" performed with other entertainments. The Evening closed with a display of "Russian mountains". When there is to be a performance of Aquatic exhibitions I shall make it a point to attend, as this place has ever been famous for representations of this sort.[1]

---

9. "Monsieur Alexandre" was the stage name of Nicholas Marie Vattemare (1796–1864). The leading ventriloquist of his time, he drew tributes and testimonials from Beethoven, Sir Walter Scott, and Victor Hugo as well as from the crowned heads of Europe.

1. *Dr. Syntax* opened in London on March 31, 1823, billed as a "comic, heroic, operatic, farcical, theatrical, poetical extravaganza in three acts." Its hero, Dr. Syntax, was a caricature created by the illustrator, Thomas Rowlandson (1756–1827) and the satirist William Combe (1741–1823), in a series of books that parodied the "picturesque" travel writing popular at the turn of the century. The "Russian Mountains" was an interlude in which the performers and

5th. The rain still continuing I did not move about much.—Dined at 5, rather earlier than usual,—then went to the "Italian Opera". This is a famous building outside, & perhaps shews as well as any other public edifice in London. The interiour is also very spacious but is not at all to be compared in point of splendour to the "Academie royale de Musique" at Paris.[2] The music was very fine & the singing in the first rate style, as also the dancing, for almost all the dancers, at least all the principal ones are French. One of the pieces performed, was "Alfred le grand, roi d'Angleterre" I had previously seen this same piece at Paris, & altho' this Evening: the decorations, the "Scenery & machinery" as they call it, were all very sumptious, yet I must give the palm to the French. They unquestionably have the most tast[e] & understand better the arrangement of all these things than any other people. The Opera is The place of amusement where none but the "nobility and gentry" attend, or at least those who call themselves genteel. The Boxes are all private property, or are hired for the Season by the "fashionables", & none are allowed to enter the Pitt, [*sic*] except in "full dress" that is to say: the gentleman with shoes and short coats, & the Ladies with as little

---

volunteers from the audience slid down inclined planes stretching from the back of the stage to the pit. Sadler's Wells Theatre also had a tank for the presentation of aquatic spectacles such as "The Siege of Gibraltar."

2. King's Theatre, also known as the Royal Italian Opera House, located in the Haymarket, had a capacity of 3,300. Box-holders paid up to £2,500 for the season. On April 5, 1823, the program included Mozart's *Le Nozze di Figaro* as well as *Alfred le Grand, Roi d'Angleterre*, a ballet danced by a French company. On the Académie royale de musique, see p. 12, n. 8.

upon their heads & shoulders as possible.[3] Here the English sit four or five hours, grinning & gasping, & no doubt do their best to enjoy an amusement of this kind.—Some even go so far as to effect to understand Italian music but it is all in vain, & tho' they lavish vast sums upon a train of Eunuchs & French and Italian whores, yet it is only for the sake of being called fashionable. While the audience were retiring a fellow was sized as a pick pocket. He was detected in the very act of stealing a Gentlemans gold Snuff Box. He was well dressed, & looked as much like a gentleman as any one in the Theatre.—He was carried off to the Watch house.[4] One ought to be very careful how they expose their money or watches in London, you will find rogues & swindlers wherever you go. For my part I generally carry but very little money about me & in the Evening always take care to tuck in my Watch chain.

6th. Sunday. Altho' it did not rain, yet it was very dark & the weather extremely chilly breakfasted late—spent 2 hours in a Bath house,—dined alone in a Chop House for ½ d. Having occasion to go into the Upper part of the Town, I passed thro' "Cock Lane", not far from Little Britain. This is famous as having been the residence of "the Ghost of Cock lane". 'Tis a long narrow, dark, dismal place, & I should suppose a fit residence only for a

---

3. Since the mid-eighteenth century fashion dictated that gentlemen wear shoes rather than boots to places of public entertainment with ladies present.

4. The watch-house was a station where night-watchmen detained disorderly persons pending arraignment.

Ghost.[5] At candlelight, I saw the Chapel of the "foundling hospitle" lit up.—Curiosity led me to go in, where I heard the Organ that was given to the Establishment by the great Handel. The little foundlings were arranged on either side of the Organ, & sung most delightfully. they were all neatly dressed, & <u>of course</u> must be contented & happy, for they know nothing of the troubles of this world, & their minds are not yet harrassed and irritated by the conflicting interest of ambition. I intend examining hereafter this humane foundation, for objects of this kind certainly deserve the attention of every traveller.[6]

7th. This Morning the rain poured down in torrents, & at 12 oclk: when I sat down to write, I could hardly see without a Candle. 'Tis now three weeks since I have been in London, & altho' I have been from home nearly a year & without any particular companion, yet I confess I sometimes feel the want of one in this immense

---

5. Cock Lane was reportedly visited by a ghost that made rapping noises audible only to an eleven-year-old girl. It created a sensation early in 1762 and attracted visits from Horace Walpole and Samuel Johnson who later exposed it as an imposture. Oliver Goldsmith and Charles Churchill ridiculed both public and literary interest.

Little Britain was a narrow, winding street, once the center of the book trade. Washington Irving described it in his *Sketch Book* (1819–1820: "Little Britain") as a quiet, run-down neighborhood.

6. The Foundling Hospital in Guilford Street, a fashionable charity, opened in 1739 for "deserted children." It later took in illegitimate children whose mothers were known. George Frideric Handel donated the score of *Messiah* as well as a pipe organ to the Hospital where he occasionally conducted performances of his music. See p. 9, n. 9.

City. Merchants & professional men to whom a stranger may have letters, cannot be of much service to you; if they return your call, & give you a dinner, they have then done what the rules of Society demand of them, but this occupies a miserably small portion, of the time you spend among them.

But I dont happen to have been even so fortunate as all this; for three of the introductory letters which I have delivered (& it is more than a week) have been taken no notice of, altho' one was to a commercial house which told me they formerly had some correspondence with B[*rown*] & I[*ves*]. The other to a Baptist minister to whom B[*rown*] U[*niversity*] has given a D.D. & the third was much more pressing than either of the others, to pay me some attention.[7] I have some other letters in my trunk, but hardly think I shall deliver any more of them.[*] In the Evening I went to Drury Lane Theatre. It was the benefit night of Miss Clara Fisher, a little girl of about 12 years old, & who I think might well be counted as one of the wonders of the age. The house was crowded to overflowing, & the audience testified how much they were satisfied with her performance, indeed it is really astonishing, how great are the powers of this child,—I might say that in every respect she was perfect, for her conception of the character she was acting was equal to that of any veteran of the stage; her articulation was clear & distinct, & she went thro' with

*Since writing the above, one of the persons referred to has called & left a card. It was Mr D—.

7. See p. 34, n. 2.

all her parts without the least hesitation. How would old Sheridan have felt, could he have been present last Evening & have seen "Isaac Mendoza" in "the Duenna" personated in so masterly a style. Besides this she sings most sweetly, danses, plays on the Castanets speaks French, all far beyond what could be expected from one so young.[8]

Miss Stephens & Braham also performed in "the Duenna" & of <u>course</u> gave us some fine singing. Miss S. appears to be a charming girl, setting aside her great vocal powers. All together I have scarcely ever been more satisfied with a Theatrical exhibition than I was this Evening. I would most willingly give a guinea to see the same repeated.

8th. Hearing that there was to be some fine cocking to day, I went at 3 oclk: to attend a match at the "Royal Cock Pit, Tufton St. Westminster".[9] There were seven matches fought & considerable sums lost & won on each. I had once before seen a cock fight at Cadiz it was not a new thing to me, neither did I go for

---

8. An "infant phenomenon," Clara Fisher (1811–1898) made her stage debut at the age of six and, while still a child, played lead roles (Shylock, Richard III) opposite some of the foremost actors of the time. In this performance of Richard Sheridan's *The Duenna*, she appeared with two of the best singers on the London stage: Catherine Stephens (see p. 12, n. 6 above) and John Braham (1774–1856), a durable tenor whose singing career lasted sixty years. On April 7, 1823, *The Duenna* was followed by *Bombastes Furioso* and *The Actress of All-Work*.

9. The Royal Cock-pit on Tufton St., displaying the royal coat of arms, opened in 1821, a testimonial to the continuing popularity of cock-fighting long after bear- and bull-baiting had disappeared as public amusements.

the sport of the thing, but merely to see how they manage such things in England. The company was pretty numerous & judging from the dress & the Sir James' & Sir Charles' who were present, it would be called "respectable," but Cock fighting is a barbarous & to me a very uninteresting amusement, yet the "Amateurs" seem to take a great relish in this kind of fun. In the Evening I went with Mr C[*oster*] of NYK to the Royal Coburgh Theatre in the Boro.' This is a very neat Play House, & in the interiour they seem to have imitated the French fashion, that is, to have a sort of balcon in front of the Boxes. The Salon of the Coburgh is adorned with the full length portraits of the Prince C—& the late Princess Charlotte, as Patron & Patroness of the Theatre.[1]

9th. Made a few calls this Morning & after 'change hours went in "Bishop Gate St. within" & presented a letter of introduction which I had to the house of Baring Brothers & Co.—Saw Mr Holland of the House, who received me very politely, much more so than any other person to who I have delivered any.[2]

---

1. The Royal Coburg Theatre was founded in 1816 under the patronage of Princess Charlotte (see p. 27, n. 7, above) and her consort, Prince Leopold of Saxe-Coburg (1790–1865), future king of the Belgians. In 1833 the theater was renamed the Victoria Theatre, later known as "Old Vic." The program for April 8, 1823, announced a "grand historical, military, melodramatic spectacle" called *The Siege of Saragossa* or *The French in Spain* and a "Russian melodrama" entitled *Lowina of Tobolski* or *The Fatal Snow Storm.*

2. Swinton Colthurst Holland (d. 1827), earlier a Liverpool merchant, became a partner in Baring Brothers and Company in 1815 and the bank's general manager thereafter. His cordial reception of JCB contrasts with his general

10th. Walked up Picadilly—into Hyde Park, &c &c.—Spent 2 or 3 hours at the "Old Bailey" during which time I saw half a dozen cases disposed of; they were all for theft, but as the Laws of this Country are very severe & make it capital to steal 40s. They were pronounced "guilty"—but recommended to mercy. In which case they will be sent off to Botany Bay—the Lord Chief Justice Abbott presided. He appears to be a mild, good natured man, & possesses great powers of dispatching business.[3]

11th. Mr D[orr?] called upon me before I went out this morning & we then walked into the City & took a look into "Lloyd's" afterwards I spent the day in the "Old Bailey Court" & heard a number of causes disposed of.

12th. —————————————————————

13th. Called at 11 upon Mr D[orr?] & went with him to attend service in the Foundling Hospital. The little Children gave us some very fine music; the chapel was crowded & as it is customary to give a shilling at the door I think the funds of the Establishment must be in the course the year be very considerably benefited.

---

reputation for hostility toward Americans. His brusque treatment of John Jacob Astor cost Baring Brothers that customer's business.

3. Old Bailey was the seat of the Central Criminal Court in London. Charles Abbott (1762–1832), after 1827 first baron Tenterden, was the son of a Canterbury barber. A legal scholar with a flourishing practice, he became chief justice of the King's Bench in 1818. His impatience with legal niceties and his moderate judgments were sometimes attributed to his humble origins.

The Expenses however of such a Charity as this, must be very heavy, as in England every thing of this Kind must be conducted in a certain Style, or it will not take, & besides the expenses of every thing in this Country are so enormously great, for a man in London with £1000 a year is on no better footing than one in Providence. with £300. After church we looked into the interior of the Building & saw the little ones at dinner, the two sexes in different apartments. The victuals were very plain (good boiled beef & potatoes) but very neatly served up, on wooden plates. their drink apeared to be a sort of beer. On the whole every thing was well conducted & the children seemed happy. The long dining halls were ornamented with different portraits of distinguished benefactors, & the names of all those who have contributed to the funds are annually painted on a board with the respective Sums affixed to their names, & hung upon the wall, so you will see the names of all its patrons for the last century. In the Evening I dined with Mr Holland of the house of Baring Bs & Co. There were only two Gentlemen present besides the family of Mr. H. a Mr R of Phila. & Mr B. an Agent for a house in Naples. The eldest daughter appears to be a fine girl. The rest are mere children. Every thing passed off as is usual on such occasions, & probably here will be an end to my acquaintance with this famous commercial house excepting that I shall make a few morning calls upon Mr H's family according to custom. On the whole it is a difficult thing even when one has first rate letters to get into good society in London, there is so much ridiculous calling & sending of cards, & even so much form & ceremony when you do meet that society is hardly worth the trouble of seeking. This perhaps may be owing in great measure to the over-grown size of the City which renders it very inconvenient getting about, & perchance when it is a pleasant day every body goes out at the Same hour. Of course, no body is found at home. As I have before observed, I shall continue as I began to see and make myself acquainted with the principal curiosities & leading features of London. I could wish that I was more particularly acquainted with some good companion, with the same views as myself. However this is not the case, so nothing more on this Subject.

14th April 1823 ——————————

15th. After breakfast took a walk into the Strand, & sat to have my profile taken in bronze; afterwards visited "the royal National Menagerie, Exeter 'Change, Strand".[4] Here are a large collection of beasts & birds, an Elephant in particular, who knows about as much as half the human species. 'Tis astonishing how tractable this animal becomes by kind usage. I also saw the famous serpent the "Boa Constrictor" from India, it is not at all of the venomous tribe, but kills his prey by squeezing them to death, & has been known to attack & vanquish even the Tygre. He swallows alive two or three fowls at a meal—At 3 oclk: called on Mr P[*rice*] of the Inner Temple, to show I had a letter from his brother in America, & walked with him all over the West End of the town. This Gentleman is just such a person that a stranger in London wishes to become acquainted with. He pointed out all the resi-

---

4. Pidcock's Menagerie was located at Exeter 'Change.

dences of the distinguished personages of the City, & gave me a great deal of other useful information. In the course of our walk, we went into the great banking house of Coutts & Co. (Mr P. having some little business there)[5]

---

5. A private bank, Coutts and Company had a well-established reputation as the bank of the landed classes. In *The Gondoliers* (1889) W. S. Gilbert's Marco sings about "the Aristocrat who banks with Coutts / The Aristocrat who hunts and shoots."

Book Two

August 21 to September 7, 1823
ENGLAND

IN COMPANY WITH Mr R. H. Ives, left London in the light-coach at ½ past 8 AM. The weather remarkably fine; passed nothing particularly worthy of observation excepting the neat Box of the Earl of Southhampton & the Devils Punch Bowl.[1] In the afternoon had frequent showers of rain, & arrived at Portsmouth at 6. After dinner we walked all around the place & took a general view of the harbour. Took a very refreshing warm salt water bath & then went to bed—slept sound. The Weather to day was as unpleasant as I have as yet known it in England—an incessant rain, yet notwithstanding this we visited the whole of the interiour of the Royal Dock yard, viewed particularly: the rope walk, nearly ¼ mile in length; the smith shops for the making of Anchors, &c, the Block makers shop; the long range of

---

1. The first earl of Southhampton, Thomas Wriothesley (d. 1550), in 1538 bought a former monastic house in Hampshire which was converted into a hunting lodge.

The Devil's Punch Bowl in Surrey had been visited earlier in August by William Cobbett who described it as "a singular space which resembles a sugar loaf, inverted, hollowed out and only an outside rim left." (*Rural Rides*, August 7, 1823). Elsewhere he pronounced it "certainly the most villainous spot God ever made."

anchors for the heaviest ship, (about 5 tons) &c, &c.—Then took a boat & sailed up into the harbour,—view'd many first rate ship's in ordinary.[2] Went on board the royal yacht & the Queen Charlotte 110 gun ship. She is moored in the harbour with chain cables & is the flag ship. Met on board Mr White, a midshipman in the navy, a gentleman with whom I became acquainted in Boulogne (sur-Mer). Rain continuing all the while we dined early. In the dry docks within the yard, I noticed several ship's of the first class, & also the Victory, the flag ship of Lord Nelson undergoing repairs—[3]

Arose early & visited the Ordnance department. Saw the Congreve rockets & other like instruments of death.[4] On the wharf were piled up the great guns of the Ship's in ordinary. Among others I noticed with satisfaction those of the Victory.— Portsmouth is a mean town & is not at all interesting: except for its being the naval Emporium of Britain. It contains about 7000

---

2. Ships "in ordinary" were those which were out of service or de-commissioned. Royal yachts were introduced to Britain by Charles II and his brother, James, when the monarchy was restored in 1660. On that occasion the Dutch Estates General presented Charles with the *Mary*, a *jaght schip*, modeled on one he had favored while in exile.

3. The *Queen Charlotte* was launched in 1810, later used as a training ship, and sold in 1872. The *Victory* was launched in 1765, rebuilt in 1801 and preserved as a memorial to Admiral Nelson. I have been unable to identify Mr. White.

4. Rockets invented by Sir William Congreve (1772–1828) were designed as a substitute for artillery in land and sea battles with Napoleon. They were also used against American forces at Bladensburg, Maryland, and at New Orleans during the War of 1812. An early and inaccurate form of missile warfare, they were abandoned later in the century.

inhabitants a great proportion of whom are females. After break-fast took the packet for Ryde in the Isle of Wight, & were landed in about an hour; distance 7 miles. Had a full view of Spithead roads, a number of Ships of war & others at anchor. Ryde is pleasantly situated & as a watering place much visited by people of fashion. At 11 AM. took a Gig for Newport, distance 8 miles.—the ride a most delightful one indeed. most of the way in full view of the sea, & the Country all hill & dale. Newport is not pleas-antly situated being low & surrounded by hills.—Visited Carrisbrooke Castle, about a mile distant. It stands on a very ele-vated spot; but is now entirely in ruins; 'tis one of the most ancient in the Kingdom, & is supposed to be built in the 6th. century. It contains about one ½ acres within the walls & 20 sur-rounded by a broad, deep ditch. Its entrance is through 2 larger portals, the outer built in the reign of Elizabeth & the other in that of Edward 4. We ascended the old battlements from whence there is a most extensive view in fine weather, but today it was very foggy.[5] The well also is really curious, being 300 ft. deep, & 220 to the water. A light was let down & tho' so far beneath the surface, the air was sufficient to preserve it. Water thrown down is 4 seconds going to bottom. An ass or Donkey is employed to drain the water. I saw one which is hob[*bled*] & has been for the last 27 years worked for this purpose. The part where was for-merly the Chamber of Charles 1st. & the window thru' which he

---

5. JCB's description of Carisbrooke Castle repeats that of Benjamin Silliman, *Journal of Travels etc.*, 3rd ed. (New Haven, 1820), II, pp. 223–226. On Silliman, see Introduction.

tried to escape is shewn, but like all the rest it is now in ruins & the halls are moss grown & covered with Ivy.[6]—After dinner we took various walks around in the neighbourhood of Newport. The scenery around is delightful & the Country well cultivated. Newport has 5000 inhabitants.

(Sunday) Augt. 24th. 1823. Having determined to make an excursion to some of the romantic spots which the Isle affords, we started in a gig at 9 AM. altho. the weather was by no means promising, & indeed in a few minutes the rain commenced. We continued however our ride & passed the village of Carrisbrook, & proceeding in a Westerly direction, passed Shorewell, but we could not enjoy the scenery much for the rain began to pour in a deluge & on our arrival at Brixton we thought best to [*illeg*]. In an hours time we renewed our junket, when the rain had stopped, & passing over the Downs of Brooke, enveloped in a cloud of fog, we arrived at Freshwater, distance 14 miles from Newport. It had now become clear, & the sun was out a little, so we continued on foot along the white chalky cliffs 3 miles to "the Needles," the most western extremity of the Island. From this point we had a most charming view of the channel & the Island, with the bay

---

6. Charles I was put under guard in June 1647 by parliamentary forces and transferred from Hampton Court to Carisbrooke Castle in the custody of Col. Robert Hammond, governor of the Isle of Wight. In March 1648, Charles tried to escape through a window but could not slip between the mullion and an iron bar. This and other failed attempts to escape, together with his continued encouragement of resistance to parliamentary authority, led to his trial and execution early in 1649.

of Yarmouth & the opposite Coast of Britain. Returning the same direction we reached Freshwater at 2, & after dinner resumed our route, passing in full view of Yarmouth on our left & thro' Calburn we arrived again at Newport at 6 P.M. The Sun was out very bright during the afternoon & the prospect perhaps as enchanting as any one could wish. So on the whole considering the unfavourable circumstances under which we started, we had a very agreeable time of it. At 7 took our seats on the coach for Cowes & just as it became dark, we entered the town, the moon rising in her strength.—The evening was enchanting: & Mr I & myself walked on the spacious wharf fronting the channel or Solent. Cowes contains 3000 inhabitants, & the whole number on the Isle of Wight are about 21,000.

Monday. 5th day out. After breakfast employed our time in walking over the town, viewing some of the pleasant villas in its neighbourhood till 11 when we took passage in the Steam packet for Southampton. The sea was perfectly calm & the sail altogether most delightful. Cowes from the water presents a fine appearance & perhaps for salubrity of air is unequald in any place in the Kingdom.—Arrived at Southampton at ½ past 12 AM. Immediately took a general view of the place & walked on the general promenade on the banks of the river; this and only this was the place of any particular interest, excepting an old gate way, said to be very ancient, accordingly after dinner at 5 we took post chaise to "Stoney Cross" in the New forest distance 11 miles. Here we saw the stone erected on the spot where William Rufus was killed by an arrow fired by Sr. Walter Tyrril. 'Tis only a common rough stone about 3 ft. high, & the inscription almost entirely defaced. We made out however that it was erected by the Earl of De la Warre in 1750 something, where had been the tree from which the arrow glanced, & on another side that George 3d. & Charlotte visited the stone in 1789. On the 3d side it mentioned that the body of William was put into a cart & conveyed to the Cathedral at Winchester.[7]—It was gratifying to have visited a place so illustrious in story, altho. after all it was nothing at all. Yet we understood—a [*illeg.*] many persons have done the same thing. The New forest is an immense royal domain, of about 9000 acres— after this at 7 oclk: we continued in a chaise to Ringwood a miserable dirty "town" of about 3000 inhabitants. We intended going to Salisbury, but rather think we have been taken in a little bit by the Inn Keeper, for on consulting our map we find we have come in quite a contrary direction however we will say nothing about it, lest the laugh should come on ourselves.

Tuesday. Aug. [6th]—Left Ringwood at ½ past 8 in a post chaise, & arrived in due time at Salisbury 18 miles. The day altogether very rainy & uncomfortable. about noon the sun was out so we had an opportunity to visit the Cathedral here It is a very ancient building & takes its date from 1225, about 480 ft. in length with a

---

7. The Rufus Stone, erected in 1745 in Canterton Glen near Lyndhurst, Hampshire, marked the site where William Rufus (William II) was killed on August 2, 1100, while hunting. According to tradition, Sir Walter Tirel, aiming at a stag, shot an arrow which glanced off a tree and fatally struck the king. The stone was ordered in 1745 by John West (1693–1766) who was created first earl De La Warr in 1761.

tower of nearly 400. Like all other builds. of this kind it is an immense mass of stone, & looks as if it would last 'till the day of judgment. The monuments are numerous but not particularly interesting. In the afternoon notwithstanding it was rainy we took a post chaise for Stonehenge distant 9 miles. This is a famous Druidical ruin & the most ancient of any thing of the kind in Britain. 'Tis certainly an interesting curiosity for any one, but more especially for the Antiquary, & tho' not one myself yet I could not contemplate such a stupendous work (& being certain too of its great antiquity) without being filled with emotions of astonishment & veneration. The description given by Mr Silliman is in most respects correct, & as he has entered largely on the Subject & has made copious extracts from various antiquaries I shall merely refer to the 3d vol. of his Journal in Europe for a full account tho' I remark at the same time that I could never from any reading have formed any very distinct idea on that Subject.[8]

Wednesday—After breakfast, Mr I & myself having provided ourselves with a ticket to visit "Fonthill Abbey" we started in a post chaise for this splendid mansion distant 18 miles from hence (Salisbury) This is the so celebrated seat of William Beckford Esq. son of the distinguished Alderman of the same name. Since its commencement Mr B. has lavished almost incredible sums upon it & it has lately been sold to a Mr Farquar of London for

---

8. The third edition of Benjamin Silliman's *Journal* (see p. 41, n. 5) was the first to appear in three volumes. But its description of Stonehenge and accompanying plates appear in volume II, pp. 207–215.

£300,000. Take it all in all it is perhaps the greatest collection of all that is rare & precious now existing in this or any other country. No expense has been spared by Mr B. (who is or has been the richest commoner in the relm of an income of rising £90,000 per annum) & he seems to have collected the most costly & curious from all the museums & collections ancient & modern, public & private. As an instance of the value of only some of the pictures, there is one which cost him 20,000 francs (quite small) & another for which the King has offered 2000 guineas. Very many of the cases & cabinets are set with gems & other precious stones of the greatest value; great number of the articles were formerly in the possession of European & eastern princes, & have adorned the most splendid palaces in Europe.—how he came in possession of many of them is a wonder to me—for one would suppose that mere money could not procure them. The Library is also equally large & costly, & judging from the Books themselves, Mr B would seem to be a man of learning & taste.[9] But I shall say no more for <u>an Octavo vol:</u> has already been published, explanatory & descriptive of the whole concern.[1]

---

9. William Beckford (1759–1844), author (*Vathek*) and recluse, son of Alderman William Beckford (see entry for April 3, 1823, above), built Fonthill Abbey on his family estate in Wiltshire. One of the most elaborate Gothic follies in England, the Abbey was sold for £275,000 to John Farquhar of London who paid an additional £25,000 for such contents as Beckford chose to leave behind. Farquhar opened the Abbey as a tourist attraction in 1822. William Hazlitt in *London Magazine* (November, 1822) described it as "a cathedral turned into a toy store" and said of Beckford: "...the only proof of taste he has shown in this collection is his getting rid of it."

1. John Rutter, *Description of Fonthill Abbey and Desmesne*, 5th ed. (Shaftesbury, 1822).

Thursday. Went to Fonthill again to day, & reviewed all the pictures & curiosities I saw yesterday. The building itself is upon the grandest scale & built purely after the Gothic Style. In the grounds belonging to the Estate are upwards of 9000 acres, 600 of which are enclosed by a wall. vast numbers of English are every day going to gratify their curiosity in viewing this wonderful place, tho' the price of tickets are 1 guinea each. In Sept. every thing is to be sold. At ½ past 5 we bade farewell to Fonthill & all its greatness, & took the coach for Bath, distant 31 miles. It soon becoming dark of course I could see nothing of the country, & arrived at a little past 11 Oclk:. Went to bed soon after but having drunk some strong Tea got no sleep 'till past 4.

Friday. Did not arise 'til rather late. Walked out to take a general view of the town, & in reality found it to be what it is generally considered the handsomest City in England[2] Bath is noted for its Springs, being the general resort of invalids & of the fashionable world at certain seasons of the year. Of course we are out of time to enter into any of its pleasures. The place is most delightfully situated in a fertile valley surrounded by very high hills, & almost the whole of it not merely <u>well</u> but elegantly built. Few Cities in the world can present such a fine Street as "Pulteney". The "Circus" St. James Square Queens Street & Landsdown's buildings are admirable, & the Cresent particularly, for the beauty of its buildings & situation, is unrivalled. We visited the "Pump room" at one end is a full length statue of "Beau Nash" & on either side

---

2. Bath was rebuilt in the eighteenth century on plans drawn up principally by John Wood (1704–1754) and his son, John, the younger (1728–1781).

is the head of Pope & Lord Chesterfield. Took a survey of the Baths. The Kings bath is very large say 60 by 40 ft. & persons of both sexes bath promiscuously. The water has a heat of 117 degrees. I drank a glass but it was like taking an emetic. Went to see the grand Assembly rooms. They are large & admirably calculated for their purpose, with card & Tea rooms adjoining. Viewed the Abbey Church—a very ancient building, in the Gothic style, & contains more monuments than any others I had seen. They were from all parts, who probably came to Bath for the Waters but died in their trial. Among others was one to "Beau Nash" & one to the celebrated Quin, with the following lines written by Garrick. "That tongue which set the table in a roar, & charmed the public ear, is heard no more. Clos'd are those ey[e]s, the harbingers of wit, which spake, before the tongue, what Shakespeare writ. Cold is that hand, which living was stretch'd forth, At friendships call, to succour modest worth, Here lies James Quin, Deign, reader, to be taught Whate'er thy strength of body, force of thought, In natures happy mould however cast, to this complexion thou must come at last."[3]

---

3. The Abbey Church of St. Peter and St. Paul occupied the site of earlier Saxon and Norman churches. Attached to Benedictine monks from the tenth to the sixteenth centuries, it was rebuilt in the late Gothic style in the fifteenth century.

Richard Nash (1694–1762), Welsh gambler and dandy, became "uncrowned king of Bath" when he was appointed master of ceremonies by the city government. His office was created to improve opportunities for public amusement and to set rules for social decorum.

James Quin (1693–1766) played lead roles at both Drury Lane and Covent Garden until he retired to Bath in 1751. While in retirement he was befriended by his former rival on stage, David Garrick (1717–1779).

Saturday August 30, 1823—The weather to day has been very pleasant & altho' not a hot sun, yet without rain. We passed the day in retracing our steps of yesterday, over this most charming of Cities & really for a Town of about 50,000 inhabitants it contains more handsome Streets & blocks of buildings than I will venture to say, almost any other City in the World. Not having any letters to detain us & it not being the fashionable season, we concluded not to prolong our stay & at 6 in the Evening we took the Coach for Bristol, distance 13 miles; the piece of road I noticed was uncommonly fine even for England & the Country diversifyed with hill & dale, & at 8 we crossed the Avon & entered the City. Spent the evening in walking about the streets & from what I could see by candle light, is a very dirty place.

mem: before dinner to day took a very comfortable bathe in the Bath waters. The markets in Bath were well stocked with fruits of every Kind but the fruits in England altho. they look very fine, have not the flavour our has for the want of a hot Sun.

Sunday. A remarkably fine day. Commenced by ascending "Brandon Cliff" from whence we had a fine view of Bristol. The lovely village of Clifton not far distant is delightfully situated on a high eminence & is well built with fine blocks.—thence on to St. Vincents rocks, which are steep precipices of 300 ft. perpendicular from the banks of the Avon, on the opposite side not so steep but cover'd with trees and shrubs. Descended the rocks where are the celebrated "hot Wells of Bristol" much resorted to by the fashionable world & as well as invalids; I drank some of the water which having a temperature of 75°.[4] N/B: the bason is very narrow say not more than 20 to 25 ft. yet so deep as to admit of a 26 gun ship, coming up to the bason. Returned to our lodgings in "Cow St" & at 3 took a chaise to the charming seat of Lord de Clifford, distant 5 miles over the Clifton Downs. We were permitted to walk around the grounds which are laid out in the usual English style of park & forest. The Estate has been for many years in the family & most of the trees particularly the oaks appeared of great age. Nothing can be more delightful than to walk over the domain of an old English family: on one side was presented a fine view of the Severn & beyond it the high mountains in Wales.[5] Returned at 6. After dinner walked in various parts of the town, but saw nothing which will detain us long in Bristol for there is hardly a handsome Street in the whole place. 'Tis purely a commercial town & indeed ranks as the 3d. in the Kingdom.—but being very old & not having any firms of consequence it is not improved like other places. The College green & the "Queens Square" are both agreeable promenades, in the latter there is an equestrian Statue. Bristol must contain at present about 100,000 inhabitants. The commerce not so extensive as for-

---

4. Springs flowing from an opening at the foot of St. Vincent's Rock near Bristol became the center of a fashionable spa early in the eighteenth century. It was chartered as "Hot Wells" in 1710.

5. Edward, twenty-first baron de Clifford (1767–1832) was proprietor of King Weston, a manor house set in a park of 500 acres. According to Paterson's *Roads*, 17th ed. (London, 1824), p. 413, "The park abounds with knolls and broken grounds, and the trees are exceedingly luxuriant, while the rivers Avon and Severn impart an interest to the views that is rarely to be equalled."

merly owing to the increase of Liverl. NB: on leaving the park of Lord de C. Lady C met us & most graciously return'd our salute.

Monday Sept. 1st. Another very pleasant day, & the Sun as hot as we have often in Rhode Island. Visited the Glass Manufactory[6] & the Ancient Cathedral of Bristol.[7] There is noting particularly worth noticing excepting that it contains the monument of the Wife of Mason the poet[1] & upon which are inscribed the so celebrated pathetic lines commencing with "Take holy earth all that my soul holds dear Take that best gift which heaven so lately sent" &c &c & also that of Mrs. Draper, the Eliza of Sterne.[2]— Walked in various parts of the Town which was very crowded being the commencement of The Fair; the number of horses & cattle were very numerous. St. James' Church yard a larger Square was filled with booths for the Show men & mountbanks—here

---

6. Bristol had been a center of glass-making since the late Middle Ages.

7. Bristol's cathedral, on the south side of the College Green, had a choir dating from the fourteenth century. The nave was not raised until 1877.

1. William Mason (1725–1797) was remembered for his *The English Garden* (1771–1781), a long poem in blank verse. When his wife, Mary Sherman, died of consumption in 1767 he and his fellow poet, Thomas Gray (1716–1771), jointly wrote her epitaph, a series of apostrophes. JCB quotes Mason's opening lines correctly except that the last word in the second line should be "gave" rather than "sent."

2. Elizabeth, née Sclater (1744–1778), wife of Daniel Draper, an East India Company official, appears as Eliza in Laurence Sterne's *A Sentimental Journey through France and Italy* (1768). With her in mind Sterne also wrote *Letters from Yorick to Eliza* (1775–1779) and *Journal to Eliza* which was not published until 1901.

especially it was dreadfully noisy. so to remove ourselves from the dust & dirt we took our same walk of yesterday to the Hot wells, where I purchased a specimen of the St Vincent rock containing the Bristol Diamonds.[3] Returned over the Cliffs at 5 & dined & at 7 took the mail for Gloucester distant 35 m. & arrived at ½ past 11.

Tuesday. 2d. Intending to proceed immediately to Cheltenham, we had only time to take a general view of Gloucester, which is a very ancient & alway a very loyal town. A little Boy acted as tour guide & took us first to a Pin Manufactory. I had never before seen one altho. I had so often respecting them; [*sic*] the simple process of making a pin employs about 20 or 25 different persons, in all its various branches, & we were told that 8 or 9d per day was as much as the most expert of those who make the head; put it on; & put them in papers could earn working industriously many hours. If this is the case & there can be no doubt, how can these poor devils find means to live?[4] Went next to the Cathedral Church, an immense pile of stone & of great antiquity, it was commenced by Hengist the Saxon in the 6th Century. The pillars are larger than any I have yet seen in England 24 ft. round. At one

---

3. These "diamonds" were a transparent rock crystal found in limestone formations near Bristol and available as souvenirs.

4. English pin factories, considered models of industrial efficiency (see Adam Smith, *The Wealth of Nations*, Book 1, ch. 1, "On the Division of Labor"), drew many tourists, including American entrepreneurs interested in ending American dependence on imported pins. Gloucester had been a center of pin-making since the early seventeenth century.

end there is an addition to the building with 2 gothic pillars, indicating that this part was built in the "dark ages" In this Church are the Monuments: of the Saxon & of Edward 2d. King of England, who is actually buried here; like the fashion of the times he lies a full length in marble with the Crown on his head.[5] At 12 took the Coach for Cheltenham distant 10 m. This is now become one of the most celebrated watering places in England & it is crowded with rank & fashion. The waters very much resemble those of the Congress Spring at Saratoga & are much used by the invalid. We immediately walk[ed] to the Spring & during the day took a general survey of the place, & saw large numbers of elegant well dressed people promenading the town & public walks.[6] In the Evening attended at the literary salon where there was a little picnic[7] &c. &c.—

Wednesday 3d. Arose early this morning & visited the Fountains. The Sun shone very pleasant & the company very numerous & highly fashionable, among others was H.R.H the Duke of Glocester. I had before seen him at the Opera & in Parliament so

---

5. Hengist, or Hengest, a Saxon chieftain of the fifth century. JCB may have confused him with Prince Osric, a seventh-century ruler of the Weicce, who founded a monastery close to the site where the present cathedral was begun in 1087. The cathedral has several images of Osric, in stone and glass, honoring him as one of the founders.

6. The spa at Cheltenham became a center of fashion late in the eighteenth century. Its Assembly Room opened in 1815.

7. A picnic in the 1820s was not necessarily eaten out-of-doors. It was any informal meal, usually with dishes provided by the participants.

I recognized him immediately. Without this I should not have distinguished him from any other Gentleman.[8] This place is at present very crowded & the shops &c. &c have as much appearance of Style as any thing in London. The Town is fast increasing & the houses are generally speaking built in an elegant style. The public walks are as good & convenient as any one could wish & take it all in all Cheltenham must be a charming residence for a few weeks in the year. Its population is about 7000 but this must include much of the surrounding Country. Intending to pay a visit to Stratford upon Avon, the birth place of the immortal Bard & finding a Coach to go at ½ past 1, we took our seats & arrived here at between 6 & 7 distant 36. The Country thro. which we passed was as most other parts of England well improved, & the roads as usual very fine.—our fare today was 6d per mile.

Thursday Sept. 4th. Arose early, & thro' the day the most pleasant I have ever met with in England. Went to the Church to visit the Tomb of Shakespeare. The building is very old & enclosed in a pleasant yard, on the bank of the Avon surrounded with "time honoured Elms". On the Stone over the body in the Chancel of the Church are the following lines, "Good friend for Jesus sake forbeare, To dig the dust enclosed heare; Bless be the man yt spares these stones, And Curst be he yt moves my bones."[9]

---

8. William Frederick, duke of Gloucester (1776–1834) was a great-grandson of George II and a son-in-law of George III.

9. The lines on Shakespeare's tombstone in the chancel of Holy Trinity

On the far side of the wall is his monument, with his bust. there are some latin lines supposed by Ben Jonson, & the following in English. ["]Stay passenger, why goest thou by so fast, Read if thou canst, Whom envious death hath plast, Within this monument, Shakespeare with whome Quick nature died; Whose works doth deck [*blank*] ys tomb, Far more than cost; Sith all yt he hath writt, Leaves living art, but page to serve his witt, Obit ano doi 1616 [*a*]et[*atis*] 53 Die 23 Ap:["]][1]

There is a book kept in the church in which we also inscribed our names. We observed many American names inserted. While in the Church we met Mr Hughs chargé to London as he was going immediately to Cheltenham, we had not much conversation with him.[2] After breakfast explored the old house in which Shakespeare was born; it is now divided into two parts: one the Maidenhead Inn & the other a butchers Shop; here is shewn the very room where he first drew breath. The house, or rather this part of it retains the same appearance it ever did, tho' the other

---

Church are transcribed exactly except for two spellings: "dig" should be "digg," and "enclosed" should be "encloased."

1. The Latin lines commonly but improbably attributed to Ben Jonson are: JUDICIO PYLIUM, GENIO SOCRATEM, ARTE MARONEM/TERRA TEGIT, POPULUS MAERET, OLYMPUS HABET. (A Nestor in judgment, a Socrates in intellect, a Virgil in art. The earth covers him, the people mourn him, Olympus has him.") JCB transcribed the English lines exactly including their obsolete spellings.

2. Christopher Hughes (1786–1849) was chargé d'affaires at the American legation in Stockholm from 1816 to 1825. When JCB met him, Hughes was returning to his post by way of England after leave in the United States. While in England he ran some diplomatic errands for Secretary of State John Quincy Adams in negotiations leading to the proclamation of the Monroe Doctrine.

part has been modernized. Here was also another Book for visitor's names, the one given some time since by Colonel Perkins of Basham has been carried off by some meddling old woman.[3]

The Town house is a very respectable building for the Kind. On the outside is a Bust of the Poet, with these lines, "take him for all in all"[4] &c &c. Within is a large well painted portrait of the Bard in the act of composing some of his final verses, & a quotation is upon the scroll—another portrait of Queen Ann, & of Garrick leaning in a pensive mood upon a Bust of Shakespeare. —At 11 left Stratford upon Avon for Warwick. Stratford is but a dull deserted place & undoubtedly is entirely supported by the Stir which is caused by strangers who visit it from its having given birth to Shakespeare. Stratford contains 3000 inhabitants (about). Arrived at Warwick in time to attend the races (2d day). Saw one very good race, but only 2 horses being entered the sport did not last long.[5] The Celebrated Castle of Kenilworth being near at hand, we took a chaise & drove to it distant 6 miles. It is all in ruins now as every body knows, & indeed so much so & for so long time (since the days of Cromwell who pulled it down)

---

3. The original visitors' book was given, around 1815, by those in charge of Stratford's library to Mary Hornby who was proprietress of the house from 1793 to 1820. She took the book with her when she moved out. Washington Irving described her as a "garrulous old woman." See *The Sketchbook* (1819–1820), "Stratford-on-Avon."

4. *Hamlet*, act 1, sc. 2, line 187: "He was a man, take him for all in all, / I shall not look upon his like again."

5. The racetrack at Warwick, long-established but not highly regarded, held meetings in February, April, September, and November.

that even with the help of drawings & descriptions, it was with difficulty we could make much out of it, yet after puzzling a good while we were able to obtain some imperfect idea of its former greatness & slendour. It is certainly an enormous pile of Stone, & is surrounded by a wall enclosing 7 acres. We made out the "great Hall" "the audience Chamber," "the Oriel" the "plaisance" "Caesars Tower," "the strong tower" "Leicesters buildings" &c &c as they are called in the guide. Some 2 or 3 pair of winding stairs are still to be seen & many vaults under ground; the walls are grown over with Ivy & present a melancholy picture of former grandeur. The Lake so celebrated is or was entirely drained by Cromwell, & there is now merely a small stream of water running at one corner of the walls.[6] The barbican is inhabited, having been fitted up for the overseer of the grounds we entered it & saw the remains of an elegant fire place, & the Arms of Leicester engravd on the corners &c. &c, the order of the garter, &c. & on the oak over the fire place is ER. carved for the virgin Queen.[7] These ruins are now in the possession of the Earl of Clarendon.[8]

Friday Septr. 5th. 1823. Visited Warwick Castle, which is said to afford the finest specimen of the old Baronial Castles now exist-

---

6. Kenilworth Castle was plundered and destroyed by officers of Cromwell's army during the 1640s.

7. Robert Dudley, earl of Leicester (1532?–1588), was a favorite of Elizabeth i who gave him Kenilworth. Both Elizabeth and Leicester appear in Sir Walter Scott's *Kenilworth* (1821).

8. John Charles Villiers, earl of Clarendon (1757–1838), whose family inherited Kenilworth in the eighteenth century.

ing in England. After entering the Porters Gate we proceeded along a road cut mostly thro' a rock for the distance of ¼ of a mile 'till we came to the Castle. Entering the port-culis is a fine spacious courtyard, with the grand entrance to the left. This part has been much modernized & is now used by the Warwick family. We view'd the grand Hall, which has its walls decorated with a quantity of old armour, brest plates; swords; spears, Helmets, &c &c, & a complete suit of the same, as when used, which would entirely cover the whole body. These were formerly made use of by the ancient Earls of Warwick. We were shown thro' the "State apartments" a long suit of rooms, well furnished & containing some fine paintings—portraits of the family &c. &c. & one of Maria Henretta queen of Charles 1st. & also some of Charles 2ds. beauties. The prospect from the windows in the rooms is remarkably fine, looking out directly upon the river Avon, which runs at the foot of the rock on which the Castle is built. Indeed the whole bed of the river is rock, which rises solid the distance of 40 ft. on this side & I should say the Castle is built 100 ft. from this In fact it is all one immense rock on which the Castle stands, & in old times was considered the strongest point in England,—so much so that in the time of Richard 2d. an injunction was laid upon the heiress of the estate, that she should not marry without the Kings consent.[9] We then were shewn around the grounds, which is full of ancient trees & shrubbery, & I noticed a great number of

---

9. Rising on a site that had been fortified since the early ninth century, Warwick Castle was built up chiefly in the fourteenth century. During the Stuart period it was converted into a country residence.

Ceders. 'Tis said there are more here than on any other estate in England. In a summer house is [*a*] large vase of marble, dug from some old ruins in Italy. 'Tis elegantly sculptured & of the largest dimentions, being 20ft. in circumference.[1] From the Grounds we ascended "Guy's tower" so called. I should say it was 200ft. from the earth, is like all the other towers attached to the walls & affords a very extensive view. Leaving the Estate by the same rout we came in, we were shown into a small room near the porters lodge, where is kept "Guy's porridge-pot" an immense copper kettle, which holds 102 gallons & is on great occasions, such as the coming of age of the heir &c. &c. filled with punch. There are a number of other articles exhibited to elucidate the fabulous history of the famous Guy.[2] On the whole this is perhaps the most interesting of all the English Country Seats a stranger can visit, & gives you the best Idea of the strong holds of the "barons bold" you can possibly have; the whole is now kept up in good repair & the walls being covered with ivy; the various high towers rais-ing their heads above the other parts of the building; the grounds almost covered with a dense forest & the flag flying from one of the turrets fills the beholder with venerable ideas & carries him back to olden times. At 12 took the Coach for Woodstock distant

---

1. The Warwick Vase was a large basin, five to six feet deep, found in a lake near Hadrian's Villa at Tivoli.

2. Guy of Warwick was the entirely fictitious hero of an early thirteenth-century romance, *Gui de Warewic*, the story of a pilgrim and dragon-slayer. His name was adopted into the Beauchamp family later in the century when William de Beauchamp, having become earl of Warwick, named his heir Guy (1278?–1315).

42m & did not arrive til ½ past 7—the most miserable piece of coaching I have met with in England. Passed thro' Leamington a small watering place & the Borough of "Banbury," celebrated for a peculiarly fine Kind of Cake.

Saturday Sept. 6th. The weather to day was equally as fine as has been for some days past, & in this we were particularly fortunate as it afforded a fine opportunity to examine & explore the prince-ly Palace of Blenheim, the seat of the Marlboroughs. This is allowed to be by far the finest estate in England. The park & gardens &c. &c. comprise about 2700 acres, 250 of which are water. The house including the court within 7 acres. Even to attempt any thing like a description of a place so celebrated as Blenheim, when volumes have been written for the purpose, would be arrogance in me.[3] What struck us with wonderful effect was the triumphal column of victory, 130 ft. in height, with a collossal statue of John the great duke. He holds a figure of victory in one hand & a marshal's baton in the other. This column is most happily situated on rising ground & is seen from every conspicuous part of the grounds. The acts of parliament passed in his favor were inscribed on the marble pedistal & on the side fronting the palace an appropriate inscription said to be from the pen of Lord

---

3. Blenheim Palace was built by act of Parliament as a national monument to honor John Churchill (1650–1722), first duke of Marlborough (after 1702), for his brilliant early victories against the French in the War of Spanish Succession (1701–1714), particularly for his success in 1704 at Blenheim (Blindheim) in Bavaria.

Bolingbrooke;[4] the distance of this pillar is exactly a mile from the center of the Nw front leading to it over a magnificent stone bridge. We took a good view of the house & bridge from Rosamonds well, so called because here was formerly the bower or rather labyrinth where Henry 2d. concealled his fair mistress. This well is now all that remains to remind us of the celebrated but unfortunate beauty.[5] At 2 Oclck: we were shown thro' the palace itself. It as might well be supposed contains a magnificent suit of appartments, hung round with an abundance of paintings of the first masters particularly Rubens.[6] Some of the rooms are wainscoted with the manufactures of the Gobelin, representing the celebrated actions of the first John. Among a variety of family portraits, I dwelt with infinate satisfaction on those of the famous Sarah the first Dutchess. All accounts agree in representing her a most beautiful woman, & so I found her. The first I saw

---

4. Henry St. John, first viscount Bolingbroke (1678–1751), statesman and political writer, saluted Marlborough as "the Hero not only of his Nation, but of his Age" because, by defeating the absolutist, Louis xiv, he "asserted and confirmed the Liberties of Europe."

5. Rosamund's Well was a spring located at Woodstock Manor in a maze-like bower. A residence of kings from Henry i to Charles i, Woodstock was where Henry ii (1133–1189) sequestered his mistress Rosamund Clifford (d. 1177?). According to a popular ballad, she was murdered by order of Henry's queen, Eleanor of Aquitaine (1122?–1204). The royal estate at Woodstock was given to Marlborough in 1704 by Queen Anne to be the site of Blenheim Palace.

6. Guide books listed some two dozen works attributed to Peter Paul Rubens (1577–1640), or to his school, that were on display at Blenheim. William Hazlitt considered them the cream of Blenheim's collection. See his article, "Pictures at Oxford and Blenheim" (1823) in *Complete Works* (London, 1932), x, pp. 69–75.

she was taken in her weeds, after the death of "her beloved husband" for so she called him.—a most sweet countenance full of loveliness yet not without a certain air of dignity. How every way suited was such a woman as Sarah to be the wife of so great & good a man as the Duke of Marlborough.[7] Among other rooms shewn was the Library, said to be the finest room in Europe its length is considerably rising 100 ft. The number of books are numerous & very valuable, but what attracts the attention most is the superb full length Statue of Queen Ann in her coronation robes of white marble & standing from the air, is as fresh as if completed yesterday [;] in front is an inscription, stating it to having been executed out of respect & in gratitude for the munificence she had shewn towards him; in the Library are also full length portraits of the daughters of the first duke.[8] From the Library we entered the Chapel,[9] which is very small & the only thing worth noticing is an immense Obelisk of marble, superbly executed; but much too large for the place it is in.—The Gates thro. Which you enter to the Park are of colossul size & of fine

---

7. Sarah Jennings (1660–1744) married John Churchill in 1677. Portraits of her by Sir Godfrey Kneller hung in the library, the small drawing room, the billiard room, and the breakfast room.

8. Blenheim's library housed a large collection of rare books and first editions acquired by Charles Spencer, earl of Sunderland, third duke of Marlborough (1706–1758), who inherited Blenheim when his grandmother, Sarah, duchess of Marlborough died in 1744. JCB's widow bought some Aldine editions from this collection (Bibliotheca Sundleriana) when it was sold off in the early 1880s.
   The marble statue of Queen Anne was by Michael Rysbrack (1694?–1770).

9. Apparently an erroneous reference to the Marlborough family tomb, designed by William Kent (1685–1748) and executed by Michael Rysbrack.

workmanship. there is an inscription on the outside in Latin & a translation of it into English on the inner, Stating they were erected by order of Sarah after the death of her "much beloved & lamented husband" who left to her care to have completed the many things he left unfinished.[1] On the whole this palace of Blenheim is indeed a most sumptious & princely establishment & in every respect a present well worthy of Queen Ann to make & John Duke of Marlborough to receive. The present Duke is said to be a miserable fellow atho. he is allowed to be the best botanist in the Kingdom. He has wasted nearly all his estates & even encroached on some of the heir-looms of the family to raise money, such as having some of the gold & silver plate melted down;[2] the Eldest son the Marquis of Blandford, has however procured an injunction from the Lord Chancellor to stay waste & a person is actually place'd in the house to see that nothing is made way with. This has of course produced great coolness between the father & son, & there is now no communion or communication betw. them.[3] The 2d son is in the Army the 3d.

---

1. The Triumphal Gate, the usual approach to Blenheim, was built in 1723. The inscription was both a personal and a political statement. The English translation says: "This gate was built the year after the death of the most illustrious John, Duke of Marlborough, by order of Sarah, his most beloved wife, to whom he left the sole direction of the many things that remained unfinished of this fabric."

2. George Spencer (1766–1840), grandson of Charles (see p. 62, n. 8), inherited the estate in 1817. He took the name Spencer-Churchill and became the fifth duke of Marlborough.

3. The marquis of Blandford in 1823 was Charles Spencer-Churchill (1793–1857) who became sixth duke of Marlborough in 1840. Because of declining

in the Navy & the 4th in the Church. In the park are kept 1500 deer & consequently every year there is a great surplus to be disposed of but the 1500 must be kept up. Woodstock itself is a miserable place & is of no consequence any further than as it is attached to Blenheim. In the afternoon after making a few purchases of gloves &c &c for which this town is noted we took post chaise for the City of Oxford distant 10 or 12 miles, & we arrived in time to get a general view of the place & its different colleges besides viewing the anatomical collection, but as I had already examined the extensive establishments of this kind at Paris, it was nothing new to me & I looked upon the preparations with a good deal of indifference. This is the first of the kind I have seen since Iv been in England & as far as this is concerned those in Paris are greatly its superior.[4]

Sunday Sept 7th. Not feeling exactly in the mood of going to Church, we concluded it was best to improve time, by seeing at once all that we could in Oxford & then to return to town. In order to facilitate our operations we took a guide & really without him it would have been rather a difficult task; for the Colleges instead of being situated all together in one spot as is the case with us in America, they are built in every part of the Town without any regard to order, & most of them stand entirely on a level

---

revenues and his father's extravagance, he lived and died in reduced circumstances.

4. Oxford's collection in 1823 was scattered and incomplete. It consisted of some skeletons, some wax models imported from Florence, and some "preparations"—specimens ready for dissection or preserved for examination.

or regular line with the other houses of the Street. I shall not think or pretend of giving an account of Oxford but merely state some of the objects that came under my observation. We at first viewed "the Theatre" a large round building used for disputations & other public occasions. 'Tis said to be the largest room in Europe or at least in G.B. that is not supported in the center by pillars;[5] the interior is admirably calculated for its purposes, & here it was that the Allied Sovereigns received their honourary degrees in 1814, with Mareschal Blucher. It must really have been a grand show from all accounts & this visit of his Majesty & his royal friends cost the University £8000.[6] There are here full length portraits of the King & also of the Emperour of Russia & King of Prussia. Afterwards we viewed the Chapels of New College, Magdalen College, Christ Church C'ge & some others, all of which have their windows of painted glass which produces a fine effect, as it cast a shade of gloom & silence over the whole, which certainly is more congenial to the feelings than a brilliant glaring light when engaged in devotional exercises.[7] All the Colleges are built with a spacious court within, & some of them have

---

5. The Sheldonian Theatre, named for Gilbert Sheldon (1598–1677), chancellor of the University, who paid for construction costs.

6. In June, 1814, two months after Napoleon's abdication at Fontainebleau and one year before his final defeat at Waterloo, Oxford awarded honorary doctorates to Tsar Alexander I (1777–1825) and King Frederick William of Prussia (1770–1840) and to their victorious generals and diplomats such as Prince Blücher, the duke of Wellington, and Prince Metternich.

7. JCB may have been reflecting on the clear windows of the First Baptist Meeting House in Providence, R.I., while stating his preference for the dim, religious light of Oxford's chapels.

extensive gardens & walks—one (New College I believe) has a park with Deer from which the fellows &c &c are furnished with venison. Notwithstanding it was Sunday we were permitted to see the Hall of Christ Church C—. This is the hall where the fellows & students dine & is also used as a banqueting hall on great occasions. It is a well proportioned room & is hung round with portraits of their distinguished men who have been educated here. Among a variety of others, I noticed that of Mr Canning[8] & the late Chancellor of the Exchequer.[9]

8. George Canning (1770–1827), was foreign secretary in 1823, later prime minister. He attended Christchurch from 1787 to 1791. His portrait is attributed to Sir Thomas Lawrence.

9. JCB's reference to the "late Chancellor of the Exchequer" is an error. He probably refers to a portrait by Thomas Gainsborough of Sir John Skynner (1724–1805) who had been chief baron of the Exchequer.

[*Editorial note: The second diary ends with the entry for September 7th, 1823. The original has a loose insertion, a page with notes probably written some thirty years later recommending sights in England and Scotland accessible by rail, coach, or lake steamer. These notes mention several towns, castles, and natural features which JCB visited in 1823–24. They also mention a few sights such as Abbotsford and the Lake District which he had not visited at that time.*]

Book Three

September 25 to December 1, 1823
ENGLAND, SCOTLAND, AND IRELAND

L EFT LONDON at 8 PM in the Royal Mail for Stamford & arrived at 7 the following morning a distance of 89 miles— Passed thro. a number of small towns of no particular note excepting Stilton famous for its fine cheese. Spent the day at Stamford & viewed the splendid domain of the Earl of Exeter, "Burleigh house." The portal is more magnificent than any I have yet seen, not even excepting the one at Blenheim—The house itself stands back from the road nearly a mile & is not at all seen when passing the Great Gate. You approach it thro. a park of noble trees & the house is said to be one of the finest in England.[1] I was shewn thro. and was much pleased with the numerous family portraits which hung among the halls. There was also a beautiful portrait of the Dutchess of Cleveland mistress to Charles 2d,[2] the State

---

1. Burghley House was built (1553–1589) by William Cecil (1520–1598) who for forty years was a principal advisor of Elizabeth I. He was created first lord Burghley (or Burghleigh) in 1571. His son, Thomas, became first earl of Exeter in 1603. The park was laid out in the mid-eighteenth century by Lancelot ("Capability") Brown (1716–1783).

2. The art collection at Burleigh House was reviewed by William Hazlitt in *The New Monthly Magazine* (April 1822). See *Complete Works* (London, 1932), x, pp. 62–69. He did not mention the portraits. Barbara Villiers (1641–1709) in 1659 married Roger Palmer who became earl of Castlemaine. As Lady

Bed of Elizabeth as it was when used by her, when she came to visit her secretary,[3] the watch which she wore at her coronation, & a hat of King William 3d. In one of the State rooms is the sumptious Bed & chairs intended for the use of the present King when as Prince of Wales he was expected on a visit to the noble marquess, but he did not arrive & the Bed has never been used. An idea can be formed of its splendour from its costing £3000 & upwards. The park grounds are well laid out & covered with ancient oaks, & are said to be very extensive—the present marquess is quite a young man, & I was informed did not like to reside much of his time at Burleigh.[4] I went into St. Martins Church to see the monument of the great Cecil 1st Lord Burleigh —he is buried here & some others of the Exeter race who have a stupendous sacophagus or monument richly sculptured in Italy.[5] I also took a look at the old monastary of St. Leonards standing some distance out of the town. 'Tis now only used as a store house for bark. Not having anything to detain me further at Stamford I took the coach at 9 PM for York direct & arrived at 12 AM distance 110 miles. As we passed along the harvest

---

Castlemaine she became mistress *en titre* to Charles II and subsequently duchess of Cleveland.

3. Elizabeth I planned a state visit to Burghley House in August, 1566, but because of an outbreak of small-pox there stayed at a nearby friary.

4. Brownlow Cecil (1795–1867), second marquess of Exeter, inherited his title from Henry Cecil (1754–1804), tenth earl, who had become first marquess of Exeter in 1801.

5. St. Martin's Church at Stamford Baron, Hampshire, built in the late fifteenth century, was chosen by Lord Burghley for the tombs of "my grandfather,

appeared to have been abundant but large quantities of corn are still in the fields.

26th Sept. On my arrival I found the whole city of York in the greatest confusion owing to the musical festival which has been held here this week, & persons from every part of the country have flocked here to be present.[6] This was the last day & the performances had already commenced in the "Minster" yet I at once purchased a ticket & went as it afforded me the double opportunity of seeing the inside of this wonderful structure & of hearing and seeing how they manage these things in England.[7] The concourse of people was immense & I understood the number of musicians & singers to be [*blank*]. Among them was the celebrated Madame Catilani whom I had never before met. On the whole I was not particularly pleased with the concert, & Madame C—was the only one that much excited my attention & she proved herself every way as powerful a singer as I had often heard her spoken of, & this Minster of York is exactly the place above

---

father, mother, and myself" and became the burial place for the Exeter line of the Cecil family. A marble sarcophagus was added in the eighteenth century.

St. Leonard's had been a Benedictine priory from the twelfth to the sixteenth centuries.

6. Music festivals in support of charity had been held at York since 1796. In 1823 the attendance was about 17,000 over a four-day period. Some 180 instrumentalists and 285 vocalists performed.

7. York Minster, or the Cathedral of St. Peter, has occupied the same site since the late eleventh century. An Anglo-Norman building was entirely replaced between the early thirteenth and the early fifteenth centuries.

all others calculated for her voice.[8] The Organ is spoken of as something extraordinary, & so it is, but I do not think it equals the great organ at Haarlem in Holland.[1] As to the Cathedral itself I shall remain silent, upon which so much has already been written. 'tis enough for me to say that its dimensions every way are of the greatest magnitude, more than 500 ft. in length & that it has probably the largest windows of any other building, say 70 ft. in height. This church is remarkable for the five painted glass windows, which are in higher perfection than in any other part of England, & taken as a whole 'tis generally allowed to be the finest specimen of Gothic architecture now standing.[2]

There seems to be nothing further in York which will detain me, indeed the "Minster" is all that gives York any celebrity above many other towns of the same size in the North of England, & so I probably shall be off tomorrow.

27th. Today I have employed in taking a general view of the city of York, & in more particularly exploring & examining the beauty

---

8. Angelica Catalani (1780–1849), soprano, was one of the reigning divas of European opera in the early nineteenth century. She sang at several York Festivals, making her final appearance there in 1828.

1. JCB traveled in the Netherlands in May and June, 1823, on business errands for Brown and Ives. The great organ in the Groote Kerk at Haarlem, built by Christian Müller in 1738, was considered the largest and finest in the world.

2. JCB evidently refers to the "Five Sisters Window" (c. 1260) in the north transept which consists of five lancets and contains over 100,000 pieces of stained glass.

of the "Minster". I ascended to the top of the "Lantern Tower" in the center of the pile from whence I had a commanding prospect of the town & surrounding country,[3] but the suburbs of York do not appear to be so variegated with their fine county seats as many other places. In the course of the day I spent many hours contemplating with wonder & astonishment this stupendous fabric, the interior contains the tombs of a great many bishops & prelates & of other persons. Among others I noticed those of Bishops Sharp & Sterne (the ancestor of Yorick).[4] Some of these old fellows have been laying here a vast many years, 500 & even more. A number of curiosities are shewn—the horn of Ulphas is the most remarkable & by this horn the See of York continues to this day to hold many valuable domains. 'Tis a piece of Elephants tooth say 1½ foot long (curving) mounted with Silver, it had gold formerly, but when it was stolen in the time of the civil wars, these were lost.[5] Some rings and a variety of other articles are also exhibited.

---

3. The height of the central tower is 213 feet.

4. John Sharp (1645–1714) was consecrated archbishop of York in 1691. One of his predecessors, Richard Sterne (1596?–1683) became archbishop in 1664. He was the great-grandfather of Laurence Sterne, the novelist, who in some of his writings assumed the name and persona of Yorick. See above, p. 51, n. 2.

5. The horn of Ulphas was a drinking vessel made from an elephant's tusk. Ulphas, son of King Canute (994–1035), according to tradition, swore by this horn when he formally disinherited his family and left all of his land to "God and St. Peter." It was therefore claimed as the legal instrument deeding property to the Archdiocese of York. During the civil wars of the 1640s, the horn fell into the hands of Sir Thomas Fairfax (1612–1671) whose son redecorated it with silver and restored it to the church in 1675.

York contains about 18,000 inhabitants & is a very irregular built town, entirely surrounded with walls & the entrances every way is thro' mossy gateways. It is situated on the river Ouse over which there is a substantial stone bridge & in fact the river divides the town, running nearly South by East. There is a fine pleasure walk along the banks of the river shaded by lime trees, & in the afternoon I amused my self promenading here & in the best streets the city could boast of, tho' by the way there are none of any considerable note. It was my intention to have called upon an English Gentleman whom I met last summer in Bruges[6] & who politely gave me his address, but as I had determined to push on the following morning I concluded it was best to forego the pleasure of meeting, as I should be able to enjoy his society for so short a time.

28th. Having taken my seat in the Coach for New Castle I arose at 6 this morning & started at 7, & altho. the sun was out very bright yet the air was cold & frosty. We passed thro a number of inconsiderable Towns viz: Easingwold, Thirsk, North Allerton, Darlington & Durham one of the richest Bishops Sees in England. As the coach stopped to change horses I had a distant view of the Cathedral Church which stands on the brow of a high bank of the river & like all the other Cathedrals in this country seemed the work of other days.[7] From Durham we continued our course to New Castle & night came on just before we entered the town.

---

6. JCB visited Bruges (Brugge) in June 1823 during his trip to the Netherlands.

7. Durham Cathedral was built between 1093 and 1133.

We could however see the fires at the numerous coal pits in its neighbourhood & at ½ past 7 I was safely landed at the "Turf Inn" Collingwood Streets in New Castle upon Tyne. We had rode 80 miles today & the air uncommonly sharp, so being a good deal Fatigued I took a refreshing dish of Tea & went to bed.

29th Did not arise 'til late; after breakfast took a guide & went out to see what might be worth seeing in New Castle. I at first (of course) was taken to a Coal Mine in the neighbourhood & did intend on descending to the shades below but it was <u>Monday</u> & from this & some other cause the miners were not at work below.[8] I however saw the apparatus for pumping out the water & hoisting the Coal which consisted of a Steam engine & as far as I could judge of the common description. They have also a convenient method of transporting the Coal from the pit to the keel boats on the Water Side. By the help of some simple machinery, carts roll upon a declining railway so that when the loaded one goes down the one that has been emptied returns—thus saving a vast deal of animal labour. On the whole I am not sorry that I did not descend today as it would have been a tiresome & dirty job, & such a thing can be done almost any where in America. From the pit my guide took me to view the quay said to be the longest but one in England. There certainly seemed to be a good deal of berth upon it for a place of this size. indeed New Castle is well

---

8. The miners may have been observing Michaelmas Day which was still a feast day in England. It was also commonly set aside for the holding of municipal elections.

situated for Commerce as the Tyne is navigable for ships of 600 tons up to the town. After this he took me to the more fashionable parts, which is to the North of the city, & Pilgrim Street & Northumberland Street, its continuation, with Saville row & Albion Place or Row may be called the court end, yet in point of beauty New Castle has very little to boast, as the houses are mostly black & dirty from the smoak of so much coal. It contains 28,000 inhabitants & as all the world knows is celebrated for its Coals of which it is said to export upwards of 600,000 chaldrons annually.[9] The river Tyne here divides the Counties of Durham & New Castle for New Castle is a City & County of itself. A substantial stone Bridge has been built across which connects the city with <u>Gateshead</u> on the Durham Side,[1] & as the river rolls altogether in a valley (of course) New Castle & Gateshead are built upon the sides of the hills, which in many points are extremely steep. I had almost forgot to mention that in my ride of yesterday 11 or 12 miles before we reached the town we passed in full view from the road "Lumley Castle" the Seat of Lord Scarborough. It appeared to be a building of great size, yet we understood the noble possessor never comes near it & his Steward only pays it a visit once a year.[2]

---

9. A chaldron was equal to thirty-six bushels, approximately a long ton.

1. A bridge over the Tyne with nine stone arches, built between 1774 and 1778, widened in 1801.

2. Lumley Castle, begun in the late fourteenth century, was named for its owners. Lord Lumley (d. 1721) became Viscount Lumley and earl of Scarborough in 1690. Richard Lumley, the sixth earl (d. 1832) succeeded to the title in 1805.

September 30th. A very disagreeable morning the rain pouring down, in torents. Left New Castle at 10 Am, & reached Alnwick at ½ past 4. in the afternoon. It became pleasant & the sun shone out very bright. Passed thro' the small town of Morpeth, only celebrated I believe as being the birth place of Admiral Collingwood.[3] Further on we had a full view of the German Ocean,[4] & saw some sail at a distance. The country appeared poor & the crops very backward & thin. On entering the villiage on the right hand stands a column erected not long since by the tenants of the Duke of Northumberland as a testimony of respect to their landlord. It is crowned with the Percy lion & on its base the motto of the family.[5] After dinner I walked out to see as much of the Castle as was possible before night. My route took me over the bridge across the river Alne & along its banks on the opposite side from whence is a commanding view of this famous seat of the Percies. Its situation is upon a high hill, & what with its extensive walls, battlements & turrets has a most imposing effect, & is allowed to be a complete model of a great baronial castle.[6]

---

3. Cuthbert Collingwood (1750–1819), a naval hero closely associated with Admiral Horatio Nelson (1758–1805), whose command he assumed when Nelson fell at Trafalgar. As member of a naval brigade, Collingwood had fought at Bunker Hill in 1775.

4. Until the late nineteenth century the North Sea was commonly called the German Ocean.

5. Hugh Percy (1785–1847) became third duke of Northumberland in 1817.

6. Alnwick Castle occupied a site that had been fortified long before it was acquired by Henry de Percy in 1309. The castle he built there was enlarged in the eighteenth century.

The Duke of Northumberland is one of the richest subjects of the relm & from this county alone his income is stated to be £100,000. He is spoken of as a very benevolent man, & in fact must be the principle support of such a place as the village of Alnwick. On my return past the great Gateway I saw it thronged with a host of ragged children & on enquiring found they all received daily a portion of Soup & bread, from the bounty of the Duke, but I was afterwards informed that the poor of the place are very ungrateful for all the good the Duke does them. Tomorrow I intend to visit the interior of the Castle & afterwards if an opportunity offers to proceed to Dunbar, as the season is growing late & I have not any time to spare. The weather since leaving London has been quite cold & a fire not at all uncomfortable. However if it continues pleasant a fortnight longer it will fully answer my purpose, & considering that there has scarcely been any summer this year, we may reasonably expect a tolerably fair autumn. Distance from New Castle to Alnwick 35 miles.

October 1st. I could not have had a finer day for my operations. I arose at 6 Oclk: & altho. the ground was covered with a white frost the sun was out bright. I took pretty much the same walk as the night before on the opposite side of the Alne, to have another good look at the famous Castle. At a little after 7 I was admitted to view it within, & was carried thro the whole suit of State apartments. None of them were particularly striking,—all well fitted up, but the furniture not over & above splendid, the banqueting hall, salon & library were very commodious apartments & in some of them were the portraits of the members of the Percey family.

The late duke makes a conspicuous appearance. He is in his military dress, with long boots & storm coat & has an expansive countenance. This is the one that fought in America at Bunkers Hill.[7] The Chapel is that which excites the attention the most. 'Tis very superb & the painted windows are finely executed, the walls are covered with the genealogy of the family & commences as Mr. Silliman says modestly with Charlemagne.[8] Prayers are read here every Tuesday Evening when the Domestics of the household are assembled. After leaving the domicile, the porter shew me into the dungeon & upon the walls & also upon the battery, for the Duke actually has on that side of the Castle looking down upon the river a battery of 7 large brass field pieces, ready mounted upon carriages & with everything fit for action. This is a touch above anything I have as yet met with, & indeed on the whole from viewing Alnwick you have the best idea of an ancient barons citadel. On the tops of the battlements are a great number of figures representing ancient warriors with spears, darts, battle axes, &c. & as this was the original stile of the building when it was repaired these were continued. In returning I had some little conversation with a person at the porters lodge, & I learnt that the family live in Great State & that the duke & dutchess never

---

7. Hugh Percy (1742–1817) inherited his title in 1785. He held the rank of general during the revolutionary wars in North America but did not accompany his regiment to the Battle of Bunker Hill (June 1775) where, in his words, it was "cut to pieces." He did, however, command an unsuccessful attack on Dorchester Heights in March 1776.

8. Benjamin Silliman's account of Alnwick and the Percys' modest claims are in *Journal*, III, pp. 165–168.

ride out without using 4 horses & a train of footmen & outriders
& when they have company a coach & 6 are sported. All however speak in high terms of their liberality & humanity. Breakfasted at ½ past 9 & immediately after took a seat for Dunbar on
the Top of the Coach. Here I once again had a view of the Castle
& bid farewell to all its greatness. Some little distance on the road
we passed Malcholm Cross, standing on the spot where the king
was killed—it was repaired by the last dutchess who was a lineal
descendent of Malcolm.[9] Most of the route we were in full view
of the North Sea, & the country growing more & more hilly. At
2 oclk passed the river Tweed & dined in Berwick, thence continued our course & arrived at Dunbar in Scotland at ½ past 6.
Towards evening the wind became very severe & we crossed
some very pokerish glens which afforded something of a specimen of the wild romantic scotch scenery. I have thought it best to
stop here all night & not to lose the finest part of Scotland by riding in the night.

2d. Arose at 6 & ran round Dunbar for ½ an hour—not finding
any thing to detain me I took a seat at 7 on the top of a 2 horse
coach for Edinburgh. The morning was cold & very windy, yet I
prefered the top so as to have a good view of the county of the
East Lothian, the best part of the Kingdom. The country was hill

---

9. The Malcolm Cross was a stone marker on the spot where Malcolm III of
Scotland was killed while besieging Alnwick in 1093. According to a carved
inscription, the cross was restored in 1774 by Elizabeth Seymour, duchess of
Northumberland. Malcolm III (b. 1031?) was the son of King Duncan, Macbeth's
victim, and appears in Shakespeare's play, act 2, sc. 3; act 4, sc. 3; act 5, sc. 8.

& dale & the soil good, judging from the crops of oats & wheat which looked well tho not equal to what I saw in the west of England. The Firth of Forth was in full view all the way & on the right hand of the road, was the little village of Preston Pans, famous as the place where Col. Gardener was slain in the Scotch rebellion.[1] At 12 AM arrived in Edinburgh & took a room at the London Hotel, St Andrews Street, St. Andrews Square. What little I have as yet seen of this City strikes me very favourably, & the upper or new town is very magnificent. After refreshing myself with a clean shirt I walked out to deliver M[r] N[evett]s introductory letter to Mr Keir, but unfortunately he is at a distance in the country, & will not be back within a fortnight so I shall not have the pleasure of seeing this gentleman upon whom I had calculated above all others to have been useful to me, however tomorrow I shall deliver my others & take what may come.[2] At any rate I shall not despair if they do procure me <u>nothing</u> but a <u>dinner</u>, for I have been too long in Europe not to know how of little <u>real</u> <u>use</u> are introductory letters. Distance from Alnwick to Dunbar 58 miles—from Dunbar to Edinburgh 27. I have said nothing of Dunbar as it is scarcely worth mentioning. It contains about 2000 inhabitants & has some trade in herrings; the port which I took a birds eye view of this morning quite good enough

---

1. Prestonpans, a village east of Edinburgh, where on September 21, 1745, the forces of the Stuart pretender, Bonnie Prince Charlie (1720–1788), defeated the army of George II. James Gardiner (1688–1745), a colonel of dragoons, was fatally wounded there after a heroic stand.

2. See Diary entry for March 19, 1823.

for the commerce of the place & a part of it is made from the solid rock. The rest of the town is comprised in one principal street at the entrance of which is a newly erected Church—a substantial building[3]—thus much for Dunbar, the first scotch town I ever slept in.

3d. Today I have changed my resolution which I yesterday formed after no small deliberation. It is now my plan to proceed immediately on my North Eastern tour & make my visit in Edinburgh on my return from Aberdeen. Accordingly instead of delivering my introductory letters I have taken my seat in the Coach for Kinross.

My time has been spent in walking about the old & new town & I have been to Leith besides. This is merely the <u>port</u> being situated at the mouth of a small river of the same name & in some parts along the Firth of Forth, & Leith is well supplied with docks for a port of its size & there is a substantial Quay running at a considerable distance into the sea. It appears to be a busy, bustling place & I should suppose there must be a good deal of trade considering its contiguity to so large a town as Edinburgh. Most of the new town I have explored pretty thoroughly; 'tis eligibly situated & the streets spacious & houses very magnificent. On returning from my walk to Leith I ascended Calton hill to view the monument of Nelson & which also serves the purpose of a signal or look out house.[4] The view from Calton

---

3. The parish church at Dunbar was rebuilt in 1821.

4. The Monument was raised on Calton Hill in 1815 in the shape of an inverted telescope.

Hill is very extensive commanding the river, the sea coast for a great distance, a large part of Fifeshire & the whole of the city & its environs—but more hereafter of all this. After dinner I went to the theatre to see how they manage these things in Scotland.[5] The building is neat & tastily fitted up, but it was playing this evenin literally to empty Boxes; the play was Goldsmiths celebrated Comedy of She Stoops to Conquer, but the actors were bad & the only character that was passable was that of Toney Lumpkin.

4th Left Edinburgh at 9 Am as pleasant a day as one could wish, nothing particular to attract the attention before coming to Queensferry 9 miles from the City, where we crossed the Firth of Forth in a sail boat the Firth is here a full 2 miles wide & perhaps even more. The country was as might be expected for Scotland quite hilly. At 2 Oclk arrived at the village of Kinross in Kinross County. Before entering the town we enjoyed a commanding prospect of the celebrated Loch Leven & of its little Island & castle in ruins famous as having been the place of confinement of the unfortunate Queen Mary;[6] the sun shone brilliantly & the view was romantic in the extreme. As I intended to explore the ruins, I left the Coach at the Tavern upon Kinross Green & after taking a slight lunch procured a fisherman to row me to the

---

5. Religious scruples inhibited theater life in Edinburgh, as they did in Providence, R.I., until the late eighteenth century. Edinburgh's first legitimate theater, the Theatre Royal, opened in 1769.

6. Mary, queen of Scots (1542–1587), after the defeat of her forces at Carberry Hill in June, 1567, surrendered to the insurgent lords and was imprisoned in an island castle at Loch Leven until her escape the following year.

island. We were about ¼ of an hour sailing over & on my arrival I walked over every part of the little island itself & also examined minutely what remains of this once strong citadel; nearly all the walls are tumbled down & only the square tower on the North West corner & the grass tower (so the Scotch guide called it) on the South East corner are standing. This last is round & here is seen the window from which Mary made her escape with Douglas.[7] 'Tis generally supposed that they bent their course to the south side of the Loch on which there is a spot called "Mary's Knoll" & here 'tis thought they landed, tho' within a few years back a bunch of Keys have been found on the opposite bank of the Loch which has induced many to think that these were the very Keys of the Castle & that this was the landing place. This supposition is very reasonable as this distance from the Island is not more than ½ a mile whereas to the South of the Loch it is at least 2 miles. This window appears to be the only place in the castle she could have used for this purpose, all the others in this & the square tower are of much too great height, tho' this is one from which she could easily have jumped without danger & 'tis so near the water edge that the boat could approach nearly under it.[8] Loch Leven is about 17 miles in circumference

---

7. The laird of Loch Leven was Sir William Douglas, Mary's official jailer. When she escaped from the island, Sir William's cousin, Willy Douglas, accompanied her in the getaway boat. Sir William's brother, George, met her on the lake shore.

8. Accounts of Mary's escape from Loch Leven vary. Some believe she walked, in disguise, through the castle gate rather than jumped out a window. Willy Douglas used the keys to the castle to lock in pursuers. According to some

& on the North & South surrounded by mountains the heighest to the North is one of the Lomonds. The water is not very clear & when the wind blows strong there is a good deal of sea. The Island itself comprises about 2 acres, is green to the waters edge & stands nearly midway between the North & South, & as I have before observed not more than ½ a mile from a point on the Eastern or North Eastern bank. There are half a dozen trees growing on the Island one of which (a haw thorn) is said to have been planted by Mary.

I have been much gratifyed with this examination & would not on any account have omitted it. I may safely say that 'tis the most romantic little spot (setting aside all historical associations) that I have ever yet met with & the view of it from the high road was so imposing that towards evening I strolled out 2 or 3 miles towards Edinburgh so as once more to enjoy the luxury of this romantic scene. This Loch has always been a favourite pleasure tour, tho more especially since the appearance of "The Abbot".[9] The fisherman said there had not been a great many visitors this summer as the weather has all along been so cold & wet, so that I have been extremely fortunate in having so fine a day particu-

---

accounts, he then threw they keys into the mouth of a cannon; according to others, he tossed them into the lake. Cf. the "Ballad of Mary's Escape:" "These pond'rous keys shall the kelpies keep / And loge in their caverns dark and deep."

9. Sir Walter Scott's *The Abbot* was published in 1820 as a sequel to *The Monastery*. Its concluding chapters tell the story of Mary's imprisonment at Loch Leven, her escape, the defeat of her partisans at Langside in May 1568, and her flight to England.

larly as it is now getting late in the season, tho from present appearances I am inclined to think we shall have a few weeks of clear good weather for travelling.

5th. Sunday. I did not go to bed at Kinross but waited for the Edinburgh mail which I joined at 2 Oclk AM & was set down at the Star Inn in Perth at 4 when I went to bed & had a sound sleep. When I awoke I found it very cloudy & raining hard, so was in no hurry to turn out. As the rain continued throughout the day without intermission I only went out once to take a coup d'oeil of the town. I walked thro most of the principal Streets, notwithstanding the rain poured so strait that there was hardly another person to be seen.

6th. arose early & took a walk before breakfast along the "hill of Moncrieff" upon the Edinburgh road, as it was dark when I entered Perth I could not enjoy the fine views which this hill affords. 'Tis worthy the high euligum which all travellers pass upon it.[1]

Perth is seen situated between hills on all sides, & the vale of the Tay with the lofty Kinnoul Craigs on the other side of the river presents a most luxurious prospect. After breakfast I crossed the grand bridge over the Tay, & ascended the Kinnoul Craigs on the brow of which there is a hole or cave in the rocks where 'tis

---

1. Moncrieffe Hill rises 725 feet from the bank of the Tay south of Perth. It is opposite Kinnoul, the southwest spur of the Sidlaw Hills which extend east of Perth.

said Wallace used to hide himself & so 'tis called "Wallace's Cave."[2] From these immense hights are also extensive views & I enjoyed it the more as the weather was as fine as any day I have seen in England altho the morning did not promise much. After descending I continued my walk along the banks of the river to have a look at "Kinfauns Castle" the seat of Lord Gray.[3] The building is not yet completed. 'Tis after the gothic stile & its situation is at the foot of Kinnoul Craig on a mound gently rising from the river side. Its approach is thro. an avenue of larch trees & in front & on each side are groves of ever greens intermixed with old oaks & elms, tho' as they are upon falling ground the Castle is seen to advantage from the high road & the Tay. It was 3 Oclk: when I returned to my lodgings & after taking an early dinner I mounted the roof of the coach at 5 Oclk: for Dunkeld. A few miles distant from Perth is seen on the right of the road & on the opposite side of the river the palace of Scone famous for having been the residence of Scottish monarchs, but as I shall probably see it again, so no more at present.[4] Night coming on soon after I could not distinguish much more than as we approached Dunkeld the country became more mountainous & it was evident

---

2. Sir William Wallace (1272?–1305), the legendary national hero, was periodically forced into hiding.

3. Kinfauns Castle was begun in the early 1820s by Francis, fourteenth lord Gray (d. 1842).

4. Scone Palace was built (1803–1808) in "Georgian-Gothic" style, designed by William Atkinson. It was erroneously believed to be a former royal residence, probably because of its proximity to Scone Abbey, the traditional site of royal inaugurations. It was, in fact, the residence of the earls of Mansfield.

we were entering the Highlands, as this place is considered the principal pass to the Highlands in this quarter of the Country.

Distance from Edinburgh to Kinross 24.
       "   from Kinross to Perth...17.
       "   "   Perth to Dunkeld. 15.

Memo: the hight of Kinnoul from the run of the Tay is 632 ft.

7th. It rained occasionally to day tho' the weather has been fine for most of the time I took a guide to conduct me over the extensive grounds of "Dunkeld House" the seat of the Duke of Atholl.[5] I found many objects well worth attention; the first I was taken to was "the Hermitage," a small pleasure house tastefully built on the bank of the river Brahan where there is a heavy Fall of water. The water is made to reflect on the top & side walls by mirrors placed for the purpose which with the noise of the fall has a very pleasing effect. This building which is about the size of a Summer house is called "Ossians Hall"; I suppose from the large picture of Ossian to be seen there & from its romantic situation.[6] I

---

5. A modest building to be the residence of the duke of Atholl, John Murray, fourth duke (d. 1830) who abandoned plans to build a grand palace on grounds north of the village of Dunkeld.

6. The "Hermitage" or "Ossian's Hall" was a belvedere built in 1758 some forty feet above a waterfall of the River Braan. Opposite the entrance a picture of Ossian playing his harp was painted on a panel which, when drawn aside, revealed the waterfall. The interior walls and ceiling were lined with mirrors that reflected the river.

did intend to go on to day as far as "Blair Atholl" 21 miles distant, but finding it would have deranged my other plans I abandoned it & employed the remainder of the day in exploring the Dukes Dunkeld domain. I had heard frequently of the vast number of forest trees which the late & present Duke of Atholl had planted. All the hills & mountains about the village (& by the way 'tis nothing but mountains) are covered over with "Larches" Oaks & firs, & in process of time must be highly valuable. Some of the forests have been standing 200 or 300 years & the timber is fit or nearly so for cutting. In going to Ossians Hall I was carried thro. the nursery of young trees all of which are raised from the seed. While walking in the forests I could not help thinking what a pity it was that so many beautiful evergreens of all sizes should be so entirely hid from the view. How much I wished to be able to transport a thousand or two to my friends in Rhode Island. My guide informed me the Duke had planted 9100 acres with forest trees.[7] I was also shewn "Ossians Cave" a mere rough pile of stones, where within is seen an illegible inscription & Ossians bed place, but all this about Ossian is only a humbug.[8] About 4

---

7. The principal estate of the dukes of Atholl stretched north from Dunkeld through river valleys to the Forest of Atholl. In 1727, the second duke introduced the larch tree to Scotland and over the next hundred years he and his heirs conducted one of the largest planting experiments on record. According to the *Encyclopedia Britannica* (11th ed.), some 14 million larches were planted on the Atholl estate between 1727 and 1826.

8. The poet James Macpherson (1738–1796) between 1760 and 1763 published three volumes of poetry purporting to be translated from Gaelic works composed in the third century by a legendary bard and warrior, Oisin or Ossian. Soon after they were published, sceptics, including Dr. Johnson, cast doubt

miles from Dunkeld is the "Rumbling Bridge" so called from the waters of the Brahan tumbling down a steep rock of 70ft. & of course making a great noise. 'Tis a good sight for those who like the sublime & beautiful, but nothing to be compared to our Pawtucket falls which if some of these "Tourists" or guide writers should see, they would describe it as if heaven & earth was coming together.[9] The village of Dunkeld is not worth mentioning, excepting that it is a great resort of strangers from all parts on account of its highly picturesque environs & it may fairly be said to have mountains on every side & from some distance is seen a range of the Grampian Hills. I before mentioned that this is one of the principal passes into the Highlands & the <u>book</u> describes its entrance as being "awfully grand."[1] I do not know the exact extent of the Dukes property in this neighbourhood, but was informed that within a circumferance of 8 or 10 miles, the pleasure walks (many of which I have promenaded to day) measure in all no less than 70 miles. These walks extend in every direction along the mountains & upon the banks of the Tay, which is here quite wide & pretty rapid.

The mansion house is very old & plain & altogether unworthy of so princely an estate as Dunkeld & of so powerful a nobleman as the Duke of Atholl.

---

on their authenticity, and in 1805 an investigating committee reported that Macpherson had fabricated them.

9. A bridge across a narrow chasm of the Braan River one mile upstream from Ossian's Hall. At Pawtucket, Rhode Island, the Blackstone River drops only fifty feet but is much broader than the Braan.

1. JCB probably quotes from a local guide book. His principal sources of information about Scotland do not mention this pass.

8th. Octr. Left Dunkeld at 8 Am & arrived at Perth a little after 10. In this ride I had the satisfaction of viewing the grand scenery at the entrance of the village which I lost when I arrived as it was then dark. Altho. the weather was cold & windy yet we had no rain till 5 in the afternoon & since that time & is now quite a pelting storm. Towards noon I took a walk about 2½ miles from Perth to see the ancient Palace of Scone the favorite residence of the Scottish Kings. The estate is now in posession of Lord Mansfield & nothing remains of the old building; the present one was erected about 20 years ago, of a kind of stone similar to our Connecticut Stone, & in the Gothic Style; the general plan is not different from all the larger houses of the English Nobility & the furniture nothing remarkable, one room however is splendid. The chairs, sophas, & wainscotting are of Beauvais tapestry.[2] I was shewn the bed of James 6th, & also the Bed of Queen Mary doubly interesting as the satin quilt & velvet Curtains were embroided by her during her confinement in Loch Leven Castle.[3] These things of course are faded from lapse of time & the velvet curtains almost falling to pieces. The palace did not contain many paintings & the only one that drew my attention was a portrait of Lord Chief Justice Mansfield, taken in his robes & wig.[4] Scone was always visited by the pretenders when they came to Scotland &

---

2. See p. 87, n. 4, above. Some of the palace's furniture was bought in France by the second earl of Mansfield when he was ambassador to France, 1772–1778.

3. James VI of Scotland was the son of Mary Stuart and Henry Stewart, lord Darnley (1545–1567). He became James I, king of England, in 1603.

4. William Murray (1705–1793) served as lord chief justice and chancellor of the Exchequer. He became earl of Mansfield in 1776.

there are still to be seen some few other remnants of furniture which was used in the old building. I was pleased with its situation which is upon rising ground about ¼ mile distant from the river Tay & the lawn in front agreeably varigated with venerable trees. Tomorrow morning I shall take my departure for Dundee by the first conveyance, which will be by steamer & which I was told is equally as interesting a route as by land. Perth is altogether a very pleasant place, or more properly speaking the neighbourhood of Perth, & the green walks called the "North & South Inches" shaded by trees afford a healthy & agreeable promenade to the inhabitants.[5]

Octr. 9th. Left Perth in the Steam Boat for Dundee at 7 Am & arrived at ½ past 9, after a delightful sail down the river Tay. After leaving Perth the river becomes very wide, the country picturesque & many fine seats along the banks. The sun was out very bright which added vastly to the scene.

    I had previously determined to spend a day in Dundee so as to make an excursion to Glammis Castle, & after having breakfasted I took a gig & drove out to it a distance of 12 miles from the town. Glammis is the seat of the Earl of Strathmore & as to its external appearance is different from any Castle I have yet seen; the turrets are all in the shape of a sugar Loaf & the build-

---

5. The word "inch" was used in Scotland to denote an island, or meadowland close to water. The North and South Inches were parklands extending west from the banks of the Tay, said to have been given to the city of Perth by the Mercer family.

ing seems to have been erected without regard to much regularity, probably owing to its having been built at different periods. From the date of 1606 upon a stone over one of the windows it would seem that this part at least of the Castle underwent a repair at that time. The interior contains almost nothing of any consequence, as the Castle is entirely forsaken by the Earl, who seldom or ever honours it with his presence.[6] Few of the rooms have any furniture in them & what there is is only a few old chairs & tables. The most interesting part that was shown me was the bed chamber wherein Malcholm 2d. King of Scotland was murdered by Mackbeth. 'Tis a small room of perhaps 10 by 12 or 15ft. & with one small window looking into the court. On the wall is the date of 1620 by which I suppose it was refitted in that year; the floor also appears to have been laid recently (say within a century past). In one of the other chambers is shewn the bedstead upon which 'tis said the bloody deed was performed, it is not more than a foot high, with oak posts.[7] In the long hall are to be seen a great Number of family portraits. I don't know how it is, but when I am in any of these famous old Establishments I take more pleasure & satisfaction in viewing the portraits of a "long line of illustrious ancestors" than any other paintings, & I should suppose

6. Thomas Lyon Bowes, eleventh earl of Strathmore (d. 1846), was descended from Patrick Lyon, eleventh lord Glamis who was created earl of Strathmore in 1677.

7. Glamis Castle was a royal hunting lodge from the eleventh to the fourteenth centuries. It was reputedly the site where Malcolm II was murdered in 1034. His successor, Duncan I (1034–1040) was killed elsewhere by Macbeth. JCB was misinformed about Malcolm II's assassination.

they could be held in great respect by the possessors. Some of the females of the Strathmore family certainly appeared very beautiful on canvas.[8] Among others hanging in the Hall was Lady Chesterfield one of Charles' beauties a highly pleasing countenance, & a portrait of Queen Mary of England much too lovely a woman to have been the cause of shedding so much of innocent blood. Glammis is now a most dreary & dismal place & would require a vast deal of money to put it in habitable condition. The park is extensive & the trees numerous & venerable, yet every thing about the Castle as within has the appearance of neglect. The Earls estates in the neighbourhood I was told were very valuable & produce him £14,000 per Annum; I returned to Dundee at ½ past 4 & spent the remainder of the day in exploring the place, which is pleasantly on the North bank of the Tay & contains about 30,000 inhabitants. The houses are built of Stone & no part of the town can be called handsome. The harbour is a good one & has some commodious docks in one of which I saw a Boston Ship. As Dundee contains nothing to interest a traveller who has no letters of introduction I have determined to leave it tomorrow. Dundee is a thriving place & has a good many manufacturing Establishments.

Distance from Perth 22½ miles by land & I believe the same by water.

---

8. One of the later females of the family, Lady Elizabeth Bowes-Lyon (1900–2002), daughter of the 14th earl of Strathmore, became duchess of York when she married in 1923 and subsequently queen-consort of George VI (r. 1936–1952).

10th. Took my seat on top of the mail at 7 am & arrived at Aberdeen at 3 PM. The ride was pleasant as the weather was very favourable & altho. we were in full view of the German Ocean all the way, yet for the greater part the soil was as good & the Country as well cultivated as in most parts of Scotland that I have seen. But for the last 20 miles it was barren & stoney enough & reminded me of some parts of the country on the New Pawcatuck Turnpike in Rhode Island where it is miserable enough God knows.[9] The road passed over a great many mountains & deep glens which made it quite dangerous in many places. After I had dressed and refreshed myself a little I called upon Messrs. Pirie to whom I had a letter from Messrs. Dickason.[1] He was not at home, so I left the letter with my card of address. The remainder of the day I walked about the new town of Aberdeen & gained a general idea of its local situation, which is at the confluence of the Rivers Don & Dee into the German Ocean. Its harbour is safe & commodious & its navigation pretty extensive, having generally a Number of ships employed in the Greenland whale fishery.

Distance from Dundee to Aberdeen 66 miles.

11th. This has really been one of the most disagreeable nay, I may say "horrifying" days I have experienced since I have been in

---

9. A road linking Providence, Rhode Island, to a steamboat terminus on Long Island Sound at New London, Connecticut. It crossed a desolate stretch known as "Hell's Half-Acre."

1. I have been unable to identify Messers. Pirie.

Europe. When I awoke I found it raining as hard as it did at the time of "the Flood" & blowing accordingly, so I did not sally fourth 'til nearly 1 O'clk: when I met Mr. P[*irie*] who was comming to call upon me. This Gentleman who is a Scotchman received me very politely & introduced me to the reading & news room, which is an Establishment highly creditable to Aberdeen & would be to any city. After this I went to call upon Dr. Glennie of Marishall College Aberdeen. I have a letter to him from his nephew in London. The Dr. is in the country, tho. I perhaps may see him on Monday.[2]

At 5 I dined with Mr. [*blank*] to whom I had been introduced by Mr. Pirie & I believe is a partner of his. His lady is a very agreeable woman, rather youthful & has a good deal of beauty. The Brother of Mr. [*blank*] was at table & likewise two ladies who reside at Rotterdam. The dinner was good & as the company were in good humour everthing passed off well. Grouse was one of the dishes & I do not remember of ever before eating of this bird—'twas excellent—they were roasted & eaten with jelly & the meat uncommonly tender & delicate. Memo. hereafter I think I shall occassionally call for grouse.

There was nothing different at this Scotch dinner from what I have before met with & indeed from what is common at any Gentlemans table in England or America <u>excepting</u> that after the meats & desert were removed, the waiter drew a bottle of porter, poured the whole of it into a large silver Cup or Goblet

---

2. George Glennie was a professor of moral philosophy at Marischal College which took its name from George Keith, earl of Marischal, who founded it in 1593.

with two handles & set it upon the table. Then the host took it & drank what he pleased & passed it round to the company, each one drinking or not as he liked, in fact it was passed about just like a communion cup. As I had never seen any thing of the like before, it struck me very forcibly & I shall never forget it.[3] The Ladies sat at table a short time after this & then retired leaving the gentlemen to their wine as in England. We sat an hour longer —port & madeira were the wines drank, after which we met the Ladies in the drawing room, took tea & returned home at 9.

12th. Sunday. The weather in the fore part of the day was fine but towards evening we had rain.

I attended Church with Mr. Pirie & heard an excellent sermon from the revd. Bishop.[4] Afterwards dined with Mr. P. at his seat in the country which is finely situated on rising ground, with a full view of the Ocean. Mrs P. is an amiable lady & still handsome tho' she has had 9 children. 2 or 3 other gentlemen were present & the evening passed off agreeably.

13th. Rather cold this morning tho' the weather was clear, passed the day in company with Mr. Thompson, who was very obliging in showing me all the Lions of the place.[5] They were few to be sure, but the public or dancing rooms are well worth viewing.

---

3. The ceremonial passing of a loving-cup at the end of a banquet was not unknown in England in the early 1800s.

4. Bishop of the Episcopal Church of Scotland, William Skinner (1778–1857) was elected by the clergy in 1816 to succeed his father as bishop of Aberdeen.

5. See Diary entry for March 27, 1823.

They are large & spacious & elegantly fitted up & are considered only inferiour to the rooms at Bath.

I also called & delivered a letter to Dr. Glennie professor of Marishal College he received me politely & shew me the Library & apparatus of the college, the latter of which is very complete, as much or more so than any thing of the kind in the three Kingdoms. The students in the Scotch Colleges do not like our own live within the walls but board out in private families.

14th. I am again favoured with good weather, & the principal part of the forenoon has been occupied in taking leave of my acquaintances, tho' after breakfast I took a walk in company with a young Scotchman to the Old town of Aberdeen; there is nothing here to interest excepting the old stone building of Kings College.[6] 'Tis vacation time & so everything was shut excepting the Chapel where some repairs are going on. We looked in & as there was nothing but some old cut up benches to be seen we soon cleared out. Indeed it looked more like the chapel of Brown University than any thing I could imagine.[7] This young fellow was quite raw from the Country & was upon his first journey to London to

---

6. Named for its patron, King James IV (1473–1513), King's College was authorized by a papal bull some ten years before it was established in 1505. In 1860 King's "fused" with Marischal College to form the University of Aberdeen.

7. The chapel at King's College was undergoing restoration and repairs when JCB saw it. It had an elaborately carved screen and canopied stalls unlike anything in the chapel of Brown University which, during JCB's undergraduate days, occupied space on the first floor of University Hall.

seek his fortune. Johnson says "the finest sight to a Scotchman is the high road that leads him to London."[8]

Aberdeen is said to contain about 30,000 or upwards of inhabitants & is a place of a good deal of trade. On the quay I saw a number of the Greenland Whale Fisherman that had just returned with full Cargoes. Holborn Street on entering the town is the principal Street & properly Speaking the only one that deserves mentioning, as most of the others are narrow & dirty. At 4 P.M: I took the Mail & arrived at Fochabers by Huntley at ½ past 11. Towards midnight it became quite frosty & cold & as the Country is altogether uninteresting I did not so much regret riding in the night. Distances from Aberdeen to Fochabers 57 miles—

15th Wednesday. It rained very hard in the morning after breakfast I sent by the porter of the Inn a small parcel to a Miss Gordon & a sealed letter to his Grace the Duke which were given me by a female relation of theirs residing in London.[9] In an hours time I received a billet from his Grace politely requesting me to dine with him at 5. As this was the first & probably the only opportu-

---

8. JCB, quoting from memory, has garbled Dr. Johnson's reply to Rev. John Ogilvie who had remarked that Scotland had a great many "noble, wild prospects." Johnson replied: "I believe, Sir, you have a great many. Norway, too, has noble, wild prospects; and Lapland is remarkable for prodigious, noble, wild prospects. But, Sir, let me tell you, the noblest prospect which a Scotchman ever sees, is the high road that leads him to England." Quoted in James Boswell, *The Life of Samuel Johnson*, entry for July 6, 1763.

9. Alexander Gordon (1743–1827), fourth duke of Gordon and Richmond. Miss Gordon was probably a daughter by Jean Christie (d. 1824), a village girl, who became the duke's second wife after bearing him nine children.

nity I should have to associate with a noble Lord & more especially with one of the highest noblemen in the realm, I readily accepted his invitation. In the mean time I walked to the Castle & was shewn thro' it by his private secretary who has been with the Duke 40 years. It is a most magnificent building outside, but the Dining room & one or two others are only worth particularizing. The first is all that remains of the ancient building which originally stood on site of the present Castle & is a grand & superb banqueting apartment. This with many others is hung round with family portraits.

At 5 Oclk: I was ready dressed & went to the castle in a post Chaise & was received in great style by a train of servants in State liveries. The company at table consisted of only the Duke, his private secretary[,] a gentleman there on a visit & myself. After tea in the Evening I was requested to take a bed, which I declined & at between 8 & 9 I was taken to my lodging at the Inn in the Dukes own carriage.

There are <u>many</u> little particulars relating to this visit which I shall forbear to commit to paper at present; hereafter perhaps I may do it when I am more at my leisure, at any rate no circumstances would be lost by lapse of time, for an affair of this kind is always <u>too strongly</u> impressed on our memories ever to be eradicated.

16th. This morning until 11 the weather was so remarkably fine that a fire was unnecessary & in fact, I breakfasted with my window open. After sending my card with a P.P.C.[1] upon it to the

---

1. The letters "P.P.C." for Pour Prendre Congé ("to take leave") were written

Castle I took post Chaise to Elgin a distance of 9 miles—N.B.: the dearest price of travelling I have yet met with, it cost me including tolls 19s. exactly.

Elgin is only famous for a remarkably fine ruin just at the entrance of the town. 'Tis thought to be the finest in Scotland & I think well worth stopping an hour to examine. The interior of the ruin is now occupied as a graveyard.[2] Continued on in the Coach at 4 & arrived at Inverness at a little past 11. Feeling fatigued I took a cup of Tea & soon went to bed. The road presented nothing deserving notice.

Some distance from Inverness & on the right side of the road is the famous Culloden Field.[3] The weather today has been very changeable, sometimes sun shine & a good deal of rain.

17th. A rainy morning & continued so to do 'til nearly four Oclk: but I was not to be detained by bad weather, so I sallied fourth & scoured all Inverness & its environs. This Town is called the Capital of the North of Scotland & contains about 13,000 inhabitants. 'Tis pleasantly situated upon the river Ness which comes out of Loch Ness & empties itself into the Murray firth running

---

on the lower lefthand corner of calling cards left at residences of hosts before leaving their neighborhood.

2. The ruin was that of a thirteenth-century cathedral, neglected since the sixteenth century. In 1640 its interior was gutted by order of the General Assembly of the Church of Scotland.

3. Site of a brief but decisive battle, April 16, 1746, where Jacobite Scots, partisans of the Stuart pretender, were defeated by the duke of Cumberland's Hanoverian army.

nearly in a Northeast direction. Here is also the entrance of the Caledonian Canal which runs on the West side of the river 'til its junction with Loch Ness.[4] Lofty Mountains are to be seen on every side of the town, & altho the Highland garb is not so common as in some smaller places, yet from the generality with which the Gaelic language is spoken & the rough, hardy appearance of the lower orders, one can easily fancy that he is far removed from London or even from Edinburgh.[5] High Street is the best & with the exception of another running at right angles is the only one of any consequence. The walks on the banks of the river must in a fine day be delightful as the width is here very considerable, & the stream rapid. As I see no advantage in continuing my journey further to the northward & having already taken a much wider circuit than travellers in general I propose tomorrow to set my face towards the South. Indeed, when I left London I hardly expected to come to the North of Edinburgh but I have continued pushing on from one stage to another 'til at last I am really surprised that I have got so far.

---

4. A waterway connecting the Atlantic to the North Sea, the Caledonian Canal cut across northern Scotland along the "Great Glen," the country's main watershed. Sixty miles long (of which thirty-four are natural lakes), the canal opened in 1822 and was considered a marvel of modern engineering.

5. Wearing "Highland garb" was forbidden to Scots by the Act for Disarming the Highlanders of 1746 (19. Geo II c.19). Among the prohibited articles were "the Plaids, Philebeg, or little Kilt, Trowse, Shoulder belts...." Difficult to enforce, the "Diskilting Act" was repealed in 1782. When George IV visited Scotland in 1822, he appeared, as announced at Holyrood in the "Garb of Old Gaul," a Royal Stewart tartan. The insignia of Highland Jacobitism then became symbolic of a broader patriotism and was much in evidence by the time of JCB's visit.

18th. Left Inverness at ½ past 11 this morning previous to which time I employed a few hours in resurveying the town & country around & in walking to the entrance of the Canal. Shortly after commencing my ride the sun came out bright & warm as on a summers day & owing to the late heavy rains every thing was fresh & verdant & if I had had the whole season before me I <u>could</u> <u>not</u> have chosen a finer day for a pleasure ride thro. "the great Glen of Scotland." The road for the first 18 miles was along the banks of Loch Ness 'til we came to the "Generals Hut" a small Inn where we stopped to wait,[6] & in the mean time I ran on a mile ahead to have a view of the "Fall of Foyers" called in this country the Niagara of Scotland, but altho I have never seen our famous cataract yet I am convinced 'tis no more to be compared to it than a mountain to a mole hill. 'Ts true 'tis a great "fall of water" & <u>said</u> to fall a distance of 100 ft tho I should doubt if 'twas even half that. for my part I have seen many falls in R I d. quite equal to it & our Pawtucket falls especially are in my humble opinion far its superior. The disadvantage—with regard to Foyers is that there is hardly any place from whence it can be fully seen without running a great risk of tumbling off the precipice, & how Dr. Johnson, such an unwealdy old fellow as he was could ever have got down such a rugged & dangerous brae to have given such a flaming description of it as he has done, is to me quite a wonder. I am rather inclined to think, he like a great many other authors described the thing without really having seen it. He probably heard the noise & saw the side rocks, & I suspect

---

6. An inn named for General George Wade (1673–1748) who surveyed the construction of a system of roads useful for military operations in Scotland.

that's all.[7] Returning to the Inn I eat a small piece of oat meal cake, which I called for by way of trial & then proceeded on the route to "Fort Augustus" where I am now writing. The Loch is immediately lost sight of & you do not see it again until arriving at the Fort which is situated at the Western end of the Loch, a distance of 32 miles from Inverness.

Whoever has a taste for the sublime, or loves romantic scenery can here be gratified to the full extent. The moon was shining quite bright when I reached Fort Augustus where I found an Inn really very comfortable & have eaten a hasty supper & tho my bed looks rather hard I think I shall sleep sound. The village of Fort Augustus is composed mostly of miserable wood huts & the fort itself is quite dismantled.[8]

19th. At ½ past 10 resumed my route for Fort William.[9] At first it was a little cloudy as it rained at 8 Oclk: but shortly after the

---

7. The Foyers fell thirty feet in the upper cataract and ninety feet in the lower. Once called the "Fall of Smoke," it was considered the most magnificent in Britain, until the river was dammed to supply power to an aluminum factory. Dr. Johnson described "its steep descent of…dreadful depth" but added that he had "visited the place at an unseasonable time and found it divested of its dignity and terror" by a "long continuance of dry weather…." See *A Journey to the Western Islands of Scotland*, J. D. Fleeman, ed. (Oxford, 1965), pp. 25–26.

8. Fort Augustus was built in the 1730s by General George Wade on the site of a barracks which had been put up in 1716. It was named for William Augustus, duke of Cumberland (1721–1765), the third son of George II. Highlanders captured it during the uprising of 1745, but it was retaken after the battle of Culloden. (See p. 101, n. 3)

9. An earthworks built by General George Monck (1608–1670), commander-in-chief in Scotland in the 1650s. It was rebuilt in the reign of William III and renamed for him.

weather cleared up & became fine. The road led thro Glengary, along the bank of the small Loch Oich 3 or 4 miles long. 'Tis a narrow but highly romantic Glen. On the opposite side are the ruins of Invergary Castle & the seat of the Chief of the McDonnell Clan.[1] These chiefs were formerly famous for the buying of Black Mail tho' I understand the present one is a Banker in Edinburgh.[2] From Glengary, Loch Lochy soon came into view. 'Tis fourteen miles in length & on its Bank stands "Letter Findley" a most miserable filthy Inn.[3] From "Letter Findley" the road leads thro the "Lochaber Country" where I think I never saw the people live in so much wretchedness. The Log houses beyond the Alleganeys are palaces to them.[4] Soon after this the Ben Nevis shew itself with its tops covered with eternal snows, & here I could perceive a sensible change in the Atmosphere, it was keen & cold very much like our Decr. weather, before the snow falls. At 5 arrived at Fort William where I am now visiting at a comfortable Inn.

20th. Having determined to remain one day at Fort William for the purpose of ascending Ben Nevis the highest hill in Britain, I left the Inn with my guide at 20 minutes before 10 Oclk: The day

1. A stronghold of the MacDonnell of Glengarry, razed by General Monck in 1654. A second castle was destroyed by the duke of Cumberland after Culloden.

2. Protection money extorted from landholders in border counties of England and Scotland and along the Highlands border by free-booting chiefs.

3. Letter Findlay was described by Robert Southey as "a single house, which is said to have been much improved of late; it is not easy to believe that it can ever have been dirtier or more uncomfortable than it is now...." Robert Southey, *Journal of a Tour in Scotland in 1819* (Edinburgh, 1972), p. 201.

4. JCB had crossed through the Alleghenies in 1819 when, as an agent of

was fair & altogether such as one could wish for an enterprize of the Kind. We commenced mounting the hill at about 10 & as the lower part is quite as steep as any & the sun shining bright I puffed & blowed a good deal & was much fatigued by the time we had got ½ way up. Towards the third quarter all vegetation ceases & the mountain is thickly covered with loose stones, this made it still the more tiresome & I began to be a good deal uneasy, feeling faint & a general tremor thro' all my limbs; here I would have given a good many guineas to have been on the level of the earth, & I hardly think I should have persevered any further had not we rested for a time & my guide done his best to encourage me. By & bye we pursued our task & I could now sensibly feel a difference in the atmosphere. About this time the wind suddenly changed & it began to grow very cold & increased as we ascended. About a mile & ¼ from the top we came to the well, a fine spring of water among the stones. At this place we made a halt & refreshed ourselves with Whiskey & cold meat & bread which the Guide very prudently took with him. This repast served to reinstate me & to put me in condition for the remainder of the journey & as it blew so hard & we suffered so much from cold we were glad to be moving. A few moments walk from the well brought us to the beginning of snow & after traversing over eternally frozen snows & thro' a dense fog we reached the summit of "Ben Nevis" at ¼ past 1 Oclk: But how much was I disappointed in not being able to see 2 yds before me, the mist was so thick & especially as every thing promised so

---

Brown and Ives, he looked into tobacco farming in Kentucky and opportunities for land purchase in Ohio. See Introduction.

fair when I commenced my labours. But it was in vain to repine, in fact the cold was so intense & we both were so stiff & chilled thro' with it, that we did not take long to consider of the business but soon began to retrace our steps, anxious to get into milder lattitudes, for I really think if we had staid up there ¼ hour longer we should never have come down alive, for we both were benumbed with the cold & so stiff that we could scarcely move. We were not long however before we got into a more christian climate, which with the exercise of walking soon thawed us out. But the descent from the mountain was long & tiresome, nearly as much so as the ascent. When ½ way down rested & refreshed ourselves once more with Whiskey &c. Finally reached the bottom in safety & arrived at the Inn at ½ past 4 P.M., when I thanked God that he had preserved me thro' so many perils in accomplishing so arduous an adventure, & altho' <u>now</u> I am pleased that I have performed the task, yet I would very unwillingly & with much reluctance undertake it again. Along the upper part of the route the Guide pointed out many deep & dangerous precipices some of which are more than 2000 ft. perpendicular. In mounting also you are forced to go near many steep & hazardous places, from which if one should slip 'twould cost him his life. After warming myself thoroughly & taking some nourishing refreshments I went to Bed, but the next morning felt a good deal sore & stiff in my bones, as the distance I had walked was computed at the least at 15 miles, the height of "Ben Nevis" being found by actual observation to be 4370 ft.[5]

---

5. Ben Nevis rises about 4,400 feet (1.3 miles). Tourists today are advised to allow four hours for the ascent; JCB and his guide took three and one-half hours.

21st. Left Fort William at ¼ past 11 in a gig for "Kings house" a solitary Inn situated alone among the "Black Mountains" distant from Fort William 28 miles. My ride to day was first along the Banks of Loch Linnhe then crossing Loch Leven, which empties into the first mentioned Loch & thro' the celebrated "Glencoe" famous for its bold & commanding scenery.[6] 'Twas moon light before I reached the Inn & altho' its situation was in such a barren district, I was comforted by a good supper of moor Fowl & a good bed, all at moderate charges.—Weather fine—

22d. rose early & took a waggon for Dalmally but finding it went so slow & so hard that I dismissed it at "Inverarnan" 9 miles ahead & after hiring a boy to carry my bundle, footed it on the remainder of the way, a distance of 16 miles, which I accomplished with great ease & was housed at a comfortable Inn at Dalmally at 4 PM. The country presented nothing particular, most of the rout was thro' the "Black Mountains" thinly inhabited by a few miserable beings living in the most wretched manner in huts built of sticks & mud.

23d. Left Dalmally at 7 after breakfasting & walked on to Inveraray a distance of 16 miles. The day was fine & the country began

---

6. Loch Leven in Inverness-shire, a salt-water arm of Loch Linnhe, not to be confused with Loch Leven in Kinross-shire. See Diary entry for October 4, 1823.

Glencoe, a mountain pass fifteen miles long, was celebrated not only for its spectacular scenery but for historical associations, such as the massacre of the Clan Macdonald in 1692 by partisans of William III of England.

to present a more cheering appearance as I approached the Duke of Argyles property. Inveraray is situated at the head of Loch Fine on the western side & is a well built, good looking village. The Castle, seat of the Duke of Argyle is a square building, built of stone, with circular towers at each corner. The grounds are extensive and well laid out, & in many parts are covered with the Larch & Scotch Fir.[7] Just at this time the town was very gay & crowded with well dressed persons, as it was the time of the County Meeting. A sloop of war was laying in the Loch & to day was dressed in all her various signals. Towards night she fired a good many guns, which resounded prodigiously among the neighbouring hills

24th Took passage in the Steam boat for Glasgow which sailed at 2 Oclk: AM; altho' the moon was out bright; yet the wind blew fresh & on the water it was quite cold. We passed down Loch Fine; around the Isle of Bute; touched at Rothsay a small watering place,[8] up the firth of Clyde & river of the same name, where we also touched at Greenock & reached Glasgow at 4 PM. The sail up the Clyde was highly picturesque from the fine seats on its banks as well as the numerous steam boats & other craft on the river. In the Evening I promenaded the city a good deal which I found not materially different from other trading towns. I put up

---

7. Inveraray Castle, rebuilt in the mid-eighteenth century by Archibald Campbell, third duke of Argyll (1682–1761), was in 1823 the seat of George William Campbell (1766–1839) who had become the sixth duke in 1806.

8. Rothesay had been a summer resort since the late Middle Ages.

at the Tontine, an extensive establishment in Argyle Street which appeared to be the principal Street in the City.[9]

25th. It being my intention to visit the Trossachs & Loch Catherine before leaving Scotland, I thought it most prudent as the season was so far advanced to proceed immediately & make my visit on my return to Glasgow.[1] Accordingly I this morning took the coach for Sterling & arrived at about 12 AM, distance 35 miles, nothing worth remarking offered itself. At 1 PM: I left Sterling with only a small bundle & an umbrella & footed it on as far as Callander distance 16 miles. Stopping a few minutes at Doune, a village ½ way, to rest & refresh a little, & it was 6 PM before I reached Callander, a neat highland village & where I passed the night at a very good Inn. This is the first entrance of the Highlands & as you approach it the high Mountains begin to make their appearance. On the road between Doune & C. I passed a number of fine estates but my time would not allow of examining them particularly. Memo. Slept sound after my walk.

26th. Started from Callander on foot for James Stewarts house 10 miles ahead.[2] The morning was remarkably fine & my walk led thro the little village of Kilmahog; thence acrost a small stream,

---

9. The Tontine Hotel, built in 1783, included an assembly hall as well as a coffee shop and guest rooms.

1. A wooded gorge extending from Loch Achray to Loch Katrin (Catherine), the Trossachs was used by Sir Walter Scott as a setting for dramatic action in *The Lady of the Lake* (1810).

2. Probably a reference to Stewart's Inn, a large hostelry, one mile from Loch

called by Scott in the Lady of the Lake "Coilantogle's ford—Clan alpines utmost guard."[3] It was near here that the combat took place between Roderich Dhu & Fitz James, in which the former was slain. Shortly after the Loch's Vennachar & Achray successively make their appearance, which to day shew to great advantage. At noon I reached the Inn which is all that a traveller could wish. Took a guide to the "Trosachs" & Loch Catherine, which altho grand & beautiful did not <u>astonish</u> me as being any thing so <u>very</u> wonderful. I took a sail on the Loch to "Ellens Island" so cald which is a high mass of rocks about 2 miles from the East end of the Loch. It is covered with trees & Lord Gwydir has built a small rustic upon it so that travellers might have some <u>object</u> in visiting it.[4] Returning from the Trossachs my guide led home by a different route among <u>almost</u> impassable rocks, where no person would ever think of going unless to conduct a Whysky Still, of which there are many among the highlands & a good deal of this Liquor is smuggled into the towns without paying the excise duty. A number of gentlemen arriving towards Evening we all dined together & what with comparing notes & agreeable conversation the evening passed off very pleasantly.

Katrin. Possibly a reference to James Stewart, a local peasant, who worked as a tourist guide to the Trossachs and Loch Katrin.

3. JCB cites a phrase from Scott's *The Lady of the Lake*, Canto IV, 786–787: "Till past Clan Alpine's utmost guard/As far as Coilantogle's Ford."

4. "Ellen's Island" at the east end of Loch Katrin was named for Ellen Douglas who was "The Lady of the Lake." The island was once used by rustlers to hide stolen cattle.

Peter Burrell (1754–1820) was created baron Gwydir in 1796.

27th. Arose at 6 Oclk: which is nearly an hour before day light. Breakfasted with my new friends & there we parted. They took the route up the Loch & I to return to Sterling the same way I came. The fine weather we have had for some time past seems now about to give place to wet & cold for before starting this morning it rained considerably. I walked on as far as Callander, but feeling a good deal unwell I stopped for an hour & eat some mutton chops to reinstate myself & then procured a highland poney, but as he went so slow & so hard that I left him at Doune & took again to my legs, which brought me the remaining 8 miles to Sterling at 6 PM & after eating a moor Fowl with toast & jelly went to bed & slept sound.

28th. Before leaving Sterling I walked up to the Castle & enjoyed for a few minutes the highly picturesque & extensive view which it affords. It is situated upon a very high rock & before the invention of ordinance must have been impregnable; but now a few well directed shots would rattle it about their ears.[5] This Castle was formerly considered a place of great importance, it was taken once or twice by Edward of England, & was also beseiged in the rebellion of 45 by the highlanders, but was not taken.[6] In former

---

5. Stirling was given a town charter by Alexander II of Scotland (1198–1249) who made the castle a royal residence. From the mid-fourteenth to the mid-sixteenth centuries it shared with Edinburgh the status of capital of Scotland.

6. Edward I, "Longshanks" (1239–1307), captured Stirling Castle in 1296. It was retaken by William Wallace (1274?–1305) the following year. It fell again to Edward I in 1304. A parliament met there in 1646 because of a plague in Edinburgh.

times it was used as a royal palace & the Scottish parliament occasionally held its settings here. Now 'tis only kept up as a barrack for soldiers & but few guns are mounted. At 9 AM: took the Steam Boat for Edinburgh but as the weather was windy & it rained some I had not much of an opportunity to be on deck & view the scenery; but from what I did see, it did not appear particularly striking. At 3 we were along side the Chain pier at New Haven & landed in a deluge of rain.[7] Took coach & came immediately to Edinburgh.

29th. After calling upon Mr. Keir & Mr McKenzie,[8] gentlemen, to whom I had letters (neither of whom I found at home) I went to visit the old Palace of "Holyrood house" situated at the foot of the Canongate. This royal residence has so often been described that I shall only mention a few of the objects which attracted my attention particularly.[1] The Chapel is in ruins & the Tomb which contains the bones of Darnley & which were formerly shewn,[2] is now locked since the remains of one of the royal family of France

---

7. Newhaven, so called because James IV (1473–1513) built a port there. It was a self-contained, Scandinavian fishing village in 1823. It was later absorbed into the metropolitan area of Edinburgh.

8. I have been unable to identify Mr. Keir and Mr. McKenzie.

1. A palace begun ca. 1500 on the site of an abbey founded in 1128. Holyrood House was ravaged by sword (1544) and fire (1650) and rebuilt in the 1670s by Charles II of England.

2. Henry Stewart, Lord Darnley (1545–1567) through his grandmother, Margaret Tudor, daughter of Henry VII (1457–1509), had, after Elizabeth I, a claim to the English throne. See p. 91, n. 3 above.

have been deposited here. (The Bourbons it will be recollected inhabited Holyrood during the French revolution)[3] It was in this chapel the lovely Queen of Scotland used to say her prayers. The long hall containing all the portraits of the kings was next shewn; the portrait of Mary has been much defaced by some bungling fellow attempting to clean it, but I doubt if it was ever a very good one. In this hall the election of the 16 peers of Scotland is always made. But what above all others was the most interesting to me was the apartments of Mary. In the State Bed room is shown her State Bed, now all in tatters, & another old Bed in the same condition in an adjoining room, called her private bed room. From this last you enter a small closet where Rizzio was stabbed as he was sitting at supper with Mary.[4] In this place is still to be seen the boots armour & a glove of Darnleys. I saw also the private stair case by which the conspiritors entered. Marys work Box is likewise to be seen, but I could not open it as Mr. Silliman says he did.[5] The spot of Blood said to be the Blood of Rizzio is yet pointed out to Strangers. Altho', all that is now to be seen at Holyrood is in fact nothing at all, yet I could not but feel satisfied

---

3. Members of the French royal family in the 1790s were provided apartments in Holyrood House where they could escape creditors as well as revolutionaries. The comte d'Artois, after 1824 Charles x of France (1757–1836), lived there until 1814 and fled there in 1830 when overthrown by the July Revolution.

4. David Rizzio (Riccio) (1533?–1566), Piedmontese courtier and musician, as secretary to Mary Stuart, in 1565 helped to arrange her marriage to Darnley who conspired to kill him the following year.

5. Benjamin Silliman says: "Her toilet remains uninjured; I opened her dressing-box, which contained her pin cushion, the little vessels for perfumes, and other articles of various kinds." *Journal*, iii, p. 179.

that I had visited the very identical apartments that were once inhabited by so interesting a personage as Queen Mary of Scotland, whose misfortunes & sufferings even at this remote period excites the pity of every one who reads her story.

30th. Breakfasted this morning with Mr. Kier, who lives a little out of the City. Afterwards, we walked out together & as the day was fine went around the Salisbury Craig & upon "Arthurs Seat" a high hill to the East or South East of Edinburgh from whence we had a good view of the city, the Firth of Forth & the Neighbouring Coast.[6] From thence Mr. K. shew the different parts of the old town some of its public buildings (including the old parliament house) & afterwards we went to visit the famous Castle of Edinburgh for it is at least famous for its elevated situation, built upon a high rock & so commands the town that a cannon ball could be fired into any mans window—'tis just the counterpart of Sterling Castle.[7] Every part of the city is seen to great advantage from this hight perhaps quite as much so as from Arthurs Seat. Within the Castle is now to be seen the "regalia of Scotland" which for more than a hundred years past has been locked up in a stout oak chest & this in a Bomb proof room until within 4 years past.[8] Indeed so long had they been laid away that

---

6. A hill, 822 feet high, "Arthur's Seat" overlooks Holyrood; once the site of St. Anthony's Chapel, a scene associated with Sir Walter Scott's *The Heart of Midlothian* (1818).

7. Malcolm III (1031?–1093) built Edinburgh castle on this elevated site; James IV (1473–1513) was the first king to make Edinburgh his principal residence.

8. The royal regalia—crown, scepter, and sword of state—were locked away

all rememberance of them had been lost, & it was finally supposed that they had been removed during the turbulence of past
times 'til finally the King gave an order for the room to be
opened. It consists of the "Sword of the State" made of [*sic*] to
James 5th by the Pope of Rome. The Scepter & the rod of office,
each with a large ball of Crystal The crown as might be supposed, composed of gold & precious stones of a large size, some
of which were very brilliant. The ermine is new, but the velvet
part is said to be the <u>original</u> & the same as when worn by the
Scottish Kings & Queens. Some of the pearls & brilliants are
lost. The crown is kept laying upon a red velvet cushion, standing upon a small table with the sword &c. laying by its side. The
table is surrounded at some distance by a strong iron railing or
cage, the keys of which are kept by the Barons of the Exchequer
& all is within the Bombproof room. Accordingly it is necessary
to light the room with lamps. As these were the first regal baubles
that I had ever seen I spent a considerable time in examining &
inquiring into the <u>particulars</u> of a real crown. The castle of
Edinburgh has now only a few guns mounted & but a small garrison. After leaving the castle, Mr. K. took me upon Calton Hill,
which however I had before ascended.

31st. Breakfasted again with Mr. K. We then walked to Leith, as I
had occasion to call upon a Gentleman to whom I had a letter.

---

after the formal union of the kingdoms of Scotland and England in 1707. By
order of George IV (1762–1830), they were put on display a few years before
JCB saw them in 1823.

Took a general survey of this "port of Edinburgh" & then returned, glad enough was I to get to my lodgings, as a more disagreeable day I have scarcely known in England; it was cold & the wind blew a hurricane.

November 1st. Did not arise very early to day, as the wind of yesterday made me quite sick. Mr. K. called upon me at 11 & we profited of the fine sun shine, by taking a pleasant walk 3 miles out of town on the banks of the canal. Returning, we came by the Castle which was formerly occupied by Napier so celebrated for discovering the Logarithms & the room where he studied was pointed out.[9] Passing over a large common to the East of the town we stopped to see them play at the game of "Goff" a game I had never seen or heard of before.[1]

Viewed "Herriots Hospital" as we came along thro' the lower part of the city. This is not really a hospital as it is called, but an assylum where boys are brought up & educated. Tis an old Establishment & munificently endowed & the building is not only spacious but elegant, & a great ornament to Edinburgh.[2] Dined to day with this Gentleman & after passing the Evening in pleasant conversation, I took my leave of him & his sisters, with

---

9. John Napier (1550–1617), a native of Edinburgh, described the invention of logarithms in *Mirifici logarithmorum canonis descriptio* (1614).

1. A variant spelling for golf, derived from a Medieval Dutch word for "club." The "large Common" was the "Links," situated between Edinburgh and Leith, near the Firth of Forth. "Link" in Scotland denoted a level or gently rolling ground near a coast-line, and its plural, a seaside golf course.

2. The hospital was built between 1628 and 1659 with funds left in trust by

but little prospect of ever meeting him again. Mr. K. was formerly of the Army & went with the expedition acrost the desert to Egypt

Novr. 2d. (Sunday) Attended divine service in the presbeterian church in "George Street" where I heard a tolerable good sermon.[3] Dined at Leith with Mr. Scath, where I met a small party of agreable gentlemen. He gave us some very good port & the evening was passed in lively conversation. Mrs. S. is a very genteel pretty little woman but it being only nine months since her marriage her situation was highly interesting. I took leave of the company at 9 & could not but regret the shortness of my acquaintance with this family[4]—And now as I am to leave the city of Edinburgh tomorrow I will only repeat what I believe I have done before, that the situation both of the old & new town is highly romantic, and that no City I have yet seen in Europe exceeds the new town in point of magnificence in its private buildings. The whole is well laid out, with spacious streets & squares & the buildings all of a light colored face stone which give it a very airy appearance.[5] George Street is nearly a mile in length, with St.

George Heriot (1563–1623) to promote the education of poor boys. Heriot was jeweler to the Stuarts, the royal family of Scotland, and after 1603, of England, and to many of their courtiers. The Heriot Trust invested heavily in land around Edinburgh and profited from the city's expansion in the eighteenth century.

3. St. Andrew's Church, 1783–1787, first church built in the New Town; designed by David Kay.

4. I have been unable to identify Mr. and Mrs. Scath.

5. In April 1766, the Edinburgh Town Council, planning to expand to the north, invited "architects and others to give in Plans of a New Town, marking

Andrews Square at one end in which there is erecting a column to the late Lord Melville,[6] & Charlotte Square at the other containing an elegant building for public worship. I had not the good fortune to see much of the society of the place. Mr. J[*effrey*]—a brother to the celebrated reviewer was out of town, which prevented me from seeing this distinguished character as I otherwise probably should have done.[7] Another letter I had to a gentleman residing in a fine house procured me no attentions, in fact he never even took any notice at all of it, either by leaving or sending his card. As the weather begins to grow cold the inhabitants from the country will come to town & every thing becomes more gay than it has been some time past. So a visit to Edinburgh a month or 6 weeks hence would have afforded me more of an insight into Scottish bon ton, than at present. However we cannot always make our arrangements so as exactly to hit the mark, & I am quite contented as it is. The "Great unknown"[8] I understand is also out of town.

---

out streets of a proper breadth, and by-lanes, and the best situation for a reservoir, and any other public buildings...." A plan submitted by James Craig was finally approved in July 1767.

6. Henry Dundas, first viscount Melville (1742–1811), member of Parliament for Midlothian, was an ally of a succession of English prime ministers. His control of patronage made him one of the most powerful men in Scotland.

7. John Jeffrey (d. 1845) was until 1807 a merchant who spent some time in Boston as partner in a family business. His older brother, Francis, lord Jeffrey (1773–1850), in addition to being a distinguished lawyer, founded the *Edinburgh Review* in 1802 and helped edit it until 1824.

8. A sobriquet, in common use after 1814, for the author of the Waverly novels which were published anonymously. By the early 1820s, authorship was widely

Novr. 3rd. Left Edinburgh at 8 Oclk AM & arrived at Lanark at 1 a distance of 32 miles. After taking breakfast I walked out to the "Falls of Clyde" 2 miles from the Inn, passing the very extensive cotton mills of Mr. Owen, in whose different establishments at this place are employed I was told 4000 persons.[9] The lower fall at this place is termed [*blank*]. 'Tis truly a fine fall of water of about 80 ft & the scenery around is picturesque, but it is thought much of by English & visited by all travellers in these parts, yet to an American it is altogether a secondary affair.[1] I had intended to have taken the coach this Evening for Hamilton but it was so overladen that I am obliged to wait 'til tomorrow. The Evening however I spent in pleasant conversation with a German traveller I met at the Inn.

Novr. 4th. A couple of Gentlemen inviting me to join them in a Poste Chaise as far as Hamilton. We started at 9 after breakfast & had a very sociable ride, & as the day was fine & the road led along the Clyde our 15 miles did not seem as long as tho' we had

---

and correctly attributed to Sir Walter Scott (1771–1832) although he refused to acknowledge it until 1827. The phrase may come from a hymn by Isaac Watts (1674–1748): "When shall we see the Great Unknown/and in His presence stand?"

9. Robert Dale Owen (1771–1858), Welsh industrialist, social reformer, and lobbyist, bought his father-in-law's cotton mills in New Lanark in 1799 and tried to make them a model community. He continued to manage them until 1825.

1. The River Clyde had three falls in a four-mile stretch of wooded, rocky terrain. One of them dropped eighty-four feet in three cataracts.

been in a lumbering Stage Coach. On our arrival at the village I walked out for the purpose of viewing the palace of the Duke of Hamilton. But I could not get admittance into the house or even into the grounds, so the only view I had of it was from the high road. It is a longer pile of buildings, built of gray stones, which gives it a venerable appearance, & the front exhibits a good deal of taste in architecture, a wide spreading lawn with ancient oaks & elms separates it from the road, on the opposite side of which is the dukes Deer park (an extensive range) where is also another residence or hunting lodge of the Noble family of Hamilton, called "Chatelherault" being built after a palace of the same name in France, as the Dukes of Hamilton were formerly peers of France likewise.[2]

After taking some refreshment I joined my companions who intended walking into Glasgow & at 5 PM, just at candle light, I entered the city by the "Canon Gate" at the East end of the town & repaired to my old quarters at the Tontine[3]—10 miles from H.

---

2. Alexander Hamilton Douglas, tenth duke of Hamilton (1767–1852), in the 1820s used money from his father-in-law, William Beckford (1759–1844), to "recast" Hamilton Palace in Lanarkshire. It was torn down in 1927 because of mining tunnels below.

James Hamilton, second earl of Arran (d. 1575), was given the title duke of Châtelherault in 1548 when, as governor of Scotland (regent) during the minority of Mary Stuart, he acceded to her marriage with the dauphin of France, the future King Francis II (1544–1560).

3. See p. 110, n. 9, above; also reference below to "Tontine C[offee] H[ouse] and exchange." From its establishment in 1783, Glasgow tobacco and cotton merchants met there to do business.

Memo. I had almost forgotten to mention that the country from Edinburgh to Lanark is the most dreary piece of country I have yet [*met*] with in the Low Lands of Scotland, & 'tis a wild swampy moor, & so black a tract that but little ever comes to perfection. As late as it is now in the season I noticed oats standing in the field quite green & which cannot be expected to come to any thing this year.

Novr. 5th. I was disappointed in not receiving [*letter?*] for this place which I expected from a gentleman in Leith, so I could only make myself familiar with its situation & its public institutions. Glasgow has within a few years owing to its commerce & its increasing manufactures risen to be the 2d. city in Great Britain & the third in the empire containing at present about 130 or 140,000 Inhabitants. Its situation is a convenient one, being nearly on a level, excepting a gentle rise at the west end & a still greater at the North on the suburbs. To day I have been continually upon the walk, & I believe have most thoroughly viewed & examined every part. Argyle Street is the leading one of the place running nearly East & West on a parallel with the quay & river Clyde, in this Street is the Tontine C. H. & exchange where I lodge.

George Street running to the north of Argyle but parallel also is a wide straight & well built Street. The most fashionable part of the town is the West End, where from the appearances of the houses the nabobs must reside. To the South East of Argyle, is "Glasgow green" bordering upon the river, an extensive & well laid out public walk; here is "Nelsons monument" a tall, clumsy stone obelisk:[4] on the opposite side of the Clyde is a small [*extension?*] of the City, & the row fronting the river called "Carlton row" is really magnificent. About in this quarter are 3 bridges, St. Andrews Square near the Salt Market is quite a retired spot & containing a large & handsome stone church.[5] At the end of St. Georges Street. which I have before mentioned is St. Georges Square filled with fine buildings & containing also a bronze statue of General Sir John Moore who was a native of Glasgow.[6] Memo—I have merely an item of the above Streets & squares so as to fix them more deeply in my memory. In the Evening was quite fatigued with my days operations & accordingly went to bed at an early hour, as I did not find that there were any amusements whatever of a public nature going on.

Novr. 6th. Before breakfast promenaded most part of the City again & afterwards as it was a pleasant day took a walk on the South side of the water to a considerable extent below the town. Between 12 & 1 I went to view the Museum of Natural History,

---

4. An obelisk erected on Glasgow Green in 1807 with money raised by subscription begun in 1805 shortly after Admiral Horatio Nelson died at Trafalgar.

5. St. Andrew's Parish Church, opened in 1756, was known as "the tobacco lords' kirk."

6. Born in Glasgow in 1761, Moore made his career as an officer in colonial and continental wars. He was killed in 1809 at Corunna, Spain, during a victorious battle with the French. His status as hero was enhanced by "The Burial of Sir John Moore," a poem published in 1817 by Charles Wolfe (1791–1823). The statue, cast in metal taken from cannons, was erected in 1819.

left to the University, by the late celebrated John Hunter of London.[7] A description of the repository of valuables would be too much of a Herculean job for me, so all I shall say is that it in every respect answered the high euligeums which I had previously heard & read of it. At his death the Dr. who is an alumnus of the University, willed it to this institution at Glasgow, where it is now deposited in a building of chaste Grecian architecture erected expressly for the purpose.

The University of Glasgow is in "High Street" running north from Argyle.[8] The principal building is venerable in its appearance & stands on a hill with the houses & shops in the street. Entering a court is a large square, & a still larger one in the rear of this. Back of the whole is an extensive field of green, shaded with elms & walled around. One is quite surprised to see such extensive pleasure grounds in the heart of so large a manufacturing & commercial city. The Number of students I understand was about 700, & most of them live without the walls. Their accademic dress struck me rather singularly, it is the usual hat,

7. William Hunter (1718–1783), an anatomist, rather than his brother John, a noted London surgeon, bequeathed his anatomical collection to Glasgow University where it became the nucleus of an important natural history collection, the Hunterian Museum. JCB may have been misled by the error in Benjamin Silliman's *Journal*: "They are erecting a magnificent Grecian edifice, for the reception of the anatomical museum of the late celebrated John Hunter of London." (III, p. 276)

8. Founded in 1451, the university, like that in Edinburgh, did little to provide collegial residences for staff or students. JCB's application of the word "useful" to the university is meant to praise its success in educating leaders in all fields rather than just the practical professions.

but a flaming red gown with flowing sleeves over their common clothes. The professors are numerous, tho' their salaries are nothing when compared with the luxurious livings of the English Universities. This seminary at Glasgow is now in a very flourishing condition & considered to be as useful as any other of the kind in the 3 kingdoms.

Having thus viewed every thing worthy of attention in Glasgow & seeing nothing to detain me further I embarked at ½ past 2 PM in a Steam Boat going to Greenock & at a little before 5 was landed from a small boat at the foot of Dumbarton Castle, having concluded to pass the night here, as I wished to investigate a little of its environs before leaving Scotland.[1] I am comfortably entertained at the Elephant Inn.

Novr. 7th. A rainy morning but at ½ past 9 it cleared up a little & I sallied forth on foot to see the monument erected to the memory of the immortal author of Roderick Random, situate 2½ miles from Dumbarton on the road to Loch Lomond. The Pillar is round, upon a square pedistal & of Gray stone. In front is a marble slab set in & upon which is an inscription in Latin, but I was sorry to find the slab so broken, as it has so much obliterated the writing.[2] Being so near Loch Lomond I was loth to leave the country without having at least one look at this romantic spot. So

---

1. A fortress and royal residence in the Middle Ages, a barracks in 1823, later a museum, Dumbarton Castle was built on a rock rising 240 feet above the Clyde.

2. The *Adventures of Roderick Random*, a picaresque novel published in 1748. The author, Tobias Smollett (1721–1771) was commemorated by a monument erected in 1774 at Renton near his birthplace.

accordingly I pushed on notwithstanding it rained & when I arrived upon its banks I was 6 miles from D. & was after all my trouble almost deprived of any thing of a view from a "Scotch mist" or what we should call a heavy rain with a thick fog. Of course I did not dwell long here, but soon retraced my steps to "the Elephant." If the weather had been fine I should have visited the interiour of "Dumbarton Castle" from the height of which there is said to be a delightful prospect. With the exception of the view, the Castle is seen to every advantage from the Clyde. 'Tis an immensely high rock rising directly out of the water & can only be approached from one particular point. In former times it was strongly fortified but, at present most of the guns are dismounted & a small garrison only is kept up. As it was necessary for me to take advantage of the Steam Boat to day for Belfast or delay my jaunt to Ireland another week I resolved to pursue my original plan & so paid my bill immediately & was put on board one of the Steam Boats passing for Greenock & was landed at the latter place at ½ past 2 PM. I had only a short time to look about Greenock, indeed altho' its population is large & trade very extensive yet there is nothing which ought to detain a traveller any length of time, unless he may have acquaintances or letters of introduction, which was not my case. The town is far from being a handsome one & Hamilton Street running nearly parallel with the river & distant from the quays, appears to be its "leading feature." In the Docks I observed some fine ships, but these are mostly owned in Glasgow as the navigation as far as Glasgow for larger shipping is not at all convenient. A large & well built Custom House upon the Quay is the only building worth particularizing.

At ½ past 5 the "Eclipse" Steamboat arrived from Glasgow on her way to Belfast & I had no small difficulty in getting on board such was the crowd of Irish labourers returning to Ireland. These people had come over to harvest it in Scotland & such a ragged, dirty crew I never before set my eyes upon, men, women & children all together, higgledy piggledy, & the deck was crowded to overflowing. At first I was undecided about going in a Boat that was so overladen, as besides the Deck load, the Cabin was full & all the births taken. But as this was the only opportunity by Steam that I should have from this quarter for a week, I determined to risk it, altho' in case of any accident to the Boat with such a number on board the scene would have been dreadful. Happily there was no wind & we were favoured in having a fine night, so calm was it that there was scarcely any motion at all in the boat, & at 7 AM we entered the Belfast Loch, tho' we did not land owing to the tide 'til about 10.

156 miles from Glasgow to Belfast.

Novr. 8th. After breakfasting & indulging in the comfort of a clean shirt, I called upon Mr. Gillies to whom I had a letter from a Gentleman I met at Aberdeen.[3] He received me politely & after inviting me to dine with him the next day, carried me to the new commercial rooms, which I think is as fine an establishment of the kind as any I have yet met with in Europe. Here are to be found news papers from every part of the united kingdoms as well as from Paris & sometimes from the U.S.

---

3. I have been unable to identify Mr. Gillies.

The remainder of the day I passed in exploring Belfast, which I find to be a town of no small consequence. The population is reconed to be between 30 & 40,000, its commerce is extensive & altogether is thought to be the most flourishing town in Ireland. Its situation is well adapted for trade; laying at the head of "Belfast Loch" 20 miles from the Channel, the Loch itself separates the counties of Down & Antrim. Belfast is mostly upon a level with hills rising in its rear. The houses are built of brick, & the town is well laid out with broad streets. High Street & Donegall Street are the most considerable, altho. Donegall Square E.N.W.&S. & Donegall place, Wellington place, & the College Green, all at the South Western part of the town are really elegant. Of the public buildings, the Academic Institution, is the most promenant, situated in a fine large Square surrounded by a high brick wall.[4] The House of Correction & particularly the Linen Hall, situated in Donegall Square are striking features in this interesting place.[5]

Novr. 9th. Attended divine service to day in the Episcopal "Chapel of Ease" in High Street.[6] The congregation was small enough & the parson gave us a tolerably fair sermon, altho. his appearance did not indicate his labouring very hard in his vocation. From the

---

4. Belfast's "Academical Institution" was established in 1810 primarily for the education of Presbyterian divines. Its building was completed in 1814.

5. The Linen Hall, after 1785, provided office and warehouse space to merchants in the linen trade. It was razed in 1896.

6. A chapel built for the convenience of members of the Established Church who lived some distance from their parish church.

"Chapel of Ease" I looked into a Catholic Church in Donegall Street. I was attracted to it from the great crowd I saw around the doors. The priest was holding forth to a crowded audience & I could not help contrasting this with the slim sleepy auditors of the Episcopalian parson.[7] The Catholic religion in Ireland is said to be gaining ground very fast, even in the North & it is attributed to the great zeal & perseverance of their Clergy as much as any thing. That this is the Fact I have no doubt, & how a stop can be put to it by the Government is a question which I am not prepared at this moment to solve. 'Tis indeed a melancholy circumstance, for the Catholic religion I consider to be totally averse to all principles of rational liberty.—At 4 Oclk: walked with Mr. G[*illies*] to his seat about 2 miles over the river Laggan in the county of Down & dined & spent the evening with his family. He is not a married man but his sisters live with him, whom I found to be intelligent, hospitable ladies. The conversation was general & many questions were put to me respecting America, all of which I endeavoured to answer to the best advantage possible.

A young Gentleman who dined at the table accompanied me to town in the Evening.

Nov. 10th. Took the coach in the morning for Coleraine, on an excursion to visit the Giants Causeway.[8] This busy little town is

---

7. St. Patrick's Church was completed in 1815.

8. A spectacular headland made up of some 40,000 basaltic columns of varying height, forming three platforms—the Little, Middle, and Grand Causeways.

   An Irish mile, mentioned below, equalled 1.273 statute miles.

40 Irish miles from Belfast, & owing to the shortness of the days & the hilly roads, it was night when we arrived. Miserable villages & Cabins of the low Irish were all that was to be met with.

11th. Early after breakfast, chartered a jaunting car to go & see the Causeway, which is 9 miles from Coleraine. The appearance of the country did not improve as approaching the coast. When I arrived a host of ragged wretches hovered about offering their services as guides & wishing me to hire their boots. [*Since*] the weather was more propitious for a sail upon the north stretch [*?*] I embarked immediately, which is the best way to have a perfect view of this singular natural curiosity. Without a visitor had a rule & compass in his pocket to take the different dimensions it would be folly to attempt a description of the Giants Causeway. This was the case with myself, & so can do no better than to transcribe the following account verbatim from a small travelling book then met with.

[*Page missing.*]

The above description is as far as I could judge perfectly correct, & should have regretted very much having visited this country & not to have seen the causeway. Resuming my Car, I rode along the N W coast of the Island to have a look at the ruins of Dunluce Castle, formerly a seat of the Antrim family, & forming one of the most picturesque & commanding objects on the Coast of Ireland.[9]

---

9. An offshore, fortified residence built on a rock-stack, connected to the main-

It was just candle light on reentering Coleraine, & at the Inn I found a jolly, good natured parson, who was ready to join me at dinner. He was an intelligent fellow & gave me a good deal of information respecting the state of the Church in Ireland, & of the country generally.[1] In the south of Ireland, in many parts it was almost impossible for the clergy to collect the tithes, their lives were often in danger, so much so that many have removed elsewhere rather than live in a country where they could not go to bed in safety. My friend for one told me he had giving up a living of 250£ Sterling in the South for one of 50£ in the North not considering it safe to live where he was. The mail for Belfast stopped at our Inn at 10 Oclk: & having finished our whisky punch (of which the parson partook very fluently for the purpose of fortifying himself in the faith as I suppose) took our seats & returned to Belfast.

12th. Nov. It was late in the day before the coach arrived & I determined to pass the remainder of it here. In the afternoon took leave of Mr. G[*illies*]—a worthy hibernian & who in the course of conversation often alluded to & lamented at the same time the ruined & impoverished condition of his own sweet Island.

---

land by a bridge. It was owned by Randal MacSorley MacDonnell, viscount Dunluce, who became earl of Antrim in 1620, and occupied it until 1642. Ownership of the ruins was transferred to the government of North Ireland in 1928.

1. The Church of Ireland, the established church, came under attack by noncommunicants who were tithed to support it. In 1823 the Catholic Association was founded to organize non-violent agitation. The Church was disestablished in 1869.

13th. At 5 Oclk, nearly 3 hours before it was light, the coach started for Dublin. 80 Irish miles from Belfast, & in no part of the 3 Kingdoms have I ever travelled faster. Passed thro. Newry, Druhugada, & a number of other towns. The road in general was good, but the county thro. which we passed exhibited neglect & great want of improvement. Very few gentlemans seats were to be seen, but in the country miserable Irish cabins in great numbers all surrounded by an idle, ragged, wretched population. 10 miles from Dublin I was taken so unwell as to determine me not to go further, so I stopped at a comfortable Inn & passed the night. The next morning feeling a good deal [better], walked into the City.

15th Novemr. Since I have been in Europe I have not spent a fortnight more pleasantly or more advantageously than in the Capital of Ireland. Altho. I had but one letter of introduction, yet such is the hospitality of the Irish, that I soon formed a round of acquaintances, & received more attention & saw more of the society of the place than in any other part of G. Britain. One dinner party succeeded another, & invitations to breakfast & to supper, came pouring in upon me so fast that I could have passed a very gay winter in Dublin, but this was incompatible with my previous arrangements, which were to go again upon the Continent. My particular friend Mr. Kiernan,[2] was extremely attentive in pointing out the various curiosities & objects worthy of notice with which his city abounds & few cities can be compared to Dublin for the grandeur & magnificence of her public buildings, & some quarters of the town. Trinity College, The Bank, The Post Office,

---

2. I have been unable to identify Mr. Kiernan.

The Customs House & the Lying In Hospital, are built of granite stone, of elegant architecture, have commanding situations, & all together efface[?] any thing of the kind in London. The river Liffey divides the City nearly in the center, adorned with substantial Quays only inferiour to those of the Seine at Paris.[3]

Among other distinguished Gentlemen to whom I was introduced, was Dr. Brinkley, distinguished as one of the literati of Dublin & one of the most eminent astronomers of the day. I had the pleasure of breakfasting with him & his amiable family, at their seat a few miles in the country. Dr. B. is president of the royal society of Dublin.[4] Another gentleman whom I frequently met in society, was Sir Charles Geisecke, a German by birth & distinguished for his science in chemistry. Such is Sir Ch[s]. thirst after knowledge that he has twice visited Iceland & Greenland & resided 2 years [?] at one time in the latter country. His stories of his travels, adventures & hair breadth 'scapes in these distant & inhospitible regions were highly amusing, & often detained the company 'til a late hour.[5] Another gentleman I dined with was Dr

---

3. The neo-classical public buildings that excited JCB's admiration were built during the "Protestant Ascendancy" of the eighteenth century. The Bank (of Ireland) in 1802 bought the Irish Parliament building (1729–1739). Trinity College's grand façade and the Lying-in Hospital were built in the 1750s, the Customs House in the 1780s. The one exception was the General Post Office 1815–20). The other "quarters of the town" he admired were private mansions built then by the Irish nobility both north and south of the Liffey.

4. John Brinkley (1763–1835), clergyman and scientist, was astronomer royal for Ireland and president of the Royal Society of Dublin. In 1826 he became bishop of Cloyne.

5. Karl Ludwig Giesecke (1761–1833), a native of Augsburg, after an early career in the theater, became a mineralogist and prospected in Greenland,

Lebatte whose dear spouse had already presented him with 28 children. This I heard from her own mouth at table. She is yet a young & beautiful woman, & to all appearances is likely to have a dozen more.[6]

The Phoenix Park in Dublin is much more extensive than either Hyde or Regents Parks. It contains a Lodge for the Lord Lieutenant & some other official Buildings. The Monument to the Duke of Wellington, stands upon a knoll & commands a grand view of Dublin.[7] No stranger can visit Dublin without observing at once the great contrast between the different edifices of the inhabitants. The extreme of luxury & fashion in opposition to the last stages of want & wretchedness seems to abound here more than in any other place & the inhabitants in the very environs of Dublin, are as miserable & ragged as in other parts of the island. It was so late in the season that I only made one or two excursions in the country. Mr. K[iernan] & myself one morning took a post chaise & drove to "the Dargle" a romantic glen about

---

1806–1813. Thereafter he was a professor of mineralogy at the Dublin Society of Arts, a school of practical arts and sciences founded in 1749.

6. I have been unable to identify Dr. Lebatte.

7. One of the largest city parks anywhere, Phoenix Park with some 1,750 acres could swallow London's Hyde Park and Regent's Park and have room for St. James Park, Kensington Gardens, and Hampstead Heath. A royal deer park under Charles II, it was opened to the public in 1747 on recommendation of the viceroy, or lord lieutenant, Philip Stanhope, fourth earl of Chesterfield (1694–1773). The Lord Lieutenant's Lodge was a vice-regal residence.

Wellington's Monument or "Testimonial," was begun in 1817, completed in 1821. The tallest obelisk in Europe, it commemorated Arthur Wellesley, duke of Wellington (1769–1852), a native of Dublin.

15 miles,[8] but the bleak cold winds of the last of Novr. reminded us that this was not the proper season to view a fine landscape, & so we were glad to get back to the Inn & enjoyed a coal fire a good dinner & a bottle of port. [Note:] Dublin is famous for its Hotels, which are upon a scale not exceeded by any city in Europe. I was first at Greshams in Sackvill Street and afterwards at the Hibernian in Dawson Street.—the last a capital House—

Thursday the 27th of Novr. I left Dublin for London, & shall always reflect with no ordinary pleasure & satisfaction upon my visit to Ireland & the many kind attentions I received from The warm hearted Irish—a people whose native talents & genius make them often rise superiour to poverty & opression.

Embarking at Hoath in the Steam Boat at 8 in the morning I was landed at Hollyhead on the island of Anglesey about 3.[1] Here the passengers took coaches on to Bangor, 23 miles distant upon the opposite fery[?], which we crossed in the dark & in a heavy shower of rain—

Friday 28. The weather was rainy & unpleasant for travelling I determined to spend a day in Wales. It was market day at Bangor & the little town was filled with country people. I was much surprised to find them speak almost all to gether among themselves

---

8. A mile-long glen located some fifteen miles from Dublin, a favorite resort of seekers after the picturesque.

1. Howth on Dublin Bay got new facilities for a packet station in 1807–1814. After steam packets were introduced in 1819, ferry service from Howth to Holyhead, Wales, offered the fastest crossing then available.

in the Welsh or Gaelic language, not a word of which could I understand, & which is as different from English as the Russian is. I attempted to converse with a number of the peasantry, but found they understood not a word of English. This is indeed singular enough, that in an Island no larger than Britain, where education is so general, & within 250 miles of London too, there should exist a race of people unacquainted with the English tongue. The Women wore round hats, instead of bonnets, had agreeable countenances, but their features appeared to me different from the English females of the rest of the Island.

Saty: 29th. Travelled from Bangor to Shrewsbury in Shropshire, 80 miles. over the government road, one of the best in the Kingdom & made at a great expense.[2]

The scenery of North Wales is grand & imposing reminding me of the Highland scenery I had so lately left. The Vale of Llangallen thro. which we passed in the afternoon was beautiful even at this later season of year but before we arrived in the Evening the weather became very cold, attended with snow & rain.[3]

Sunday 30th, I passed at Shrewsbury & attended devine services. It rained hard all the day. Shrewsbury has rather a mean appearance & would not have detained me but the indisposition.

---

2. The roads from Holyhead to Shrewsbury and from Shrewsbury to London were much improved after 1815 under the supervision of Thomas Telford (1757–1834).

3. Llangallen is a picturesque valley of the River Dee in north Wales.

Lieutenant General Lord Hills is a native of this place & the inhabitants have erected at the entrance of the town a lofty stone column, commemorative of his services in the pininsula & at Waterloo.[4] At 10 Oclk Sunday Evening I took the royal mail for London, passing thro. Birmingham in the dark, where we merely changed horses, & dining at Oxford, reached town at 8 in the Evening of Monday the 1st. of Decr. 1823—150 miles.

---

4. Rowland, first viscount Hill (1772–1842), a native of Shropshire, distinguished himself in the Napoleonic wars, in Egypt and the Peninsula, and at Waterloo. He succeeded Wellington as commander-in-chief of the army in 1828.

Book Four

December 17, 1823, to March 31, 1824

FRANCE AND ITALY

AFTER HAVING made all the necessary preparations for a journey into the South of France & Italy, I left Paris in the Malle Poste in company with my friend Mr. Ives the Evening of the 17th Decr. 1823, for Lyons & stopped only twice on the road just sufficient time to take dinner until we arrived.[1]

Altho I had rode for three successive nights & travelled a distance of 340 miles nearly, in the space of 60 hours, I felt but very little fatigued. This was owing in a great measure to our precaution in taking the whole of the interiour to ourselves instead of being troubled & crowded by a third person. We entered Lyons on the morning of the 20th, & took lodging in the "Hotel du parc" in the place des Turceaux, for which we paid 6 francs per day & the other charges were not extravagent excepting wood which is always dear in France.[2] After refreshing ourselves by a good shave & indulging in the luxury of a clean shirt, we took

---

1. The "Malle Poste" was a stage coach used primarily for carrying mail, usually faster than ordinary passenger coaches.

2. The Hôtel du Parc was long established as one of the best hotels in Lyon. The Place des Terreaux was built on earth (*terreaux*) used to fill in an ancient Roman canal connecting the Rhône and the Saône.

breakfast & then sallied forth to view the 2d city in the French Empire. Our attention was first directed to what constitutes the chief celebrity of Lyons viz: her silk manufacturers. Our valet de place[3] took us to one of the principal establishments where we saw them at work upon the richest & most costly description of silk & satin stuffs, particularly some that was specially intended for the Dutchess of Berri[4] the machines upon which it is wove is similar to those upon which common cloths are made & the looms & [*blank*] are worked in a similar manner.[5] The wages for a person working 12 or 14 hours was not more than a franc & ½ or 2 francs, from this we see upon how small a sum the poor & labouring classes in France are obliged to live. Besides silk, cotton is manufactured to a very considerable extent at Lyons, & the local situation of the place, upon the deep and rapid Rhone & at the junction of the Saone with the Rhone is very favourable to internal industry. We visited the Musé,[6] but there is nothing particular in it to attract the stranger & after having seen similar collections in Paris & elsewhere one feels very little zest for anything

---

3. A manservant, or factotum, who served travelers visiting his city.

4. Marie-Caroline de Bourbon (1798–1870), granddaughter of Ferdinand I of the Two Sicilies (see p. 156, n. 9), married in 1816 to Charles Ferdinand, duc de Berry (1778–1820), who was in line of succession to the French throne. She was reputed to be the only popular member of the royal family in the 1820s.

5. The mechanization and prosperity of Lyon's textile industries were furthered after the turn of the century by Napoleon's protective "Continental System" and by the inventions of a Lyonnais silk-weaver, Joseph Marie Jacquard (1752–1834).

6. Probably a reference to the Palais des Arts, or to the Palais Saint-Pierre.

of the kind till he arrives in Italy. The Churches in Lyons are hardly worth noticing,[7] & having made ourselves acquainted with the local situation, we took measures the following day to continue our journey, to the South as we had no letters to any one & no acquaintances to detain us. Altogether I was disappointed with the general appearance of Lyons, it is not so fine a City as I expected to have found it & with the exception of the quays, the place royale & one or two smaller squares the whole town is composed of narrow, crooked, dark & dirty streets. Its environs in the summer season must be fine & indeed in the immediate vicinity there are some points from which there is an extensive & commanding prospect, particularly the terrace of the Church of Fourvière.[8]

I have as yet hardly mentioned my route from Paris for in fact it was so rapid that I had scarcely an opportunity to make any observations. We passed thro as might be expected a great number of small towns, but none of any considerable importance, but what was quite a novelty to me & in the summer must be a luxurious scene was the vineyards on both sides of the road nearly all the way from Paris. We passed thro' the fine Burgundy Country, so celebrated for its wines. Towards the morning of the 2d day

---

7. The Cathedral of Saint-Jean (twelfth to fifteenth centuries) had been badly damaged by Huguenots during the Reformation and by revolutionists during the 1790s, and had been badly restored.

8. The Fourvière is a granite spur rising above the Saône. JCB refers to the Chapelle de Notre-Dame (1746–1751), which today is over-shadowed by a basilica (1872–1896).

we crossed the range of mountains extending from the borders of Switzerland & for a few hours had a smart touch of the cold of Winter. The tops of these Mountains were all covered with snow, & on one of them for a few moments we were envelloped in quite a heavy snow storm.

Memo: Dined the first day out at Auxerre the 2d at Chalons sur Saône & passed thro Macon, famous for its winery. The Evening. of the 21st we left Lyons at 10 oclk having taken the Coupé to ourselves.[9] This mode of travelling would have been quite as convenient as a post chaise, had it not been for its slowness, & we did not reach Nismes til 6 the Evening of the 23d. The day after leaving Lyons we could perceive a very sensible change in the climate & the appearance of the Olive trees, with everything in full verdure reminded us that we were entering the charming country of the Languedoc. The sun was bright & the air as warm & mild as spring. We took lodgings at the Hotel du Luxembourg, facing the esplanade.[1]

Decr. 24. As Nismes is particularly remarkable for its remains of Roman antiquities, we of course improved the first opportunity to view them. The most celebrated are the "Maison Carrée" the Amphitheatre & the fountain; the last is still in good repair, hav-

---

9. A "coupé" was a small, closed carriage, a truncated diligence. The latter was a common model of stagecoach in France. "*Carosse de diligence*" meant "express" or "speed" coach.

1. Centrally located, the Hôtel de Luxembourg continued to be one of Nîmes's principal hotels into the twentieth century.

ing been in a great measure rebuilt by Louis 14th.[2] The Maison Carrée is justly called the glory of Nismes & is said to be the most perfect of any of the Ancient Temples remaining at the present day. It is altogether of the Corinthian order with 9 Columns in each front & 4 on the sides, the whole upon a basement story, about 5 feet from the ground. The columns on the sides & those on the North form a portico, the whole length of the basement story is 117 feet by 37. Altogether this temple is allowed to be unrivalled by any work of the kind North of the Alps. Very considerable repairs are now making upon it, to preserve it in its present state, & the interiour is fitting up for a repository of paintings. Mr Girards banking house at Philadelphia is a model of the "Maison Carrée."[3] The Amphitheatre is also said to be one of the best works of the kind that has been preserved its magnitude is immense; the circumference being about 1100 feet & hight 70. The whole structure being entirely detached from all other buildings, can be seen to great advantage. It was during the

---

2. Nîmes had several exceptionally well-preserved Roman buildings. The Maison Carrée since the first century A. D. had served as a temple, fort, private residence, and church, before it became a museum. It was restored in 1824. The Amphitheatre (first to second centuries) was cleared of private dwellings in 1809. Restoration began in 1813. JCB gives approximate measurements for both buildings. The Fontaine de Nîmes rises at the foot of a hill and flows into basins built on ancient foundations restored in the early eighteenth century.

3. JCB refers to a building in Philadelphia, dating from 1789, which had Corinthian columns and a portico similar to those of the Maison Carrée. Originally occupied by the Bank of the United States, it was taken over in 1811 by the Bank of Stephen Girard.

time of the Saracens very much damaged by fire, otherwise in all probability it would have remained perfect to the present day, for any effect that time could have upon it; such are the immense masses of Stone of which it is built. One can easily judge of its size when told that it was capable of containing 17,000 persons. At present in Summer the Amphitheatre is used for a sort of Bull fight but which are quite inferior to those celebrated spectacles of Spain.

25 of Decr. the Atmosphere was as warm as our summer without its burning heat, the sun was bright & the sky without a cloud. As far as respected weather, it was the most delicious Christmas I had ever passed. At 11 AM we took a Cabriolet with post horses & went to view the "Pont du gard," distant about 18 or 20 miles from Nismes. This was built by the old Romans for an aquaduct across the River Gardon, & is situated in quite a solitary spot. It well deserves the particular attention of every traveller, as well on account of the magnitude of the work as its being at present one of the most perfect monuments remaining of Roman grandeur. "It consists of 3 tiers of arches, making in all a hight of nearly 200 feet above the river the length at the top is 800 feet." The lower tier is composed of 6 arches, 2 of which only are over the waters of the Gardon the other four rest upon its banks & upon rocks, & are for the purpose of supporting the superstructure. The middle tier is the principal one & has 11 arches. The hight of which is 80 feet in the center. The upper tier has 35 arches & upon those is the channel thro' which the water runs. Their height is 20 feet. There has been erected a <u>bridge</u> connected with the Ancient work for carriages; formerly it was only for foot passengers, but the modern work can easily be distinguished from the other, such is its inferiourity.[4]

During our stay at Nismes, we also paid some attention to the manufactures of the place. Silk is one the principal & we saw them at work making gloves & Stockings; but the machinery appeared so intricate that I would not attempt a description. Shawls made of cotton & silk & particularly a manufactory of printed cottons; this last is very curious & I was very glad to have so good an opportunity to view one as similar establishments in France & England are very difficult to be seen.[5] We also saw the process of making Olive oil which is here made in great quanties The olives are simply mashed by a large stone turned by an ass. They are then put into vats, hot water poured over them & pressed. The oil is afterwards skimmed off & filtered thro' a sieve then it is fit for use. On the following day after having resurveyed the Antiquities of Nismes we took our places in the Diligence for Marseilles at 1 Oclk.—The climate of Nismes I think must be very delightful for a winter residence, at times the North West wind blows with violence & makes it extremely disagreeable,

---

4. The Pont du Gard, spanning the Gardon valley, was part of an aqueduct which brought water from the Eure some 26 miles from Fontaine d'Uzes to Nîmes. Built in three tiers, the bridge is 295 yards across and 160 feet high. A road bridge was added in 1743–1747. JCB probably quotes from a guide-book bought for the occasion.

5. Foreigners were not universally welcome in factories such as the print works in Nîmes. Industrial espionage was common.

accordingly it would not be an advisable place for an invalid.[6] Good wine is to be had there & particularly the Muscat, which comes from Lunel a small town between Nismes & Montpelier. We drank some of a most delicious flavour & which cost but 2½ francs the bottle. Living I think must be cheap & I have seen no inland town in France which I should prefer as a place of residence (provided I wanted to economize) to Nismes. The town itself is miserable & dirty, but it abounds with pleasant walks, such as the Boulvards, the Esplanade the field of Mars & the fountain & its gardens above mentioned. Distance from Lyons to Nismes about 180 English miles,

I can say very little of our ride to Marseilles. The fields were covered in many places with Olive trees & the view, & the general appearance of Provence was very little different from that of Languedoc. About sunset we passed the Rhone over a bridge of boats, & entered the village of [*blank*] where all the population were in high glee as it appeared to be a fête day. We took a walk thro' the "promenade" which was crowded with folks all in their best bib & band[7] & I could not help observing that I saw more handsome girls among the peasantry than I had before met with in any village in France. The dress of all was the same as is the case in every particular section of the Kingdom, each province having something to distinguish itself from the rest. Here the

---

6. The mistral, a strong, cold, dry wind, common in southern France. JCB later identified it as the "Mistrial."

7. The "bib and band" were neckpieces, here used as a synecdoche for finery. Cf. "best bib and tucker."

fashion, or rather custom was to wear a cloak, flowing open in front, & the Cap was bound with a wide flaming yellow riband tied in a large bow. At this village we took up a Number of passengers & at 11 PM stopped to sup at a miserable Inn. The Country taverns in France are execrable, at least all such as I have seen. Instead of the neat, tidy "travellers room," with a blazing coal fire such as you are shown into in England, you find nothing but a nasty appartment, cold stone floors, often times no fire at all, & generally bad attendance.

We passed thro Aix in the Morning & about 11 Oclk. entered Marseilles. Our lodgings were at the Hotel Beauvau, in a street of the same name.[8] The remainder of the day was employed in refreshing ourselves & rambling about the Town to get a general idea of the place, as was also the following day Sunday.

Monday Decr. 29th. Delivered some of our letters of introduction which were received very politely & during our stay at Marseilles we made a number of agreeable & pleasant acquaintances. Dined with Mr. Fitch & with Mr. Rogers. These gentlemen are Americans & regular established merchants. The Messrs. Rabaud one of the most respectable French houses, & whose families are among the most genteel in the City, were very polite in their attentions.[1] On Newyears day after dining with Mr Rogers, he politely took us to the Mayors Ball, which afforded an opportunity of seeing the "beau monde." The ladies were dressed with the usual taste

---

8. The hotel was located at 4, rue Beauvau.

1. Mr. Fitch, Mr. Rogers, and M. Rabaud remain unidentified.

of French fashions & many were really beautiful. Here I will remark that at Marseilles I have seen more female beauty, than in any other part of France, no place that I have as yet visited in <u>any part</u> of the world surpasses & but few I think can be compared to it.

With respect to commerce, Marseilles is admirably situated, being about equal distance between Spain & Italy, & may be considered the first port in the Mediterranean Sea. Her commerce, however is vastly less than what it was formerly, as during the long wars in Europe it was nearly destroyed. At present it is again reviving, tho' it will be a long time before it can (if ever) entirely recover.[2] During the last year, nearly a hundred sail of vessels from the West Indies alone entered the port. No place can boast of a more secure harbour: tis' one immense bason, which can be entered at all times as there is no tide & when once in, nothing can be more safe. Long & high ranges of buildings surround this bason, in front of which is a broad & well paved causeway. This walk is one of the principal promenades in Marseilles. Tis always kept unusually clean for such a quarter & on Sundays particularly is crowded with fashionable, well dressed people. This scene is then enlived by a display of the flags of almost every nation floating from their respective vessels & Greeks & Turks; Jews & Christians are all huddled together, as if there was no distinction. The "Course" which runs about East & West is also another of

2. The commercial recovery of Marseilles was slowed in the 1820s by the royal government's trade policies as well as by unsettled conditions in the eastern Mediterranean. There would be no boom until the 1850s.

the principal points of the City & always affords a busy & often times an amusing scene.[3] The "Allées de Meilhan" are likewise agreeable resorts in the summer, but during the winter months & especially when the "Mistrial," or Northwest wind blows the quay is preferred. As to fine views, few cities can boast of one like that of "Notre Dame de la Garde" on the South from whence is a most commanding view of the city; the environs (covered with "Bastides" or country houses) & of the whole Gulph of Lyons.[4] Marseilles is famous for no other manufacturers than those of soap & coral; the former are very extensive & as to the latter, it the only place in the French dominions where that kind of manufacture is carried on. We examined them both.[5] On the whole I was very much pleased with my visit to Marseilles as I expected to have been. The climate is altogether delightful & the fruits of almost every country are in plenty & cheap. The inhabitants judging from what I saw myself & the information of others are polite & hospitable & had our time allowed we could have spent 2 or 3 months very pleasantly at this season of the Carnival, but

---

3. The Cours Belsunce and the Cours St.-Louis joined at a broad thoroughfare running northeast from the "Old Port" to the suburbs, the Allées de Meilhan.

4. In 1824, Notre Dame de la Garde was a medieval chapel located at the top of a steep hill rising some 480 feet above the harbor. Forty years later the chapel was enclosed by a Byzantine Revival basilica also called Notre Dame de la Garde.

5. Soap manufacture using olive oil was established in Marseilles in the thirteenth century. The city dominated the Mediterranean coral trade until the 1790s, when it was overtaken by Genoa and Naples.

as our plans were to go immediately into Italy by water, it was necessary to improve the first opportunity; accordingly we took our passages on board the French Brig [*illeg.*] of 110 tons. Captain [*illeg.*] to sail for Naples the 6 Jany.[6]

January 6th. 1823. Having previously taken leave of our friends, we went on board this morning at 6 Oclk: & with a good wind were soon in the Gulph of Lyons. Nothing but calms & head winds attended the first part of our passage & it was with great difficulty we made any head way at all. The French are such miserable sailors & so cowardly with all upon the water, that they kept close under the land & really seemed to be afraid to venture out at all into deep water. The weather has been such as might be expected upon the Mediterranean Sea, soft & mild & a bright sun shine every day.

Jany: 13th. Yesterday morning when going on deck found we had made considerable progress during the previous night & where there is full view of the Island of Corsica. This morning we were up with the Isle of Elba, & felt the effects of a burning sun, tho' in the midst of winter. At 12 AM, hung out Mr. Ives's Thermometer, in the shade it stood at 56°: in the Sun at 76°, & hanging on the side of the vessel, which was painted black it rose as high as 102°. In fact ever since we sailed the weather has been delightful & I cannot help thinking how much better such a climate as this is to live in, than our own, where we are frozen to death half the year round.

---

6. The names of the brig and of its captain are indecipherable.

Jany: 14th. We are now moored in the harbour of the Isle de Ponza, or Pontia, a small island in the Mediterranean & with a good wind not more than 10 or 12 hours sail from Naples. We arrived the day before yesterday, as the wind was ahead & blowing strong, it was impossible to make the bay. The place is only celebrated as being the exile to which illustrious Romans were formerly banished. At present it is used by the Neapolitan Government as a kind of State's Prison or Botany Bay & a small garrison of Soldiers is kept up. We were immediately put into quarantine & have only been allowed to go on shore for a few moments yesterday when we mounted the hill & standing before the door of a house saw the natives amusing themselves in dancing. Some of the girls are quite pretty & graceful in their movements. The Island itself does not appear very productive considering the climate it is in. Some few vines & fig trees were growing, but generally speaking, I should say it was rather rocky & barren. The population I have not heard, but altogether cannot be much. A large proportion are occupied in fishing.[7]

Jany: 21st. Our quarantines being finished we went on shore to day & rambled over every part of the Island, on this subject I have nothing more to say than that it is altogther a miserable abode & nothing makes it even tolerable but the climate which is all that man could wish.

---

7. Pontia was one of a group of volcanic islands some seventy miles west of the Bay of Naples. Traditionally a penal colony or place of exile, it was used as such until the 1940s.

23d. Last night the wind becoming favourable our Captain got under weigh about 12 or 1 Oclk: & it continued to blow during the day, at 4 PM we were at anchor in the Bay of Naples. For the first day since leaving Marseille it was cloudy which in some measure deprived us of the splendid view in entering the harbour. We passed in full sight of the Island of Ischia & under the tower on the Island of Procida.[8] Vesuvius we saw rising at a distance but the top was so enveloped in clouds as not to be distinguished. To say that the City & Bay presented an almost unrivalled view would be to repeat what all others who have visited Naples have said before me. During the night it rained very hard & the following morning 24th inst: it still continued cloudy, we however went on shore & during a very heavy rain got our luggage landed & after being spunged of a dollar at the examining offices got it admitted.[1] Took lodgings at the "Hotel villa di Londra" in the Strada Santa Lucia, an expensive house, but every thing clean & tolerably comfortable.[2] Paid 9 Dolls. per week for two rooms & 4 Carlins for breakfast each.[3] Engaged a valet de place & in the afternoon called upon Mr Ramsey, to whom we had a letter from Mr. N.[4] Dined at the restaurate au ville de Naples

---

8. Ischia, sixteen miles southwest of Naples, was famous for its mineral baths. Procida, two miles offshore, had a castle on top of a steep rise on its eastern side.

1. "Spung," a Scottish verb meaning to rob.

2. The Villa da Londre, near the waterfront on the via Santa Lucia, catered to English travellers, as did its rival the Gran Bretagna.

3. A carlin was a small silver coin current in Naples, worth about four pence in 1824.

4. I have been unable to identify Mr. Ramsey (sp.?).

nearly opposite the palace: a very good establishment & the only one of any note in the city.[5] The Italian cuisine is tolerable, but by no means to be compared to the French.

Jany: 25th The weather still cloudy & some rain fell. We employed the day in rambling at large about the city & in obtaining a general idea of its situation. Looked into a number of the churches (which are very numerous) most of which are filled with marbles & paintings. In the afternoon promenaded in the public garden & upon the Chiaia which is the fashionable resort for carriages.[6] Towards evening as the sun shone out we took a ride about 3 miles out of the city, upon the road built by Murat & which leads out of the Mergelliana presenting at every turn a delightful view of some part of the city & Bay & of the surrounding country.[7]

In the Evening went for the first time to the great Theatre San Cárlos, considered the largest & most splendid of any in Europe.[8] It in every respect answered our expectations as to size

---

5. Here, as often in his Italian journal, JCB uses French equivalents for Italian words and spellings. Because he had some fluency in French, it is likely that his guides used French forms of Italian proper nouns.

6. The Riviera di Chiaia was a thoroughfare just north of the waterfront by a public garden. The name was derived from "plaia," Spanish for "beach."

7. Joachim Murat (1767–1815), son of an innkeeper, Napoleonic cavalry commander, married Caroline Bonaparte in 1800 and was named king of Naples by Napoleon in 1808. One of his public works was the road, Via Mergellina, which ran along the coastline from the eastern end of the Chiaia.

8. The royal opera house, Teatro San Carlo, built in 1737, destroyed by fire in February 1816, rebuilt within a year by the king's command, a reconstruction

& decorating. It contains 6 rows of Boxes, but without any gallery, & the pit is better arranged than any other I have yet seen. The seats are all numbered so that there can be no crowding & dispute on the subject & you are as comfortably seated as if in an arm chair. The theater is ornamented with a profusion of gilding & raised work. The Kings Box is in front of the stage & is admired as being a very stately affair. The only fault I found was that it was badly lighted, having only one small chandelier from the center but there are however an almost innumerable number of side lights which when they are light on great occasions must make the Theatre a blaze of light. The King & some of the royal family were present this Evening in private Boxes near the stage, but we were at a considerable distance off & saw them but imperfectly.[9] The pieces performed were an opera which gave us some very fine singing & a pantomime where dansing was introduced. Both were splendidly got up & went off with great eclat. The dancers were not equal to those on the French Opera altho', I

---

which, according to Stendhal, did more to rally Neapolitan morale than the granting of a constitution in 1820. See his *Rome, Naples et Florence*, Daniel Muller, ed. (Paris, 1919), I, p. 380.

9. The king was Ferdinand (1751–1825), third son of Charles III, king of Spain. Ferdinand had title to two Bourbon possessions, the kingdoms of Sicily and Naples, and while Murat reigned in the latter, was protected in Sicily by the British navy. In 1816, he unified the kingdoms, as authorized by the Congress of Vienna, and assumed the title "Ferdinand I of the Two Sicilies."

Ferdinand rarely occupied the royal box at the center of the opera house, preferring to sit closer to the stage where he had a better view of the dancers. Marguerite, countess Blessington remarked that "this love of dancing in a septuagenarian has something unseemly in it." See her *The Idler in Italy* (Paris, 1839), p. 268.

thought the ladies if they did not shew so much grace, were even more sprightly & flexible than those at Paris.—Called upon Mr. Rogers who received us very politely—[1]

26th. As fair a day as any we have in May: the air soft & balmy & the sky without a cloud. Mounted to the Top of the "Castel Saint Elmo" from whence is one of the best & most extensive views, & every part of the City can be distinctly seen. This was formerly a palace, & afterwards a Convent of Carthusians. It was an exceedingly rich establishment but Murat turned out all the monks & transformed it into a Hospital.[2] The chapel is well worth the attention of any one visiting Naples. 'Tis crowded with marbles & statuary of the most costly description one of the blessed virgin with the infant jesus in her arms struck me particularly as being an exquisite piece of sculpture. The paintings also are celebrated: one of Peter denying our saviour & another of Christ just taken from the cross by Spagnioletti are of the first order.[3] Visited the garden of the palace Belvedere[4] & others on the hill back of the Chiaia afterwards The Tomb of Virgil, or rather

---

1. I have been unable to identify Mr. Rogers beyond noting that the Rogers firm in Naples had long been a correspondent of Brown and Ives.

2. The Castel Sant'Elmo, built in the mid-fourteenth century on a promontory in central Naples by Robert of Anjou (1278–1343), king of Naples, adjoins the Ceterosa (Charterhouse) di San Martino.

3. Jusepe, or Giuseppe, de Ribera (1588–1652), born near Valencia, therefore called "lo Spagnioletto" or "little Spaniard," became court painter to the Spanish viceroy in Naples. Famous for his violent treatment of violent scenes, he softened his style for scenes from Christ's passion.

4. A grand villa overlooking the Chiaia which from the summer of 1823 to the

where tradition says he was buryed. There is now nothing in the Sepulcher & the urn that contained his ashes is gone. It is quite a romantic spot, & such a place as one would suppose Virgil would have wished to have been buryed in. As for any laurel growing on the top of it, I could find none & in fact nothing else but pig weed.[5] In the evening dined with Mr Rogers & afterwards attended the Theatro del Fondo where was performed an Opera Buffa;[6] the singing was good & particular that of Seignora Feodor [*blank*].[7] This is also one of the Royal Theatres.

27th. Made a call upon Mr Falconetti the Banker[8] afterwards visited some of the curiosities among which were the Chapel of San Severo belonging to the palace of a nobleman of ancient family.[9]

---

fall of 1824 was rented from the Prince di Belvedere by the Countess Blessington. See p. 156, n. 9.

5. The poet Virgil (70–19 B. C.), revered in medieval Europe as a prophet and magician, became the subject of many myths made around Naples where he preferred to live. One of these located his tomb on a rise of ground at the end of the Via Mergellina. Here Petrarch (1304–1374) and King Robert (see p. 157, n. 2) were supposed to have planted a laurel.

6. A secondary theater in Naples, the Theatro del Fondo opened in 1779; it was in 1824, like the San Carlo, under the direction of Domenico Barbaja (1778–1841), the greatest impresario of his day.

7. Josephine Fodor (1778–1870), soprano, performed in Europe's leading opera houses before retiring in 1833. Daughter of a French composer and virtuoso, Josephus Fodor (1752–1828), she assumed her husband's name, Mainvielle, in 1812.

8. I have been unable to identify Mr. Falconetti.

9. A family crypt, built by Giovanni di Sangro (1590), the Sansevero Chapel was periodically redecorated by his descendants.

Here are some of the finest pieces of sculpture to be seen in all Italy. The figure of Modesty by San Martino, covered with a thin veil & a dead Christ by the same person covered in the same manner.[1] This Kind of sculpture was entirely unknown to the ancients & the two pieces I have mentioned above will never fail to <u>please</u> & <u>astonish</u> all who have any taste for these things. I confess for my part I looked upon them with wonder & admiration. Looked into the Church Saint Clare adjoining a large & celebrated convent. It appeared blazing with gold & rich in marbles. We were permitted to look thro' the grating into the Chapel of the Sisters & here I saw one old lady telling her beads & mumbling over some catholic nonsense to save her soul from purgatory.[2] Walked out to the great Burying place of Naples. This is curiously & admirably contrived & well deserves to be imitated by all great cities. A large space of ground is walled in & 365 deep vaults are dug, covered with stone. One of which is opened every day in the year. Those who are buryed on that day are thrown in, 'tis then shut & sealed, so that on the same day the following year, when opened the bodies are consumed. This is owing to the dampness of the place & quick lime is not made use of as

---

1. *Modesty* (1750) is attributed to the Venetian sculptor Antonio Corradini (1668–1752) who was commissioned by Raimondo di Sangro in the late 1740s to work on the family crypt. His unfinished *Veiled Christ* was altered and completed by Giuseppe Sanmartino (1720–1792), a Neapolitan, whose countrymen also claimed *Modesty* for him.

2. Church of Santa Chiara, built in the early fourteenth century by Robert of Anjou and his queen, Sancia. Badly damaged by bombs in 1943, it has since been restored.

asserted by Eustace.[3] Passed the remainder of the day in promenading the city & the Evening for a few moments looked into one of the minor Theaters.[4]

Wednesday 28th Jany: One of the finest days I ever witnessed any where & at any season we improved in making an excursion to the delightful coast of Baiae & its environs. Leaving the city we took the route to Pozzuoli by the Grotto of Pausilippo. This is a road cut thro a mountain of the same name of about ¾ mile in length & of sufficient breadth to admit two carriages abreast. What was the original cause of this excavation seems to be doubtful. Some think it was for the purpose of obtaining stone for building, as was the case of some others tho' on a smaller scale, at its entrance from the side of Naples; at length the thought of converting this into a highway pleased the fancy of some roman Emperor by which a short & commodious passage was opened thro' the mountain. It is just at the entrance, on the left hand side, about 20 feet above the pavement where is seen Virgil's Tomb. The Grotto of Paussilippo is lighted at each end by an apperture thro' the top, but notwithstanding this it is so dark in the center as to require the light of lamps at midday. The whole is paved

---

3. J. C. Eustace, *A Classical Tour Through Italy*, 6th ed. (London, 1821), II, pp. 350–355. Eustace deplored the practice of spreading quicklime over corpses to hasten decomposition. But he admired the Neapolitans' hygienic system of burial in an isolated site.

4. Minor theaters in Naples included the Nuovo and Fiorentini as well as the Fondo.

with lava from Vesuvius.[5] Nothing attracted our attention til we arrived at Pozzuoli (distance 7 miles from the capitol). Here we took a general guide for the coast & proceeded on immediately. Shortly after we passed the Lake Avernus on the left[6] & soon entered the brick Gateway of the Ancient but now entirely destroyed city of Cumae; here stopping a few minutes we ascended the hill on the right to enjoy the fine view which it affords. A castle on the sea side & the above mentioned wall (or gate) are all that afford any traces of its existence.[7] Not that far from Cumae is still to be seen an excavation of an ancient amphitheatre; even the stones of this immense structure have mostly been removed & the whole is converted into a vinyard. Continuing our ride the Lake of Fusaro soon presented itself. This is only famous for its oysters & is the only place from which Naples is supplied. Formerly the Oysters from the Lake Lucrinus were more esteemed, but at present there are none there to be found.[8]

---

5. Baia and Pozzuoli, favorite resorts of the ancient Romans, were located on the Gulf of Pozzuoli, east of Naples. The Grotto of Posillipo was a tunnel cut through a mountain to shorten the route from Naples. In 1823 it was about one-third of a mile long and "three carriages wide," with light shafts at either end and lanterns and votive lights in between.

6. A volcanic crater five miles in circumference and 110 feet deep. Surrounded by woods in ancient times, it was described in the *Odyssey*, Bk. xi, and the *Iliad*, Bk. vi, as the dark and menacing location of a cave which led to the underworld. JCB visited the site later in the day.

7. Founded ca. 750 B. C., perhaps the first Greek settlement in Italy, Cumae was depopulated after its defeat by the Neapolitans in the thirteenth century A. D.

8. The Lake of Fusaro, once known as Acherusia Palus, or Acherusian Swamp, was a marshy area separated from the sea by a sand bar. It became a center of

From Fusaro in a few minutes we began to descend the hill heading to the coast. Here we viewed the ruins of the Temples of Diana, Mercury & Venus the latter stands quite upon the shore & the water must reach it in a high wind; that of Mercury is rather curious on account of its singular echo.[1] A boat was in readiness to convey us to another part of the coast towards the Baths of Nero These as every thing else in this quarter are all in ruins, the hot springs however are still boilling, which are said to be good in cases of rhumatism &c. &c. Coasting it on still farther along the shore leading back to Pozzuoli we landed the 2d time to view the Lucrinus Lake which is connected to the sea; this is now a near puddle of water, owing to the earthquakes which raised the "Monte Nuovo" out of it. Traversing some distance on foot thro' a vinyard, we came to the Lake Avernus so celebrated by Virgil in his 6th Eneid. This lake is nearly surrounded by hills & on the south side is the famous grotto of Sybils; we entered by the light of torches, but as there was nothing to be seen, we soon made the best of our way out again.[2] In fact all this is interesting in no other respect than for its being the scene of classic story.

---

oyster-culture in the eighteenth century, replacing nearby Lake Lucrinus whose ancient oyster beds were disrupted by volcanic action.

1. A large complex of baths and public buildings, put up between the first century B. C. and the second century A. D., included buildings dedicated to or named for Diana, Venus, and Mercury.

2. An aperture on the south side of the lake leads to a cavern once thought to be the sanctuary where Aeneas consulted the local Sybil (*Aeneid*, Bk. VI, ll. 42–51). Its claims were dismissed when another sanctuary was brought to light in 1932.

Returning to the sea side, we embarked again & traversed a space of water the distance of about 2 miles, where we were landed not far from the Castle of Baiae.³ A few steps from the beach, we were shewn into the Tomb of Nero's mother Agrippina.⁴

A short distance upon a rising ground is the little village of Baulis, inhabited by none but the most miserable of beings. Here we descended the "Cento Camerelle" or hundred chambers where are dark apartments opening one into the other. They are generally small & have doors in proportion. Why they are called the 100 apartments I do not know, for in fact there are not more than 20 or 35 in all. Tis' supposed it was formerly used as a prison.⁵ The "piscena mirabili" which is not far from the Cento Camerelle, is the most imposing work I saw during the excursion. Tis composed of 5 arcades of huge pillars & unites solidity with grandeur. Some suppose it was anciently used as a fish pond, others that it was a reservoir for the roman fleet, when in the port of Miscenus.⁶ From hence a short walk brought us in sight of the Elysian Fields, but how Virgil could have described them as

---

3. The Castello di Baia was built in the mid-sixteenth century by the Spanish viceroy, Don Pedro of Toledo, and enlarged in the seventeenth century.

4. The actual burial place of Agrippina, the Younger (d. 59 A. D.), is unknown. The ruins shown to JCB were probably those of a small theater.

5. Baulis was a collection of luxurious villas built during the time of Augustus (63–14 B. C.) at or near present-day Bacoli. The *cento camerelle*, made up of numerous small chambers or cisterns, is believed to have been part of a two-story waterworks.

6. The *piscina mirabili* was built in 41 B. C. as a reservoir to supply the Roman naval base at Miseno (Misenum).

being the abode of the blessed, one can hardly conceive, unless they were directly the reverse of what they are at the present day. "They lie at the foot of a semicircle of sloping hills" which are covered with vines, & there is nothing at all in them any way attractive.[7] At the foot of the fields is the "Mare Morto" upon which sea old Charon was ferry man as the fable runs.[8] In the time of Virgil this was a healthy & delightful spot, as was the whole coast of Baiae & Misenus, as it contained a [*blank*] population & was the resort of the wealthy & luxurious romans. Now it is deserted & all those fine villa's are laid desolate, & from its being a spot favourable to the health 'tis become deadly & few places in all Italy is more shunned than this. Only a few poor, miserable beings at present inhabit it. Such is the change which this part of the country has undergone since the Christian aera. We once more took to our boat & was soon rowed over to the other side of the Bay—to Pozzuoli. This place was formerly called Puteoli & it was here Paul touched going to Roma (Acts 28:13.14.15). It was anciently a place of great commerce & had a fine port & quay. Now almost everything is in ruins & it has dwindled into an insignificant village.[9] We returned to Naples by

---

7. According to Virgil (*Aeneid*, Bk. VI, ll. 541–542) the home of the righteous dead.

8. Lake Miseno is one of two basins that formed the harbor at Miseno. It was once called the Stygian Lake and identified as the body of water where Charon ferried the souls of the dead to their final resting place.

9. Founded by Greeks, ca. 528 B. C., absorbed by Rome, 194 B. C., Potuoli became a principal Italian port for trade with the eastern Mediterranean. St. Paul landed there in 60 A. D. en route to Rome to be tried as a Roman citizen

the same route & arrived about sun set, after a pleasant & highly interesting excursion.

Thursday 29th. Took a ride to Portici to see the Museum at the Palace. Here in fact there is very little of any thing worthy of remark. You are shewn into a number of small sized rooms, the walls of which are covered with pieces of plaster taken from the ruined houses at Herculaneum & Pompeii, there extant the rude paintings of the Ancients, & are interesting in no other respect than for their antiquity & the high state in which their colors are preserved.[1] We did not think it worth while to look at the interiour of the palace (which is built immediately over the ancient city of Herculaneum) so after ranging over the gardens returned to Naples.

Saty: 31st Jany: Started in good season after breakfast on an excursion to the antient city of Pompeii, the distance is about 14 miles & the road led through Portici, & Torre del Greco which last town has repeatedly been distroyed by the eruptions of Vesuvius & as often rebuilt.[2] Many vestiges of ruins & lava are seen as you pass the road. Although the City of Pompeii was dis-

---

for inciting to riot in Jerusalem. JCB's reference to the Acts of the Apostles is exact.

1. Portici was a royal palace (1739) some six miles southeast of Naples. It was used to store antiquities when Pompeii and Herculaneum were first excavated. By 1820 most of these, except for some paintings, had been removed to Naples.

2. Torre del Greco was probably named for a tower built by the Emperor Frederick II (1194–1250). The town was buried by volcanic eruptions in 1631

troyed about 1800 years ago, yet until the reign of the late king of Naples, no part of it I believe was laid open to gratify the curious.[3] King Ferdinand however has conducted the business with much spirit & certainly to the credit of his government.[4] We examined attentively every part of it, a minute discription of which would fill a volume. We commenced first our investigations of the environs, where a whole villa is laid open. After going thro' many of its apartments, we descended into the cellar where are still laying upon the ground a number of amphorae, which were used by the ancients to keep their wine in. To this villa are joined gardens, with baths & pleasan[t] walks; all of which are still in good preservation. Opposite to this villa is the tomb of its former proprietor. We afterwards walked thro the principal streets (the paving of which is still in high order.) Rainged over the various private dwelling houses & shops. On the latter is still seen the name of its possessor, or the emblem of his calling. The Forum, the Temples of Jupiter & Venus, the Basillica, the public promenade, can each be as distinctly traced as in a modern

---

and 1794. Its motto was *"Post fata resurgo."*

3. The ancient port (pop. 20,000), subject to Roman rule ca. 200 B. C., was shaken by an earthquake in 63 A. D. and covered with volcanic ash and cinders from Mt. Vesuvius in 79 A. D. It remained buried until the mid-eighteenth century. Systematic but sporadic excavations, begun in 1763, were given fresh impetus by the French government (1806–1814). The "late King of Naples" is a reference to Joachim Murat.

4. Ferdinand, who had ruled Naples during the early efforts to uncover Pompeii, renewed the work with fresh vigor after regaining control of Naples from the French in 1815. On Murat and Ferdinand, see p. 153, n. 7 and p. 154 n. 9, above.

city.[5] In the square where the Roman Legions were quartered we partook of a light refreshment. Near to this are the two theatres Tragic & Comic, both in high preservation the former, must have been magnificent as the marble seats are mostly remaining.[6] The great Amphitheatre near the wall finished our view of Pompeii. This is as high a state of preservation, as anything in the city, & its dimentions are even larger than that at Nismes, tho' the latter is far its superior in point of solidity.[7] The appearance of Pompeii is that of an unroofed house, for in this respect they are all destitute & I believe not one has yet been found with any signs of a roof remaining. All probably were destroyed at the time of the great eruption which overwhelm'd the city. The size of which can be imagined when it is known that the walls are 4 miles in circumference. I had a very confused & indifferent idea of Pompeii, before visiting it. It was just such as I found Herculaneum after I had explored it which I did the same afternoon on my return from Pompeii.

Herculaneum was overwhelmed by seas of lava, which is like so much rock heaped upon the city, & of course has rendered

---

5. The west side of Pompeii, including the forum, the basilica or law courts, and adjoining temples, had been excavated by the early 1820s.

6. A large, open-air theater (ca. 200 B. C.) with a capacity of 5,000 was joined in 75 B. C. by a smaller, roofed theater with a capacity of 1,500. The latter was also known as the Odeon or singing-hall.

7. The amphitheater at the east end of the city (cap. 20,000) was begun in 70 B. C. and completed not long before its destruction. Built of tufa, lava, and limestone, shaken by an earthquake, it lacked the solidity that JCB noticed in the amphitheater at Nîmes.

it next to an impossibility ever to recover it, on the contrary Pompeii was only covered by a shower of ashes & cinders, so easy to be removed, that it only excites surprise how it should have remained so long unexcavated.[8] We descended to the theatre of Herculaneum, the only part of the city that is shown, or that is worth seeing. This is at distance of 70 feet below the surface of the earth & such is the difficulty of excavation, that only sufficient has been done to shew the general outlines of the Theatre, & even what there is is seen very imperfectly by the feeble light of torches. On the whole as to my visit to these famous Cities, I cannot say that I felt all the ardour of Eustace & others, or even the indifference of Berrian.[9] My curiosity certainly was very great on this subject & one of my greatest wishes to visit Italy was that I might explore these antient cities, the sad fate of which has rendered them doubly interesting. We returned the same night to Naples, only stopping a few moments to look at the late palace of Favorita. Tis a most pretty establishment & in some respects splendid. This situation looking immediately upon the Bay must render it a delightful residence.[1]

---

8. Buried up to a depth of forty feet by a flow of volcanic mud in 79 B. C., Herculaneum was covered over in 1631 by a flow of lava. Discovery of remains in 1709 led to excavations which continued for some seventy years until attention shifted to Pompeii where digging was easier.

9. See Eustace, *A Classical Tour*, III, pp. 53–57, and William Berrian, *Travels in France and Italy in 1817 and 1818* (N. Y., 1821), pp. 170–178. Berrian scoffed at the remarks of Eustace and other visitors to the ruins (including Mme. DeStael) who were inspired to imagine life as it had been in ancient Pompeii. He found their fancies "idle and extravagant."

1. One of several seacoast villas located on the "golden mile" east of Naples,

Monday Feby: 2d. Made a short excursion to Pozzuoli to view the ruins of the Temple of Jupiter Serapis situate to the Northwest of the town. Some immense columns are still to be seen, which are of themselves sufficient evidence of the magnificence of this estab-lishment.[2] Surrounding the same are a number of small apart-ments, supposed to have been the dwellings of the priests. Some of these are now used for bathing rooms, as there is a hot spring in the immediate vicinity of the Temple. which was probably used for the same purpose by the luxurious romans.

Not far from this temple is seen the remains of a very ancient amphitheatre & between this & the Solfatara are a range of cham-bers very much resembling the "piscina Mirabile" tho' not near so extensive. The Solfatara as it is called or in other words a vol-cano of Sulphur is to the North Northeast about ½ a mile. It an area of about 1000 feet surrounded with hills. The ground seems to be very hollow, as a stone thrown in some parts causes a trem-bling of the earth for some minutes, with a reverberating sound. From a hole in one part of the area arises a dense smoke strongly impregnated with a sulphurious smell.[3] Larger quantities of brim-

---

"La Favorita" was built in the late eighteenth century by a Neapolitan prince but had become a royal residence by 1823.

2. A market-hall (first century B. C.) erroneously identified as a temple and named after a statue of Serapis found during excavations begun in 1750. All but three of its great Corinthian columns were removed to the royal palace at Caserta or to a museum.

3. The *solfatara* was a large elliptical crater in a dormant volcano. The hole or jet noted by JCB was probably the "boca grande" which emitted a sul-furous steam that reached temperatures over 300° F.

stone are made at this place & the process appeared very simple. Alum is also dug here & there are works for preparing it as well as the sulphur.

After taking a passing look at the Lake of Agnano we continued our route to the city.[4] The weather to day was rather cloudy & by no means so fair as could have been wished tho' on the whole it was good winter weather.

Thursday Feby: 5th Left town at 8 AM to visit the Aquaduct & Palace of Caserta. The former is one of the most substantial works of modern times, & was built by Charles 3d. of Naples, who in all his undertakings seemed to entertain the same magnificent ideas as Louis 14 of France. The length of this Aquaduct is about 2000 feet & 200 in height, having 3 tiers of arches, one above the other, like the one at Nismes: the lowest 19, the middle 27 & the top 43. These however are by no means so well proportioned, as the old Roman Structure, & in point of grandeur & duribility, not to be compared to it. Bricks & stones of a foot in length compose its material. This aquaduct is for the purpose of conveying water to the palace of Caserta, which is at a distance of 4 miles from it. Caserta is a sort of 2d Versailles, tho' the gardens & [*illeg.*] palace itself are much inferiour to it. Tis evident that Charles in undertaking this royal establishment wished to imitate in some measure his relative of France. In point of size I am not sure but what Caserta is even larger than Versailles, it being about

---

4. A large volcanic crater filled with water until drained later in the nineteenth century.

750 by 550 feet with 4 courts & containing 1800 rooms. The materials are of brick, tho' in the interiour, an immense quantity of marble is used, one flight of steps alone containing 100 pieces all 18 feet in length. The Chaple is almost entirely of marble & gilding & is compared with the one at Verseilles. Not a half of this huge pile is yet finished: a few rooms are furnished for the Royal Family, but as the Government is so much in want of money & the undertaking so vast tis probable many years will elapse before it is completed if it ever is at all.[5]

Monday 9th Feby: We had now only one more excursion to make, which was to ascend the so celebrated Mount Vesuvius, & as the weather to day was propitious we were determined to improve it. Leaving Naples at ½ past 9 we took the usual rout thro' Portici to Resina, where leaving our carriage we mounted on donkeys & ascended the "Hermitage" as it is called.[6] The distance is nearly 4 miles & the ascent very gradual, most part of the country at the immediat foot of the mountain presented a dreary, desolate waste, where rivers of lava had rolled down during the various eruptions. From the Hermitage (a single house, where one poor soli-

5. Charles III planned this grandiose palace not just to rival Versailles but to provide office space for his ministries. Begun in 1752, never completed as planned, it was transferred to the Italian state in 1921 by Victor Emmanuel (1869–1947). In World War II, it was headquarters for the Allied Command in Italy.

The aqueduct was one of three that brought water from Monte Taburno some twenty-five miles away.

6. Resina was a common point of departure and the Hermitage a common way station for the ascent of Vesuvius.

tary monk lives & who keeps some trifling refreshments for travellers) we continued on our asses about a mile further, till owing to the steepness of the Mount it was no longer possible to make use of these animals. Here alighting we commenced ascending on foot & were in some measure assisted by holding on to a leather strap, one end of which was slung over the guides shoulder. For my own part I found little or no difficulty at all in getting up the mountain & can hardly conceive how the ascent should have been so much exagerated. In comparing with Ben Nevis it is really nothing.[7] The ashes & Stones give way a little under your feet; which of course makes it the more tiresome, but then on the contrary this facilitates the descent in an astonishing degree. We were ¾ of an hour before reaching the crater & such a horrible, yawning gulph cannot well be conceived by any one who has never looked into the mouth of a Volcano. The circumference at the top we were told is about 4 miles & the depth say 2000 feet the sides of which in most places were nearly perpendicular, from the crevices of the rocks & earth below & on the sides we could see volumes of smoke ascend & sometimes I thought I could even hear a rumbling from this (I had almost said) bottomless pit. The general appearance of Vesuvius is quite changed since the last eruption in 1820[8] & it is now not so high as formerly & since that time our guide informed us no one has descended into the crater. Our descent from the mountain was short & easy. Mr I[ves] was just 4½ minutes. I took it more leisure-

---

7. See JCB's diary for October 20, 1823.

8. The last eruption of Vesuvius before 1824 was in February 1822.

ly.[9] Remounting our asses we returned to the Hermitage & after partaking of some good wine, with bread, cheese & fruit, resumed our journey, to the village where we found the carriage ready to take us to the City.

Feby: 10th. During my short stay in Naples I visited most of the interesting curiosities the city affords. The Studio well deserves the attention of every traveller. Its collection of Bronzes is considered the finest of any in the world & many pieces might be mentioned as deserving the highest praize.[1]

Among the statury the Farnesian Venus & the Antonius are the most remarkable, the former is justly considered a second only to that of Medicis such are the exquisite proportions of all its parts. The colossal statue of Hercules with a remarkably fine head of Homer are well worthy of remembrance. All the prints we see of Homers head are copied from this.[2] The Galleries of paintings are numerous & among the number are to be found

---

9. Guide books advised allowing ten minutes for the descent from the summit to the Hermitage.

1. The Studio, officially named the Royal Bourbon Museum in 1816, was built as a barracks in 1586 and occupied by the University in the seventeenth century. It was remodeled in the late eighteenth century to receive antiquities from Herculaneum and Pompeii, as well as the Bourbon art collection, especially that brought from Rome and Parma as the inheritance of Charles III from his mother, Elizabeth Farnese (1692–1766).

2. Three of the sculptures admired by JCB were ancient copies of Hellenistic originals: the bust of Homer; the Farnese Hercules, found at Rome during the reign of the Farnese pope, Paul III (r. 1534–1549); the Farnese Venus found at Capua in the mid-eighteenth century. The colossal bust of Antoninus Pius dates from ca. 140 A. D.

some of the best pieces of the greatest masters. The Virgin & the Infant jesus by Raphael, & the Magdalen by Titian, are among the best.[3] In the other rooms of the Studio are various articles taken from the ruins of Pompeii &c. &c. Articles of household furniture & such like apparatus & a glass bottle was shewn containing some liquid (wine I believe) preserved during the long space of 2000 years.

I saw the manuscript apartments and the mode of unrolling them. Most that have as yet been found are in Greek & very much injured. Very little has thus far been found to add to the stock of knowledge.[4] The churches in Naples are very numerous & some are interesting. The most so of any we saw was the Church of Saint Januarius, the tutular Saint of Naples. In point of riches this exceeds all the others. We were shown into one of the inner apartments where is kept all the argenterie of the Church. The immense quantity of plates far exceeded any idea I had previously formed of the wealth of the Catholic church. Many of the Saints were as large as life all in solid silver & adorned with precious stones. Large candelabrias & even the altar itself was of massey silver. The Bottle containing the Blood of the Saint being locked up, we could not see it. This church like most of the others at Naples contains some fine pieces of paintings.[5]

---

3. The Farnese Collection of paintings (moved to Capodimonte in 1957) included several madonnas attributed to Raphael or his school, as well as the Mary Magdalen by Titian.

4. Rooms devoted to the preservation of thousands of scrolls uncovered by the excavations in and around Naples since the mid-eighteenth cenutury.

5. The Cathedral of St. Januarius (San Gennaro) was begun by Charles of

Having purchased our travelling carriage & made the other necessary arrangements for our departure for Rome we shall take leave of Naples tomorrow & after a pleasant sejour of 18 days bid adieu to this charming spot.

The most of our time at Naples, we were lodged at the Hotel "Crocelle" upon the Chiatamoine a very good house & very well situated. Our rooms looked out upon the Bay, & we paid 1½ Dollar [*per*] day, & 4 carlini each for breakfast, having quit the Villa di Londra, where we found the master & all concerned great rogues & rascals.[6] While at Naples visited the Catacombs, of which hereafter I may say something.[7]

Wednesday 11th. at ½ past 2 PM we left the city of Naples in our carriage & post horses. Just at night we reached Capua, but as there is little or nothing to be seen upon the road between Naples & Rome we made no stop whatever but travelled on post haste during the night & at 4 PM we reached the "Eternal City." The moon shown very clear which made it pleasant & finding the

Anjou in 1272. Its precious objects were kept in a chapel (Capella di Tesoro), built in the seventeenth century, which displayed gold and silver vessels and silver busts of saints other than Januarius and paintings by Domenichino (1581–1641). Vials containing the congealed blood of Januarius were kept there to await liquefaction on three annual occasions. Patron saint of Naples and bishop of Benevento, Januarius was martyred in 305. The first recorded liquefaction was in 1389.

6. Both hotels were close to the waterfront. Casanova stayed at the Crocelle, June – September, 1770. See Giacomo Casanova, *Histoire de ma Vie*, ed. intégral (Wiesbaden & Paris, 1960–1962) XI, pp. 263 ff.

7. Burial vaults for early Christians were cut in the hills to the north of Naples. The most important were those of St. Januarius and St. Gaudioso.

road well lined with soldiers we felt no fear of Robbers. We passed thro a number of small towns & villiges of not much importance. Came to Terracina the frontier town of the Romagna about day brake; here our luggage was overhauled.[8]

From Terracina took the route to rome over the Pomptine marshes, a celebrated work of Pius 6th & enough to immortalize the name of any crown'd head. This is called the "Linea Pia" & is constructed upon the ancient "via appia".[9] At Cisterna on leaving the town we had the first view of the Dome of Saint Peters. This place is distant 2 posts or about 16 miles & from thence the whole way leads over a perfectly level plain. We entered the city thro' the gates of the via Appia, but long before reaching it the road on both sides presents a series of ruins which formerly made a part of the magnificence of ancient rome. We found the roads very fine all the way from Naples & posting is quite as good as either in France or England. Our lodgings were at the Hotel de l'Europe in the place d'Espagne, a good house & the best in this place, but abominably dear 2½ Dollars were charged for apartments & other things, in proportion.[1]

---

8. Nautical slang for "taken apart and inspected."

9. Giovanni Angelo Brasci (1717–1799), elected pope in 1775, patronized the arts and promoted public works such as road-building and the draining of the Pontine Marshes, a project not completed until the 1930s. According to William Berrian (*Travels*, p. 162), the road showed few traces of the Appian Way. "It is hard, wide and smooth, and scarcely deviates in a straight line in five and twenty miles."

1. The hotel was located at the Piazza di Spagna, a tourist hub then as now. JCB's use of French names for Roman landmarks may have resulted from his reliance on a French-speaking guide. See above p. 153, n. 5.

After dinner as the Evening was fine we took a turn in the city & of course our attention was first directed to that first of Christian temples, the Church of Saint Peters. Of the splendour & magnificence of this wonderful building I had heard & read so much that my expectations were raised to the highest pitch, & in truth I cannot say they were disappointed. We could only take an outside view of the building, but such an impression it made upon my mind can never be lost. Perhaps the stillness & silence which every where surounded it added even more to its grandeur. Not a single individual was to be seen in any part of the court & more than 2 hours elapsed ere I returned home from viewing this first of <u>earthly</u> edifices.

Friday 13th. After calling upon the [*blank*] to deliver our letter of credit, visited the Capitoline hill, all the buildings upon which are entirely modern & nothing of the ancient Capitol so renowned in Roman story is now to be seen.[2] In the center is a bronze stat[*u*]e of Marcus Aurelius. Back of the Capitol is the ruins of the Forum, here & there a few broken columns & an arch or two only remain to shew the fomer grandeur of the Imperial & how low it is now fallen. For this place where once Cicero charmed the multitude by his eloquence is now converted into a cow market.[3] Some dis-

---

2. The citadel and religious center of ancient Rome, the Capitoline remained its political center in the Middle Ages. From the sixteenth century on, it was rebuilt according to a design by Michelangelo.

3. Used as a stone quarry during the Middle Ages, the "Forum Romanum" became the "Campo Vaccino" where cattle were pastured.

tance behind the Forum are the Triumphal arches of Severus & Constantine & not far from the latter stands the Coliseum the wonder of the world.[4] This is upon the same plan as all other amphitheatres only that in size it is superior to any other upon record. Tis' a ⅓ larger than the one at Nismes, being 1600 feet in circumference, but in point of durability is far its inferiour. That at Nismes being built of huge blocks of stone, & the Coliseum only of brick, the hight of the C. is 150 feet.

My view of these ruins was quite hasty, merely to obtain a general idea of their situation & of the City at large. Hereafter I shall view them more attentively. During the day rambled in various parts of the City. Examined the grand northern entrance thro the "porta del popolo" in the "place" of which stands one of those immense granite columns or Egyptian obelisks, so numerous in Rome.[5] Viewed the triumphal columns of Antoninus, standing in the "Piazza Collona" upon the "Corso" & of Trajan, the shaft of this latter is about 90 feet & the whole more than 120.

---

4. The arch of Septimius Severus (146–211), built in 203, celebrated the emperor's success against the Parthians in Mesopotamia and Assyria (195–199). That of Constantine (274?–337) was built in 315 to honor his defeat of a rival claimant to the imperial title.

The Flavian Amphitheater was begun under Vespasian (9–79), founder of the Flavian dynasty, and completed by his son, Titus (39–81). JCB's measurements are approximate.

5. The oval-shaped Piazza del Popolo, designed and developed between 1814 and 1823, had at its center an obelisk placed there in the late sixteenth century. The oldest and tallest in Rome, the obelisk had been brought to Rome by Augustus (63–14 B. C.) from Egypt. It commemorated Rameses II (1304–1237 B. C.).

It was after the column of Trajan that the famous bronze column at Paris was model'd.[6]

Saty: 14. Immediately after breakfast hasten to Saint Peters to take our first view of the interiour. All that has or could be said in its praise would be far short of what it deserves. In fact no <u>description</u> can give a just idea of this astonishing master piece of human art, & its beauties & riches <u>must</u> be seen to be appreciated. The best & most accurate description that I've seen is to be found in Eustace,[7] but after all, the best description or most perfect drawings of a building convey but a confused idea, & more especially to an American who has never yet seen any of the Catholick Cathedrals of Europe. We spent more than 2 hours admiring the beauty & grandeur of Saint Peters; examing its almost matchless pieces of sculpture; lingering under its golden Domes to view & compare its fine proportions, & to wonder how mortal man could conceive, much less execute so stupendous a structure. Returning stopped at the Pantheon or as it is called in Rome the Rotunda. This has always been the pride & glory of the city & at present stands the most complete & magnificent of

---

6. The column "of Antoninus," erected late in the second century, was in fact dedicated to Marcus Aurelius (121–180) to celebrate his victorious German campaigns. JCB was misled by a sixteenth-century inscription saying that Marcus Aurelius had raised it to honor his predecessor, Antoninus Pius (86–161). Trajan's column, erected in 113 A. D., commemorated that emperor's conquest of Dacia at the turn of the second century. See diary entry for March 26, 1823.

7. See J. C. Eustace, *Classical Tour*, II, pp. 122–160.

all the ancient temples. The portico is as all the world knows the model of perfection, being supported upon 16 columns of oriental granite. This portico was formerly covered with gilt brass, but this has long since been removed. The sides of the pantheon are 18 feet in thickness; the floor inlaid with variegated marbles & the sides of the interiour are ornamented with beautiful fluted columns of "giallo antico." Its diameter is 149 English feet 185 including the walls, & it is of the same [*height*] having an apperture on the center by which light is admitted. Agrippa is said to have built the pantheon tho' it is doubted whether the portico was built by him or not. It is now used as a church & the popes have consecrated the pantheon as they have the colisium & other ancient buildings in Rome for the purpose of preserving them which is highly praiseworthy in the holy fathers.[8]

Sunday 15th. Visited the Basilica's Santa Maria Maggiore & Saint John Lateran These both are among the most celebrated churches in Rome. Santa Maria stands upon a long & straight street heading from the porta Tiburtina, on the highest spot of the Esquiline hill, in the center of two squares. Immediately in front rises a corinthian column & in the rear an Egyptian obelisk of

---

8. JCB's description follows William Berrian's, but whereas Berrian refers to the "spoilation of the popes" (*Travels*, p. 109) who removed parts of it, JCB praises those pontiffs who tried to preserve ancient buildings. "Giallo antico," literally "ancient yellow," refers to marble of a deep yellow color found in Italian ruins.

Marcus Vipsanius Agrippa (ca. 63–12 B. C.), military hero and son-in-law of Augustus (63–14 B. C.), built the Pantheon in 27 B. C. Destroyed and rebuilt in the second century, it was converted into a Christian church in 609.

red granite 60 feet in height. The interiour is remarkably imposing having on each side 18 marble pillars the ceiling is covered with a profusion of gilding & the pavement like most of the Roman churches composed of variegated marbles. The chaple belonging to the Borghese family is described as decorated in a very sumptious manner, & so we should judge from its appearance as thro the brazen gateway. But as it was during services that we were there, we did not enter.[1]

Saint John Lateran is the patriarchal church of Rome & bears the title of parent & mother of all the churches. Altho rich in gilding & marbles it did not strike me so favourably as the last basilica; but the Corsini chapel, which I examined pleased me much & indeed it is considered one of the most perfect of its kind, tho' in many respects not so rich as the Borghese. The walls are covered with alabaster & other fine stones & the niches are filled with masterpieces of sculpture, one of penetence, a side of the altar will always be noticed for the plaintive expression of countenance. The body of Clement 12 of the Corsini family lies in a sumptious urn of porphyry. As the city is now built this cathedral church stands quite in the country, near to the gates of Saint John which we entered coming from Naples.[2] Close by the church is a

---

1. Rome's third-ranking basilica, St. Mary Major (Santa Maria Maggiore) was built on orders of Pope Liberius (r. 352–366). Notable among later additions was the Borghese (or Pauline) Chapel built by Camillo Borghese (1552–1621) who became Pope Paul v in 1605.

2. Rome's cathedral, the first-ranking church in Roman Catholicism, the Basilica of the Savior became commonly known as St. John Lateran, because it neighbored a monastery of St. John the Baptist and stood on ground once

small building devoted to worship, but which hardly deserves the name of church in which is to be seen a number of white marble steps, said to have been taken from the palais of pilate at Jerusalem & upon which Jesus Christ ascended when brought before the judges. In so Catholic a country as Italy, & even in the Holy See itself, it could not be supposed otherwise than that they would be held in high veneration by the people & the poorer classes in particular. Accordingly they have always been mounted upon the knees & so long & so often have they been used in this manner that altho of the hardest marble, they are quite worn away, & unless they should be entirely lost, the Pope has ordered them to be covered with plank (in which state we found them). While viewing them we saw a number of miserable devils floundering up upon their marrow bones, but as we were not quite so warm in the faith we did not follow their example.[3]

Monday 16th. Passed the most of the day in ranging in the museum & in the galleries of paintings in the palace of the Conservatori. The museum is well supplied with ancient sculptures & tho' in no way to be compared to the Vatican, yet even in Italy it must hold a high rank, & in any other country be superior to most other

---

owned by Plautii Laterani. Over the centuries the church was repeatedly restored and rebuilt. The Corsini Chapel was added by Lorenzo Corsini (1652–1740) who became Pope Clement XII in 1730.

3. The Scala Santa, or sacred staircase, consisted of twenty-eight marble steps reputedly brought from Jerusalem by St. Helena (255?–330). They were installed in a building designed for that purpose by Sixtus V in the late sixteenth century.

collections.[4] To attempt to enumerate all that are at all distinguished would be to give a catalogue of most that the museum contains. I will however notice a few of the most prominent. The hall of the Emperors is lined with the busts of most of the emperors & kings in cronological order. Then comes the hall of the Philosophers. Like the above the walls are lined with the busts of most of these ancients. In the hall of the Fauns (so called) the most interesting inscription is the decree of the Senate which gives to the Emperor Augustus the imperial power.[5] The hall of the gladiator contains the choicest of any in this collection, that piece which gives name to the hall; called the dying gladiator, is well worthy of admiration. This is said not to be a gladiator, but a gaul, & to make part of a group which represents the expedition & defeat of the Gauls in Greece.[6] The fine statue of Venus in high preservation will of <u>course</u> engage the particular attention of all ameteurs of female beauty. I should suppose it would even vie with the Medicis Venus such is the fine contour of all its

4. A complex of museums and galleries on the Capitoline had long been a collecting point (or dumping ground) for objects found in the ruins of ancient Rome. In 1824 it included the Capitoline Museum (1644–1654) and the Palace of the Conservatori (rebuilt ca. 1450) which had a collection of modern paintings on its second floor.

5. The Hall of the Faun, named for a marble figure found at Hadrian's villa in 1736, had on its wall a bronze tablet with an inscription from the *Lex Regis*, a decree of the Roman senate transferring power to the emperor.

6. A Roman copy of a Hellenistic statue found in 1622 and identified as *The Dying Gladiator*. Byron in 1817 (*Childe Harold's Pilgrimage*, IV, l. 141) nearly immortalized this misnomer which had already been rejected by several generations of classical scholars and art historians.

parts.[7] In this appartment are also two pieces of bronze, a wolf suckling young Romulus & Remus & a shepards boy sitting & picking a thorn out of his foot. Not[*hing*] can be more natural than this last.[8] In the galleries of the opposite building the collection of pictures is not numerous, but among them are some of the productions of the first masters—perhaps the most striking is the vanity of Titian, represented by a Venus lying quite exposed, & thinking I suppose that "all is vanity": vanity or no vanity, who can look upon such a glowing canvas & not acknowledge sweet womans charms? A supurb picture of Rubens representing Romulus & Remus sucking the Wolf is also among the best. I will only mention the Magician by Salvator Rosa, as one more among the many which pleased me.[1]

Tuesday 17th. On our way to the Baths of Dioclisian stopped to visit the fountain of Trevi, one of the finest falls of water in this city & which above all others in this particular, seems to be supplied most abundantly. A large figure of Ocean sitting upon a large sea shell & drawn by two sea horses each guided by a triton has a fine appearance, all around floods of water are falling into an immense marble basin.[2] The Baths of Dioclesian are or

---

7. The *Capitoline Venus*, a marble statue found in the seventeenth century and believed to be derived from the *Cnidian Aphrodite* of Praxiteles (fifth century B. C.).

8. A collection of ancient bronzes given to the Roman people by Sixtus IV in 1471, included the *Spinario*, the figure of a boy picking a thorn from his foot.

1. On the paintings in the Palace of the Conservatori, cf. Charlotte A. Eaton, *Rome in the Nineteenth Century*, 2 vols. (London, 1860), II, p. 84.

2. The fountain in the Piazza di Trevi was originally a simple basin designed

rather were situated upon the hill. Some remains of the brick walls are yet to be seen enough to give an idea of the magnitude of these celebrated works of the Romans.[3] All that part of the city called the Piazza termini with the space on which many of the neighboring houses stand was formerly covered by the Baths & indeed two churches are built adjoining the ruins which have been the means of preserving them thus far. We did not to day explore the remains so thoroughly as we shall do hereafter, but the church of "Sainte Marie des Anges" attracted our attention, not so much for its fine columns & marbles (for these are met with every where) as for the monument of Salvator Rosa. This however is nothing more than a simple slab, & only deserving attention recording the death of a celebrated artist.[4]

From hence we went to the extreme part of the city, to the Vatican; & for the first time entered this princely residence of the holy fathers. Three to four hours only afforded time to examine the numerous halls & galleries containing the ancient & modern statuary.[5] Here are to be found most of those pieces which are celebrated throughout the world, such as the Laocoon, Apollo of

---

by Leon Battista Alberti (1404–1472). The giant figures, as described by JCB, were added in 1762.

3. Ruins of the largest bath in ancient Rome, built by Diocletian (r. 284–305) and Maximian (r. 286–305).

4. The church of Santa Maria deglia Angeli was built in the 1560s when Pius IV (1499–1565) commissioned Michelangelo to find some use for the ruins. More than a "simple slab," the monument to Salvator Rosa, commissioned by his son, was adorned with figures carved by Bernardino Fioriti (fl. 1640–1675).

5. Vatican Palace became the pope's official residence in the late fourteenth century when the papacy returned to Rome from Avignon. Clement XIII (r.

Belvedere both found among the ruins of the city.[6] Many of the finest pieces of Canova adorn the collection such as the "Persius" with the Medusa's head, & the two Boxers all of which when once seen can never be forgotten. These with many other of the masterpieces contained in the Vatican were in the time of Bonapart carried to Paris, but restored in 1814.[7] Besides the statury, the salons which contained them are fitted up in a style of wonderful magnificence, floors inlaid with mosaics, the finest of marble pillars distributed around with the utmost profusion, in fact many of these literally cased with marble, leave the visitor to wonder at & admire the magnificence of the Roman pontiffs. We did not see the library, or any other part, but intending to revisit the museum with the rest of the palais another time—shall have occasion to speak again on this fruitful & interesting subject.

Wednesday 18. Today we went to see the workshop of the late Canova, which is still continued by his pupils. We saw some of

1758–1769) founded the Vatican's Museum of Pagan Antiquities; his successors, Clement XIV (r. 1769–1774) and Pius VI (r. 1775–1799), converted the Belvedere Pavilion into a museum.

6. The *Laocoön* was unearthed in 1506 on the Esquiline Hill and purchased by Julius II (r. 1503–1513). It dates from ca. 50 B. C. and was restored once on advice from Michelangelo, and once again in 1960.

The *Apollo Belvedere*, a marble copy of a bronze original from the fourth century B. C., was brought to the Vatican in 1503.

7. In 1824 these sculptures by Antonio Canova (1757–1822) stood in the same court as the *Apollo Belvedere*. The two boxers, *Creugas* (1801) and *Damoxenes* (1806), were conceived as a pair and meant to replace a classical *Wrestlers* which in 1800 had been moved to Paris by the French.

them at work finishing various statues, but I believe there were none remaining which were commenced by Canova himself. Many of the casts of his best pieces are still remaining the shop & among others I particularly noticed that of Washington which was made for the State of North Carolina. The General is sitting clothed in the Roman toga & just commencing his celebrated farewell address to his Countrymen. A very great blunder is made in heading the address in the Italian language—rather than the Latin or English as it should be. Thus what with the roman dress & Italian language no one could distinguish it from the John Doe or Richard Roe & as to the head itself, as far as I can judge from the pictures of the hero, 'tis no more like him than I to hercules. Yet after all these mistakes it is certainly very fortunate that we have in the U. S. at least one piece of sculpture from the chisel of this late distinguished artist, unquestionably the first of modern days.[1]

From hence we spent an hour or two looking at the painting in the private palace of Sciarra, situated upon the Corso. The collection is quite extensive & all are good; many from the first masters, those which pleased me most were two pictures of a Magdelen each in the same stile & by Guido, so much penitence expressed in the countenances, that none could forbear pardon-

---

In 1815 Canova, as curator of the papal collections, went to Paris to reclaim art works taken from the Papal States and other Italian territories during Napoleon's ascendancy.

1. Canova, after his mission to France in 1815, executed a marble statue of George Washington in Roman battle dress. Widely viewed as a public extravagance, it was installed in the state house at Raleigh, N. C., destroyed by fire in 1831, and recreated from plaster casts in 1970.

ing them their fault. Vanity & modesty by Leonard di Vinci, & the beautiful mistress of Titian, will be noticed by every one.[2] As yet we had taken no general view of Rome from an elevated situation, accordingly we went expressly for this purpose to the top of the belfry upon the Capitol, there you have a commanding view of the city & its environs, & we passed an hour or more viewing its present extent & comparing it with its ancient limits as far as we could judge from the ruins pointed out by our guide.[3] Many of the 7 hills upon which ancient [*Rome*] was built are almost leveled with the surrounding country, & as we looked in the direction of the Alban Mount & the Quirinal hill, the ruins of the forum, with the Colisium, Baths temples & arches, presented nothing but one series of ruins. Descending we walked thro' the forum towards the Colisium passing at the same time the Arches of Titus & Constantine. To have a more perfect view of this first of Roman Amphitheatres we ascended its ruins to the 2d & 3d, galleries. This building could contain 100,000 people. This fact alone is sufficient to convey an idea of its greatness. The Baths of Titus are not far from the Colisium, to the left, going out of the city. We stopped a few moments to examine this fine ruin, for it is still in sufficient preservation to shew the formation. Many cor-

2. The Sciarra family, allies of the powerful Barberini and Colonna, had been reduced to sharing their sixteenth-century palace with other tenants. But they continued to house an impressive art collection, much of it on loan from the Barberini. A *Magdalen* painted by Guido Reni for Francesco Barberini in the 1620s was listed in the Sciarra inventories of 1812 and 1818.

3. A tower, built on the summit of the Capitoline in 1572, afforded a panoramic view of Rome and the Campagna.

ridors & chambers which were used for bathing are yet to be seen, & on the ceiling of some of the arches, are paintings. as fresh as if the colors were just put on. Some further excavating within a few years past have been made & the bricks have all the freshness of new mason work.[4] On our way home we looked in to "Saint Peter in Vinculis." This is a middling sized Church. One piece of statuary in particular deserves notice a colossal statue of Moses sitting upon the tomb of Jules 2d. This is by M. Angelo Bonarrotti & is considered one of the first pieces of modern sculpture.[5]

Thursday 19th. Most of the ruins we have visited today have been without the Walls of the City & altho' numerous & in general interesting for a stranger the first time he sees them, yet in themselves of but little consequence & hardly deserving a second visit. We first mounted the extensive ruins of the palace of the Caesars. Upon one part is now built the Seat of an English Gentleman & the remainder is in fact nothing more than a "huge pile of old bricks" this however serves to shew the great extent, & magnificence of the palace which was taken down by [*blank*] as being too sumptious even for a roman Emperor. It was built by

---

4. JCB refers to the baths built by Titus (r. 79–81) and extended by Trajan (r. 98–117). They were built over the wreckage of Nero's palace, parts of which they sealed and so helped to preserve.

5. According to tradition, the Church of St. Peter in Chains (*Vinculis*) was founded in 422 to enshrine chains used to fetter the apostle. The building was restored in 1475 by Sixtus IV.

Michelangelo's *Moses* was conceived as a part of a grandiose tomb for Julius II (r. 1503–1513). The scale of the monument was drastically reduced by Julius's executors before it was installed in 1545.

Nero & the Colisium near which it stands was built of a part of its materials. We saw the room in which Nero caused Seneca to be put to death, in the center of the room is a round basin of bricks, which probably contained the water.[6] Near to the palaces, or more properly adjoining it were pointed out the remains of the Circus. 'Tis recorded 'twod hold 30,000 persons. The immense ruins of the Baths of Caracalla are not far from the palace, but like most of these once famous structures, the walls of a part are only standing.[7] Some distance towards the Appian Gate on the left is the Tomb of the Sipios the most celebrated family of the roman republic. By the light of torches we descended into this abode of the dead, but the Sarcophagi are removed to the Vatican & the original inscriptions also.[8] Passing under the Arch of Drusus we left

---

6. The emperors' palace once occupied land expropriated from public use by Nero (r. 54–68). After his death, Nero's buildings were razed and the land was used for public buildings—the Coliseum and the baths.

The "English Gentleman" was identified by A. C. Pasquier (pseud. Valery) writing in the 1820s "the *Vigna Palatina* situated on the summit of the hill…is at present occupied by an Englishman, Mr. Charles Mills who does the honors with infinite politeness." See *Voyages historiques et littéraires en Italie*, Eng. Trans. (Paris, 1839), p. 524.

Seneca (4 B. C. – 65 A. D.) killed himself on Nero's orders not in the imperial palace but at his own villa on the Appian Way. After his veins were cut, he was placed in a tub of water to ease his pain. The "round basin of bricks" in the ruins of the palace may have inspired the story that Seneca died there.

7. The Circus Maximus, the first and largest Roman Circus, dated from the fourth century B. C. Its capacity grew through successive reconstructions. The last public games were held there during the reign of a Germanic king in 549.

The Baths of Caracalla, built between 212 and 217, could accommodate 1,600 patrons.

8. The Tomb of the Scipios was built in 298 B. C. by the great-grandfather of

the city by the Appian Gate & rode to the Tomb a Cecellia Matella.[#]

This is in very good preservation & is as well worth noticing as almost any of the Antiquities in the neighborhood of Rome, its diameter is 86 feet & it is of a conical form. The nitch is over the port of entrances but what has become of the coffin I did not learn. Like most of the works of the romans 'tis built of large rocks of stone & seems as if it would last as long as time.[9] Leaving the

[#]The Circus of Caracalla is on the left hand side going to the Tomb, & is the only Circus [*which*] can give any idea of their ancient places of amusement. 'Tis about 1500 feet in length and 400 in breadth, & being a private establishment <u>only</u> contained 20,000 people.[1]

road and returning towards the gate & a little on the right the Temple of Baccus (as 'tis now called) was pointed out. 'Tis built of brick & has nothing in its appearance or even its history as far as I could learn, deserving attention.[2] Descending into the Vale of Caffarella, we stopped a moment to look at the fountain, or

---

Scipio Africanus (237–183 B. C.), the most famous member of the family, who died and was buried near Naples.

9. A massive round tower built for Caecilia, daughter of Metellus Creticus who conquered Crete in 68 B. C. The "coffin" (sarcophagus) had been moved to the Farnese Palace.

1. The Circus of Maxentius (r. 306–312), once attributed to Caracalla, was built in 309 and dedicated to the emperor's son Romulus. Its capacity was ca. 10,000.

2. A brick building, formerly consecrated to various Roman deities, the "Temple of Baccus" was converted into a church and re-named for Pope Saint Urban (r. 227–230). It was restored in 1634.

more properly the Grotto of Egeria & a short distance from it another little red brick house, termed the "Temple of Ridicule."[3] All these temples are converted into churches, which doubtless have been the means of preserving them. Regaining the high way again, we entered by the same gate & taking the road to the left, we alighted to view the foreigners burying ground, & near it the Tomb of Caius Astus, built after the form of the pyramids of Egypt, & in <u>perfect</u> preservation, tho after so many centuries of storms & barbarism. Its height is 130 feet & built of huge masses of stone & covered with blocks of white marble 1 foot in thickness.[4] For a few moments we meditated among the tombs & most of them seem to have been buried quite recently, say since 1815. Among the number was a Mrs Temple of Massachusetts[,] Lady of Sir [*blank*] Temple[,] an English baronet[,] one from N York were all the Americans I noticed.[5]

---

3. A brook, the Almone, also known as the Mariana Caffarella, was a site where priests of Cybele gathered to bathe the goddess's image. The Almone also watered the Grotto of Egeria, a nymph whose royal husband, Numa Pompilius (715–672 B. C.), reportedly came there to consult her.

According to legend, a temple was built to mark the spot where the god Rediculus persuaded the Carthaginian invader, Hannibal, to halt his march on Rome in 211 B. C. More probably, it was built by a philanthropist of the second century B. C. as a tomb for his wife.

4. Commonly called the "Protestant Cemetery," the *Cimetero degli Stranieri*, or Foreigners' Cemetery, was ground set aside in the early eighteenth century for burial of non-Catholic Christians. It was enlarged in 1822. The tomb of Gaius Cestius, a Roman official (d. 12 B. C.), lay just outside its wall.

5. Eliza Watson, native of Massachusetts, wife of Sir Granville Temple, was buried in Rome in 1809.

From this mournful scene we return'd to our lodging, only stopping a few moments on the banks of the Tiber near the pont palantine (a part of which, from some cause or other has been thrown down) the Temples of Vesta & of Fortuna virilis.[6] The first is now called "The Church of the Sun," & is as tasty as any other of the kind in rome. The "Maxima Cloacina" ought not to pass unnoticed by any one who delights in viewing any of the substantial works of the Ancients.[7] On all the above ruins much has & could be written & if I was to act the part of an antiquary, could fill volumes with <u>suppositions</u> & <u>doubts</u>, & perhaps be as near the truth as most of those who have preceded me, in ascertaining the time & the purposes for which these buildings were erected. In the course of our excursion to day we stopped at the Church of Saint Sebastian, & descended to the Catacombs. They are immense excavations in the bowels of the earth & form numerous long & winding passages & were used by the primitive Christians as a refuge in time of persecutions, & contained the bodies of an innumerable number of persons nothing now remains but fragments of old bones, & no use at all is made of the Catacombs at present.[8] We did not venture far, although conducted by one

6. The first stone bridge across the Tiber (179–142 B. C.), originally the *Pons Aemilius*, was built where the current is particularly strong. Frequently washed out, repaired, and renamed, it was abandoned after collapsing in 1598.

7. The "great sewer," which still functions, was a stream to the Tiber draining valleys between three of Rome's hills. It was first canalized, then in the second century B. C. arched over.

8. A Christian basilica, originally named for the Apostles, after the ninth century acquired the name of St. Sebastian (d. 288) whose remains were sepul-

of the monks on account of the great danger, & in fact I was very glad to see the day. For cases have happened of persons being lost the relation of which 'tis said would "harrow up the Soul".[9] The splendid Church of Saint Pauls, one of the Basilica of Rome, but which is now in ruins from a fire which took place a few years since attracted our attention among others.

Its materials were of the most rare & costly description having 132 Columns, each of a solid block of marble, not one of which remain uninjured. As far as it went, it might vie even with the Vatican itself.[10]

20th. Feby: Left Rome at 7 Oclk: in the morning on an excursion to the far famed Cascades of Tivoli.[1] The wind blew rather fresh at first, & soon after it began to rain, so we were deprived of the fine prospect the ride presents, particularly on approaching the mountains upon which Tivoli stands, for in fact an hour before we reached the Inn, it poured down in torrents. The rain continuing throughout the day, we only succeeded in getting a sight of the water falls, the beauty & grandeur of which, were however very much heightened by the flood of water which had fallen. To

---

chered there. The catacombs of St. Sebastian were dug nearby in an abandoned stone quarry.

9. JCB quotes from *Hamlet*, act 1; sc. 5; lines 29–30.

10. A basilica built by Christian emperors of the late fourth century, St. Paul's was Rome's largest church until the building of St. Peter's. Gutted by fire in 1823, it was rebuilt and reopened in 1854.

1. At the "Great Cascade" the river Aniene (the ancient Anio) fell 354 feet through a gorge in the Sabine Hills.

get the best view, it is necessary to pass down the side of the hill, thro' the Garden, from whence you have at once a commanding view of the falls on both sides of the banks of the Anio.*

*Immediately upon the brow of the hill & overlooking the Cascades stands the Sibylls Temple, of a small rotund form, with a colonnade of the Corinthian order & from its peculiar situation is quite appropriate to so romantic a spot. It was this temple of Sibyll that a late English[*man*] intended to transport to England, but was prevented by the government as all ruins are considered as public property & not to be disposed of—[2]

I have seen nothing of the kind superiour or even equal to the falls of the Anio since I have been in Europe. The fall of Fyers in the Highlands of Scotland altho' highly romantic cannot, when the surrounding scenery is taken into consideration be compared to this, altho' the fall of water of the latter is greater & attended with double the noise.[3] The following morning we arose very early & made what is called "the tour of the hills" on foot. The sky was cloudless & the sun shining in his strength & the rain of the following day added a degree of "fraicheur" to every thing around & I seldom ever enjoyed a pedestrian tour more than the one at

2. The Temple of Sibyll (a.k.a. Temple of Vesta) built in the first century B. C., later became the church of Santa Maria della Rotunda.
   The "late English[man]" was Frederick Augustus Hervey (1730–1803), fourth earl of Bristol, who reportedly bought the temple from an innkeeper on whose property it stood.

3. See entry for October 18, 1823, above.

Tivoli. Our walk led over the bridge, across the Anio, along the high & mountainous banks on the other side of the river, thro' groves of Olive trees. Gradually descending the side of the hill, we found ourselves in the vale of the Anio & at a short distance from the Villa of Maecaenus we recrossed to view the ruins of this celebrated spot. It is situated on the Tivoli side, standing on the edge of high rocks commanding a fine prospect of the vale, the neighbouring country & even of the Sabine Mountains. We ranged thro' this ancient mansion, many parts of which are now as it was when inhabited by the friend of the Roman poets. It is now converted into a forge, & directly under its windows are there streams of water. These were not originally so, but are the outlets of water from the Anio, which has served for mechanical purposes. From the roof of the Villa, we could plainly see the Dome of the Vatican towering to the skys, when its surrounding objects were scarcely visible.[4]

In the direction of the mountains were three conical hills, one of which is Monticelli. From this hill I suppose it is that Mr Jefferson named his delightful seat in Virginia.[5]

After breakfasting (for which our mornings walk of 5 or 6 miles had given us a good appetite) we left Tivoli to return to

---

4. Maecenas (d. 8 B. C.), celebrated patron of the arts, had a villa near Tivoli which may have been the one visited by JCB. The forge was installed by Lucien Bonaparte in 1814 as a pretext for importing iron ore from Elba and so keeping in touch with his exiled brother, Napoleon.

5. A common Italian noun meaning "little mountain," the name "Monticello" was first applied by Thomas Jefferson in 1767 to a property in Virginia that he had inherited from his father in 1757. It is doubtful that Jefferson had this particular "monticello" in mind in 1767.

Rome. The road (the same one we came) is the ancient "via Tiburtina" many parts are still running & even in good repair.[6] Like all of the other celebrated "ways" of the Romans it is composed of large masses of rock, instead of the little pebble stones used in the U.S. & even in most parts of Europe. Descending the hill, the wide spread "Campagnia" was in full view & at the foot of the Mountain turning a little from the main road, we left our carriage to view the once renowned Villa of Adrian, from the ruins of which many of the finest statues which now adorn the Vatican, were taken, & many more might be, & are still found, where excavations are made.[7] The circumferences of this extensive establishment is 7 miles but none need wonder at its immense size when told that the Villa embraced not merely an imperial palace, but three theatres: barracks for soldiers (horse & foot) a library: temples of the muses & of Venus & Diana, with buildings for various other objects. The whole is entirely in ruins, altho' many of the walls are still standing, while the appartments are filled up with bushes & briars. Resuming our seats we proceeded on towards rome passing the Solfatara or petrifying Lake & some distance from the latter we crossed the bridge over the Teverona (ponte Lugano).[8] We stopped a moment to observe the

---

6. The ancient route from Rome eastward to Tivoli (Latin: "Tibur").

7. Hadrian's Villa, a spacious estate where the emperor (r. 117–138) duplicated favorite historical sites and buildings, had a Temple of Venus modeled on her shrine at Cnidos. It once housed a copy of the Aphrodite of Cnidos. See p. 184, n. 7.

8. The Ponte Lucano, a bridge over the Aniene, may have been named for the

Tomb of the Plautian family—Its shape is conical, very much resembling the tomb of Cecelia Metella, & is built of large blocks of Teverous stone. It is still in good preservation, being used by the romans as a fortress during the wars of the middle ages, the upper part was built at that period as the work itself shews.

We reached the Holy City about 2 pm, after an agreeable excursion. We arrived from Tivoli just in time to witness the commencement of the Follies of the Carnival, which were kept up with but 2 or 3 days intermission until the 3d of March. About 2 Oclk a lively & brilliant promenade of carriages commenced in the Corso[9] which continued 'til past 4 all were engaged in pelting their friends with sugar plumbs & those strangers who had no acquaintances, took the same liberty with all the pretty women they met. Masks were in great Number in the Streets & also in the Carriages, & on this occasion all were "hale fellows well met" —"like master, like man."[1] The sport always ended with a horse race. A horse race at rome however is a very different thing from one in England or elsewhere. A parcel of horses were started from the place populo not with riders, but with burning caustic on their backs & bells & thorns hanging on their sides. These excite-

---

Lucanians, an ancient people who once lived in the area, or for Lucanus, a member of the Plautian family whose tomb was built nearby by Marcus Plautius Silvanus ca. 12 A. D.

9. The Corso connected the Piazza del Popolo with the Piazza de Venezia.

1. The Roman carnival, marking the arrival of Lent, began as early as eight days before Ash Wednesday and, except on Sundays and Fridays, allowed masking and partying in the streets. The "sugar plumbs" were often *confetti de gesso*, plaster pellets resembling candy.

ments forced on the miserable beasts, added to the shouts & uproar of the mob on the Streets & the ladies in the windows. But after the novelty of this mode of racing is over it becomes a very stupid piece of business. Almost every night there were masked Balls at the Theatre, which <u>together</u> with the private ones, made the Carnival at Rome a very gay scene, & particularly so for a sober yankee.

In the morning our time was occupied in revisiting many of the antiquities & other curiosities of the City, & in visiting many of the private palaces which we had not yet seen. Most of these contain extensive & invaluable collections of paintings of the most celebrated masters Italy has produced. The galleries of the Borghese palace pleased me as much & perhaps even more than any other. Among the vast number, all of which would be called good, three painted by that sweetest of all artists, Carlo Dolce gave me the greatest satisfaction, & whenever I think of pictures, I shall never forget the two small heads of Christ & Mary Magdalen & another of the Virgin with the Infant jesus, in her arms, the mild & heavenly expression the leading feature of them all, cannot help pleasing the most indifferent beholder.[2]

I have never yet seen any pictures that I should so much desire to possess as one of these three. The Farnese Palace, which belongs to the King of Naples is now stript of all its ornaments. It can yet boast however of the finest paintings in fresco of any in

---

2. The palace, built in the late sixteenth century, was bought by Camillo Borghese who became Pope Paul IV (r. 1605–1621). The *Madonna with the Infant* by Carlo Dolci (1616–1687) dates from ca. 1630.

Rome. The ceilings of one of the grand appartments is painted by Annibal Carucci & "the subject is drawn from the elegant mythology of the heathen" which Mr Berrian thinks are rather too bawdy subjects for a modest man to look at. Exceptionable or not I thought there was no harm in viewing what all the world had seen before me. The execution of these paintings it must be confessed are unrivalled.[3] The Rospigliosi Palace also contains the Aurora by Guido, a fresco & one of the most celebrated of the kind. Berrian attempts to call in question the direction given by the painter to the hair of the Angel & to the flambeau but, 'tis not at all probable so great an artist as Guido should have done this without some particular design.[4] The Corsini Palace contains also another fine collection. The Ecce homo & the head of Christ, one by Titian & the other by Carlo Dolce, are the most conspicuous. The same softness & sweetness of expression is perceived in both, but I should give the preference to the pro-

---

3. In 1824 the Farnese Palace was owned by the royal family of Naples and was occupied by the Neapolitan ambassador to Rome. The fresco celebrating the triumph of Bacchus was painted by Annibale Carracci (1560–1609), assisted by his older brother, Agostino (1557–1602). See p. 210, n. 7, below.

Rev. William Berrian (*Travels*, p. 154) declared Carracci's painting "without comparison the most exceptionable exhibition in Rome," warning that its "beauty and grace" were such that "if disgust does not immediately chastise the imagination, purity and innocence are sullied." On Berrian, see Introduction.

4. Now known as the Pallavicini-Rospigliosi, this early sixteenth-century palace had a fresco of *Aurora* by Guido Reni (1575–1642) in its summer house. Berrian (*Travels*, pp. 238–239) objected that Reni had contradicted nature by making Aurora's torch flame forward instead of backward as did the draperies of her nymphs and the manes of her horses.

duction of the latter.[5] The Farnesene palace contains a celebrated fresco by raphael.[6] The apartments of the Doria Palace situated in the Corso, are more splendid than any of the others we visited. Gilding & mirrors are lavished in profusion throughout the lengthy apartments & the walls are hung with an almost infinite number of the best of paintings. The large picture of "Gerard Des Nuits" (as he is called) of Lot & his three Daughters is I think the most striking of any in the whole collection; such brilliancy of coloring given to the ruby & other precious stones in the hair of one of the daughters, I never saw before in any picture.[7]

The famous palace of the Vatican we did not fail to visit often. The collection of paintings in the Vatican is not extensive, as it is quite a new appendage to the papal residence. No one however would fail to see the masterpiece of all other paintings the Transfiguration by Raphael, & to dwell with pleasure upon

---

5. The Corsini, a notable Florentine family, moved to Rome in the early eighteenth century where they became prominent in ecclesiastical government and art patronage. The Corsini Palace was rebuilt in 1728–1732 from a fifteenth-century structure, and its contents were sold to the Italian state in 1883. Subsequently, much of its extensive art collection was moved to the Barberini Palace.

6. The Villa Farnesina, built 1508–1511, was acquired by Alessandro Farnese during his reign as Paul III (r. 1534–1549). Ownership passed through his family to the Bourbons of Naples in 1731. Raphael's famous fresco, *Galatea*, was commissioned by the original owner in 1510.

7. The so-called "Doria Palace" was built in the fifteenth century and became the residence of the Doria Pamphilj in the seventeenth century. Its rich art collection was entailed by the government in 1816. The painting of *Lot and his Three Daughters* was attributed to the Dutch artist Gerrit van Honthorst (1592–1656) known in Italy as Gherardo delle Notti because of his predilection for darkness.

its matchless beauties.[8] Before taking our final leave of Rome we revisited the Vatican & wandered among the many ruins of the Sacred City & however numerous, the impressions these objects have made upon my mind will never be effaced, above all the matchless Saint Peters. The day before leaving I spent I may say hours, lingering under its golden domes, & yet unwilling to bid a final adieu to this first of christian temples.

Every arrangement being made for our departure for Florence we left the far famed city of Rome (& for myself I can say with no small regret). Most of the time we spent at Rome we were in private lodgings in the Strada Carrozze, a small street extending from the place d'Espagne to the Corso. We breakfasted in our apartments & sometimes dined there, at others at the Table D'Hote. In the Evening we generally spent an hour in the Caffé Neuf, the greatest establishment of the kind at Rome.[1]

Sunday Morning. March 7th. at 6 Oclk: The weather was as fine as could be wished for travelling & we stopped at Tirny at ½ past 5 in the evening a distance of 8¾ posts.[2] Nothing to detain the

---

8. The Vatican's picture gallery, founded by Pius VI (see p. 185, n. 5), was forced to surrender its best-known works to Napoleon in 1797. Some seventy-seven of them were returned in 1815. The entire collection was moved to new quarters in 1932. Raphael's *Transfiguration* was commissioned by Cardinal Giulaiano de Medici in 1517 and nearly completed before Raphael died in 1520.

1. The Caffe Nuovo was near the Piazza di Spagna where JCB and his cousin had rooms.

2. A misspelling for "Terni" which JCB gives correctly below. He begins here to measure road distances by "posts"—the intervals between changing coach horses. A post in Italy was eight miles.

traveller on this route & very little worthy of observation, excepting the dreary & deserted Campagna which streaches itself for many miles around the City. We to be sure passed thro' a number of insignificant villages, even the names of which I have mostly forgotten. At Terni we put up at "La Posta" a very decent house for such a town. We were well entertained & the charges not extravigant, for dinner, sleeping & breakfast with fire & lights, we paid 28 pauli.[3] Terni is celebrated for its cascades & the wild & romantic senery in its neighborhood we visited it the following morning & found everything quite equal to any description I had before read of it. After desending into the dell the walk leads thro' a grove of orange trees along the Nera, & then after traversing some of as grand scenery as any I saw during the whole of my scottish tour you come to the fall itself, or rather the falls, for properly speaking there are three. They are formed from the Velino precipitating itself from the summit of the mountain on the [*blank*] side of the Nera; the whole hight of the three cascades is about 300 feet & the water afterwards unites itself with the Nera. Some travellers have remarked that the fall of water was not large enough & did not correspond with the grandeur of the surrounding senery. There perhaps may be sound reason in this observation, but viewing the tout ensemble it must be confessed that it is a grand & imposing coup d'oeil.[4] A walk to & from the cascade distances more than 8 miles gave us a good appetite for breakfast.

---

3. A "paoli" or "poule" was a silver/copper coin minted in Tuscany and the papal states.

4. The Marmore Falls were engineered as a flood-control measure to divert the Velino into the Nera and spare the Rieti plain its overflow.

As early as 10 we were again in our carriages. The 2 or 3 posts carried us in the midst of the Appennines. Many of the mountains were so long & steep that oxen are obliged to be attached to draw you up. We passed thro' the town of Foligno, but it is not of sufficient importance to delay the traveller. At 9 in the Evening we reached Perugia, a clean well built town situated upon the summit of a mountain. Stopped at "La Posta" which in every respect I pronounce an excellent Inn. Our apartments were carpeted & in many respects splendid, fare & bedding very good. The land-lady demanded high prices, but by bargaining sharply, we got the whole for 30 pauli. The weather throughout the day was remarkably fine & the moon shown very bright. Owing to the many mountains we passed we only rode 6 posts to day. Left Perugia at 6 the following morning. Early in the day we came to the "Lake of Perugia" a clear and beautiful sheet of water, of about 10 miles long by 7 wide. We rode many miles along its banks, & passed over the plain, where the Consul Flaminius was defeated by Hannibal the Carthigenian.[5] Shortly after ascending a hill, we entered the territory of the grand Duke of Tuscany & were supposed to pass on without any molestation.[6] We found a difference in the roads after leaving the States of the Pope. Altho' good yet they are not in such high order as in the holy fathers

---

5. The lake was Trasimene near which Hannibal ambushed and slaughtered a Roman army in 217 B. C. See Livy, *History of Rome*, XII, 4–7.

6. The Grand Duchy of Tuscany, returned to the Habsburgs in 1814, had passed by secundogeniture to Ferdinand III of Lorraine in 1790 when his father Leopold became emperor. Ferdinand was replaced by the French between 1802 and 1814. He died in June 1824.

dominions. Thus far I have nothing to complain of the travelling in Italy. Fine roads, with as good posting as in any other country, things well regulated & not dear. In the afternoon we reached Arezzo but stopped only to change horses. From Arezzo to Florence the road leads thro' the charming Val D'Arno & altho' night soon overtook us, yet the moon was so bright it almost made up the absence of the sun. We drove on with great rapidity, & about 1 Oclk: in the morning we were set down in "Pungo l'Arno" on the northeast banks of the river.[7] This day we rode 13 posts or about 100 miles. Few cities can boast of a finer situation than Florence, & for an inland town it perhaps is second to none. Situated in a delightful vale, with the Arno passing thro' it, surrounded nearly on every side by mountains, the senery is of such a description that all must be pleased with it, & altogether Florence is such a city as would be chosen by a man of leisure for an agreable sejour. I now only speak of its local advantages, for of the society of the place, I may say I am entirely unacquainted. The city is divided by the Arno, a rapid stream when not too much dried by the heats of summer. This river rises among the Appennines & empties itself into the mediterranean at Leghorn. 4 stone bridges unite the city, all substantial, but that of "la trinita" can boast of some architectural taste.[8] There are not many curiosities to detain a traveller a long time in this place, more especially just

---

7. Perhaps a corruption for "Ponte Lungarno."

8. The bridge of "Santa Trinita" was built in 1564 at a point where several bridges had previously been destroyed by floodwaters. It was blown up by German mines in 1944, rebuilt in 1952.

coming from Rome. The Gallery however, is well worthy of attention, for it contains some of the most celebrated specimens of
sculpture & painting that any country can boast of. It is situated
between the Piazza Grand Duck & the river; built after the form
of the Greek letter π & is between 4 & 500 feet in height & 100
in breadth, the exteriour is heavy, but the interiour is well arranged,
a multitude of busts & statues & pictures line the walls, whilst
the Choef d'Oeuvres of the arts are kept in small side rooms
which are not entered but with the keeper.[9] It is in the Tribune
(so called) a small octagon, furnished with crimson silk & the
roof inlaid with pearls, where is to be seen that wonder of the
world, the Venus de Medicis, an ancient Greek statue & found
among the ruins of Hadrians Villa. It has been broken into 16
pieces but is so well prepared, that none of its fine proportions
are lost. On either side hang two other Venus lying at full length
both of which are from the pencil of the inimitable Titian & one
is almost at a loss which most to admire the paintings or the statues. One of the former with all its beauties invites a degree of las-
civiousness, while the statue only presents to the admiring beholder, the finest & most exquisite features of the female form.[10]

---

9. The art gallery was in the Uffizi Palace designed by Giorgio Vasari (1511–
1574) and begun in 1560. Today's Piazza della Signoria was in 1824 the Piazza
del Gran Duca. JCB's substitution of "Duck" for "Duke" may have been meant
to mimic a guide's pronunciation.

10. The Tribuna, a showcase gallery completed in 1587, was reserved for the
exhibition of highly prized objects. The *Medici Venus* (first century B. C.?)
was brought to Florence from the Villa Medici in Rome in 1638. Titian's
Venus was painted in 1538 for the Duke of Urbino and added to the Medici
collection in 1631.

Other rooms in the gallery contained collections of paintings arranged according to the respective schools. Others besides contain Raphaels, Titians, & two pictures of Carlo Dolci, (a Magdalen & a Mary) which subjects it would seem he particularly excells in.[1] Another room contains among a great variety of ancient & modern bronzes, the celebrated Mercury of John of Boulogna, one of the master pieces of this distinguished artist.[2] But t'would be writing a volume to mention a half that the gallery contains & I will only say that next to the unrivalled Vatican, no city can boast of such a magnificent collection of the fine arts as the Gallery at Florence.

We spent a few hours in <u>walking thro'</u> the museum of natural history. Few cities or universities can produce any thing equal to this establishment as respects its extensive collections of objects from the animal, vegetable, & mineral kingdoms. Besides them there are a number of rooms filled with preparations in wax of every part of the human. This last is the work of M. Fontana. There is nothing of the kind equal to this, in any part of the World.[3]

The Palazzo Pitti altho' it is the residence of the Grand Duke, is not very imposing in its outward appearance, but I suspect no <u>royal</u> palace in Europe can equal it in the number & exe-

1. Carlo Dolci (1616–1686) painted several *Magdalens* and *Madonnas*. JCB probably refers to a *Madonna* of 1630 and a *Magdalen* of 1660, both of which were in the Medici collection and shifted between the Pitti and Uffizi galleries.

2. A Flemish sculptor, John of Bologna (1529–1608), usually called Giambologna.

3. The Museum of Natural History was founded in 1775 by Grand Duke Leopold (r. 1765–1790). Felice Fontana (1730–1805) had been a professor of physiology at Pisa and Rome before being called to Florence in 1765 by Leopold.

cution of the paintings it contains. A larger suit of rooms are filled with I may say hundreds & most of them from the most celebrated masters Italy has produced. It is particularly rich in pieces from the pencil of Carlo Dolci, one representing Saint Louis & his wife, finely executed, another of the head of Christ & many others of the holy virgin with the infant jesus. Some indeed are better executed than others but the same softness of expression & finish in the execution are visible in all. One of the apartments in this palace is appropriated to the Venus of Canova, one of the best pieces of sculpture that artist has produced. It is in a different style from the Venus of Medicis, representing the Goddess about ¾ naked, holding a robe falling in folds in front to cover her charms.[4] The Cathedral of Florence is another of those vast edifices most every where to be met with in Europe which always creates wonder & astonishment in an American. It [is] about 420 feet in length & 300 in breadth, the interiour is almost too dark even for a place of worship & presents nothing of that richness so common to most of the churches in Italy. Its exteriour is covered with small slabs of white, black, & red marble. Before the building of Saint Peters, this Cathedral stood unrivalled for its Dome & it would even now make no mean appearance side of the Vatican.[5] At one corner of the Cathedral stands

---

4. Begun in the fifteenth century, the Pitti Palace was from 1550 to 1859 the official residence of the grand dukes of Tuscany. Canova's *Venus* (*Venus Italica*) was commissioned to replace the *Venus de Medici* after it had been seized by French authorities in September 1802.

5. The cathedral, begun in the fourteenth century, was dedicated to Santa Maria del Fiore in 1412. Its octagonal dome was designed by Filippo

the Campanile, or Belfry, rising to the height of near 300 & covered with marble in the same manner as the Cathedral.[6] We ascended this tower & from the top enjoyed a fine view of the city & environs of Florence, rendered doubly delightful by a soft, balmy air & a blazing sun. The Baptistry standing in the same square (plazza Duomo) is of an octagon form & is mostly celebrated for its huge bronze gates, the work of [*blank*] & which enraptured Michael Angelo so much, that he called them the Gates of Paradise.[7] The Church of San Lorenzo has quite a rough, unfinished exteriour, & would be hardly worth noticing was it not connected to the Mausolium of the house of the Medicis—a chapel of an octagon figure, & wonderfully rich in the most rare & costly marbles & precious stones from every country. Altho' it was commenced years since yet 'tis now not half finished & from the costly scale in which it is thus far completed, it is probable the finances of Tuscany will never admit of [*blank*].[8] The Church of Santa Croche in the square of the same

---

Brunelleschi (1377–1446).

6. The bell tower, begun by Giotto (1267?–1337), completed in the 1350s, was faced with white, green, and pink marble.

7. The Baptistery of St. John, built in the early Middle Ages, was faced with polychrome marble in the eleventh and twelfth centuries. The first set of doors, by Andrea Pisano (1295?–1348), was installed in 1336. The second and third sets were the work of Lorenzo Ghiberti (1378–1455). Michelangelo's pun on the word "paradiso" was reported in Vasari's life of Ghiberti. (See Giorgio Vasari, *The Lives of the Most Excellent Painters etc.*, trans. J. C. and P. Bondanella [Oxford, 1991], p. 98; or *Le Vite etc.*, 9 vols. [Novara, 1967], II, p. 193.)

8. The sculptural program of the Medici Chapel was never completed as planned.

name, presents also an unfinished front. 'Tis a large & spacious edifice & particularly remarkable as containing the Tombs of Michael Angelo, & a number of other distinguished Italians.[9] We paid a visit to the Academy of the fine arts, situated close to the square Saint Mark. The particular objects of this establishment is to afford instruction to pupils in drawing, painting, & sculpture, & is directed by one of the most eminent artists in Florence. We witnessed a great number of students, labouring in their vocation, but there are no pictures which should detain one a moment.[1] Florence has besides a number of other squares, such as the Piazza Trinita, in which there is a granit column adorned with the figure of justice. The Piazza of the Grand Duke contains a number of colossal statues, & in its center there is a huge figure of Cosmo 1st, on horse back.[2] I was particularly pleased with the delightful walks around Florence more especially the "Cassinos" extending along the banks of the Arno for miles. The Boboli

---

9. A Franciscan church, begun in 1295 and consecrated in 1443, Santa Croce was the burial site of Michelangelo, Ghiberti, Machiavelli, and Galileo, among other distinguished Italians.

1. The Accademia di Belle Arte, founded in 1784 by Grand Duke Leopold, was intended to consolidate and replace schools that had grown out of medieval guilds and companies as well as state-sponsored institutions for training artists and artisans.

2. The Piazza Santa Trinita's column of *Justice* was brought from Rome in 1560 as a gift to Cosimo I de Medici (1519–1574) from Pius IV (r. 1555–1559). The Piazza of the Grand Duke (see p. 204, n. 9) had an equestrian statue of Cosimo I executed in the 1590s by Giambologna. JCB, strangely, does not mention other figures on the Piazza's margin, celebrated works by Michelangelo, Donatello, and Cellini, all on view in 1824.

Gardens in the rear of the "palace pitti" but during the winter the fashionable resort is upon the quay, where the houses afford a shelter from the North wind.[3] I cannot say anything of the society of Florence, for in fact, we saw nothing of it, & the only <u>Italian</u> we were acquainted in the place was the American Consul.[4] As a place of residence, I have no doubt it is a very agreeable one & would be found as pleasant as a "séjour" as almost any other place in Italy. While at Florence we were at the "Hotel des Quatro Nations" on the north side of the Arno. Our apartments were good, & charged <u>not exorbitant,</u>—there is no better situation at Florence.

Thursday March 18th. We bid adieu to Florence at 6 Oclk: in the morning the weather was not so clear & pleasant as could have been wished, but with the exception of a little sleet upon the Appennines, we had no rain. The road all the way to Boulona[5] is dreary & mountainous & not one object presents itself worthy of notice. The Appennines are here crossed in their greatest breadth, altho the distance is only 60 miles we did not reach Boulona 'til 9 PM & were drove to the Pilerna in the "Via Venturini." This is

---

3. The *Cascine*, named from an Italian word for farm building, was a stretch of open land extending almost three miles along the northwest bank of the Arno. Once used for farming and pasture, it was converted into a public park in the eighteenth century and became a favorite promenade for the leisured classes. The more sheltered, formal Boboli Garden was laid out for Cosimo I in the 1550s.

4. The American consul in 1824 was Jacopo Ombrosi, a native of Florence.

5. JCB's phonetic spelling for "Bologna" which he later corrected.

called the best house in the place. We found it to be a good one & not <u>extravigantly</u> dear.

Friday March 19th. This was fête day at Bologna[6] & all the shops were shut, which was a favourable opportunity for a stranger to see the populace of the city as they were all going to mass in their best bib & band. Boulona is a part of the Popes dominions & is still a populous town, containing about 75,000 inhabitants. It is built different from any other city I have seen in Europe, as all the houses have porticos, so that a pedestrian is equally sheltered from the rain & sun. 'Tis generally well built & some of the palaces present a considerable degree of magnificence. The academy of fine arts is one of the principle institutions which attract the attention of the traveller. The gallery of painting containing many from the first masters particularly the 3 Carrachi who were natives of the place. The picture of Saint Cecilia playing on a harp, by Raphael is the one which more particularly pleased me. She is represented with her female train & the painter is here especially happy in his "grouping & expression." They all possess that same smallness of features for which Raphael was so famous.[7] The palace of Maris Kalki contains the best collection there is in

---

6. The feast of St. Joseph, patron saint of Italy, had been celebrated as a holy day of obligation since the thirteenth century.

7. The *Accademia di Belle Arti* was reorganized in 1803 by the Bonapartist government. Its predecessor, the *Accademia Clementina* had been established in 1710 by Clement XI (r. 1700–1721) as the first official art school in Bologna.

On the Bolognese Carracci family, see p. 198, n. 3. The "third" member JCB refers to here was Ludovico, a cousin of the brothers Agostino and Annibale.

Bologna, but one becomes fatigued with seeing such an innumerable number of pictures as are every where to be met with in Italy, & we are apt to pass over with a hasty glance those which would deserve a minute attention. The Saviour of Correggio is the first piece in the whole collection & generally allowed to be one of the first productions in the art of painting. The picture is remarkable for its high coloring, but I did not think that the countenance of the Saviour possessed all that softness & mildness which I had seen in other paintings.[8] The copy of Leonardo di Vinci's bella Feronia—Mistress of Francis 1st. which by some is thought to be most lovely of mortals, did not seem to me to be in point of beauty any thing so very exrtaordinary. Perhaps, however my taste in these matters is not sufficiently improved to allow me to be a judge.[9] The most curious subject for a picture that I have almost ever seen is to be met with in this gallery. 'Tis Legazzi's picture of the final dissolution of the human body. Two beings a man & woman are seen in the last stages of corruption & each by way of variety are surrounded with all the concomitants of beauty & pleasure. 'Tis a disgusting & sickening picture

---

8. The palace had belonged to Count Ferdinando Marescalchi (1754–1816), descendant of Bolognese senatorial nobility and prominent Bonapartist. Napoleon made him minister of foreign affairs for the "Kingdom of Italy" in 1808.

The *Saviour* mentioned by JCB was possibly a cartoon for the fresco painted by Antonio Allegri da Correggio (1494?–1534) for a church in Parma. The only painting by Correggio owned by Marescalchi was the *Four Saints* now in New York's Metropolitan Museum of Art.

9. The original of Leonardo da Vinci's *La Belle Ferronière* is in the Louvre.

& one is very glad to turn from it to a pretty venus hanging above it.[1] Bologna has always been celebrated as one of the most eminent seats of the Arts & sciences. The Instituto di Bologna is of modern date established by the Count Marsigli, it has a library of 150,000 volumes & in every other respect is well [*illeg.*] for the promotion of knowledge.[2] This, with the Clementini Academy for the promotion of the fine arts & the "University of Bologna" offer such advantages to a student as few citys can boast of. We visited particularly this latter institution, but altho it is in a flourishing state, has at present only about 600 students whereas in former times it is said to have had 10,000.[3] The environs of Bologna are rather interesting from the high eminence just without the walls are seen on one side the Appennines we had just past & on the other the plains of Lombardy extending as far as the eye can reach. The day after our arrival we took an early walk to view the Campo Santo or burying ground, which is highly deserving of notice & after that of "Pere la Chaise" at Paris is perhaps the most curious of the kind in Europe. It certainly is the most so I have seen. It formerly was a monastery but converted by the Government to its present use. The tombs & sarcophagi of the great are very elegant & some are fine pieces of sculpture.

---

1. The macabre painting by Jacopo Ligozzi (1547–1626) was hung behind folding doors. The *Venus* exhibited above it was attributed to Titian.

2. The Institute of Science was established in 1714 by Count Luigi Fernando Marsili (or Marsigli) (1658–1730). It shared a building with the Clementine Academy. See p. 210, n. 7, above.

3. The university, founded in the late eleventh century, had some 10,000 students by the mid-thirteenth. Modernized by Napoleonic reforms, in 1803 it was moved into a sixteenth-century palace.

There is no distinction between protestant & Catholic & the Jews only have a separate spot. In one corner is to be seen the skulls of the Capuchin Nuns, brought from the Capuchin Convent & arranged in form & order with the names of each inscribed.[4]

The Church of Notre Dame della Guardia is 5 miles without the city, but such is the religious character of the inhabitants of Bologna that they have build a portico of brick & stone from the city leading to it, & which must necessarily have been erected at great expense & labour.[5] The churches in Bologna are not very remarkable. The cathedral of Saint Pauls & Saint Peters in the center of the town is a large building & is only attractive as containing the famous meridian of Cassini the Astronomer who was a native of this place.[6] The fountain of Neptune executed by John of Bologna, is by some thought to be a work of merit, & stands in the great square.[7] There are two towers Asinelli & garisenda

---

4. A Carthusian monastery, or *Certosa* (1334), had been converted into a public cemetery in 1801. The *Recinto degli Israeliti* was a segregated enclosure near the *Certosa*.

5. The church, Madonna di San Luca, built in 1725 on the Monte della Guardia, took its name from an icon of the Virgin, reputedly painted by St. Luke and brought to Italy in the twelfth century by a pilgrim from Constantinople. The arcade, over two miles long, was built in the late sixteenth and early seventeenth centuries.

6. The Cathedral (*metropolitana*) of St. Peter, dating from the tenth century, had been destroyed by fire in the sixteenth century and later rebuilt. JCB confused it with the Church of St. Petronius, begun in the fourteenth century, the largest church in Bologna, which contained the meridian (a model of celestial spheres) designed by Giovanni Domenico Cassini (1625–1712), professor of astronomy at Bologna from 1650–1669.

7. A bronze *Neptune* executed in 1566 by Giambologna.

which of course cannot be passed unnoticed from their hight & their deviation from the perpendicular. The first is 327 feet. They are the remaining monuments of barbarous ages.[8] Bologna is also said to be famous for its "beautiful & amiable females," of the latter quality I do not pretend to be a judge, but of the beauty of the girls I saw at the church & parading the street I can readily give my testimony. They were dressed with a great deal of elegance & neatness & most of them wore "pantalettes" a fashion I had not yet seen in Italy.

In the afternoon of Saturday the 20th March we continued our journey to Ferrara & arrived about sun set, a distance of 3½ posts. The road was nearly a level & which became more & more so as we approached the region of Lombardy. The most considerable town was Malabergo. Nothing worth noting on the road excepting the large & neatly built farms—a sure indication of the fertility & productiveness of the soil. Ferrara was formerly a very flourishing city, but is now fast falling to decay, & the celebrated manufactory of sword blades is almost entirely lost. Our survey of Ferrara was rather hasty & the most interesting place we saw was the dungeon at the hospital of Saint Ann where Tasso was confined. The tomb of Ariosto is at the Lycée, but it was so late that we did not see it.[1] The three Crowns at Ferrara, where we were well [blank].

---

8. Brick towers built by rival families, Garisendi (late eleventh century) and Asinelli (early twelfth century). The former rose 320 feet and was 4 feet out of perpendicular; the latter rose 163 feet and was 10 feet out. See Dante, *Inferno*, Canto XXI, l. 136.

1. Torquato Tasso, epic poet (1544–1595), was confined (1579–1586) in the

Sunday the 21st March we were off at a very early hour on our route to Venice. We crossed the great river Po at a distance <u>of</u> <u>about</u> 6 miles from Ferrara, which is the last town of importance in the Popes dominions. The Po is by far the largest river in all Italy & at the place we crossed was perhaps ½ mile wide. We were now in the Austrian dominions & found the police much more rigid than heretofore in Italy. Passing thro' Rovigo we travelled along the banks of the river Adige & shortly after crossed it in the same manner as the Po, upon a bridge of boats, which were propelled by the current alone—the most complete labor saving machine of the kind I have ever seen. Proceeding on, we rolled along over the plains of Lombardy passing thro' Montesilici 'til we reached Padua, 7 posts from Ferrara, but as we were anxious to reach Venice, we only changed horses & continued our journey, leaving the examination of Padua 'til our return. 3 posts more took us to Fasina the road running along the river Brenta & thro' a number of populous villages, & which are connected by rows of magnificent palaces, many the work of the celebrated Palladio the architect.[2] This was much the most agreable part of the days journey & I believe as delightful a ride as can be found in any part of Italy. It was quite late when we arrived at Fasina,

---

Ospedale Sant' Anna by Duke Alfonso II d'Este. He was celebrated by later generations as a rebellious lover and victim of despotism. See Goethe's play, *Tasso* (1790), and Byron's *The Lament of Tasso* (1817).

Ludovico Ariosto, mock epic poet (1474–1533), was originally buried in the monastery church of St. Benedict near his residence. His remains were moved to the Biblioteca Communale Ariostea during the French occupation of Ferrara.

2. Andrea di Pietro della Gondola, "Palladio" (1508–1580), architect, designed

where we left our carriage & took a Gondola to Venice which is 5 miles, so that is was some time after candlelight when we entered the city & were rowed up the Grand Canal to the Hotel Grand Britania.

One can form no distinct idea whatever of Venice without having seen it, for as to its situation & construction, it is altogether sui generis & can be compared to no other city that I have ever seen or read of. It rises majestically out of the Adriatic, built upon 70 or more small islands The grand canal intersects it in the form of an **S** & innumerable other smaller ones run in every direction. The Streets are very narrow & what seems peculiar to strangers no such thing as a carriage, cart, horse or any other cattle are to be seen. The Gondola is the only mode of conveyance, & houses are so separated from each other that next door neighbours are obliged to use a gondola if they wish to have any intercourse. From these circumstances alone, it may well be supposed Venice cannot for a long time be a very agreeable residence for a stranger, accordingly we heard of fewer English & other foreigners having taken up their abode here than in any other part of Italy. Mi Lord Byron who spent 3 or 4 years here, says that "Venice in the language of scripture is dying daily" & never was there a more correct remark.[3] Every thing seems to be going to decay & general ruin & desolation is fast overtaking this once proud & spledid

---

many private country villas in northern Italy as well as public buildings in Venice and his native Vicenza.

3. George Gordon, lord Byron (1788–1824), arrived in Venice in November 1816 and made it his base of operations until 1820 when he moved to Ravenna.

republic. We found it really melancholy to be rowed around & see so much fallen grandeur. The quay & the great place of Saint Marc still present a busy scene, & these with the grand canal are the principle points of the city. The "Place di Saint Mark" is a large square, surrounded with buildings of different orders of architecture & the on one side the sumptious Church of the Saint upon the front of which over the great doors stand the long cele- brated Venetian horses of bronze, 4 in number.[4] Upon the quay mar which stands the palace of the famed Doges of Venice, are two columns upon one of which is the winged lion, the coat of arms (as I believe) of the republic.[5] This part of the city in the Evening especially is very gay. The coffee houses under the piaz- zas are brilliantly lit up & thronged with beautiful females & fashionable company. The Grand Canal is or rather was lined (for many of them are now pulled down) with marble palaces & many elegant churches. Over this is the "Rialto" well known to every one who ever read or heard of Shakespeare. 'Tis what we should call a bridge, built with one arch only & having upon it a number of dirty, insignificant shops, but with all these objections to it, we walked frequently over this celebrated promenade of

4. The Basilica of St. Mark, rebuilt in Byzantine style, 1043–1071, was conse- crated a cathedral in 1807. The bronze horses were brought from Constan- tinople in 1204, removed to Paris in 1798, restored to Venice in 1815.

5. The Doge's Palace, begun in the ninth century, often rebuilt, took its pres- ent form in the fifteenth century. The two monolithic columns were brought either from Constantinople or from the Near East. St. Theodore, an early patron of the Venetians, stood on one column; wings were added to the Assyrian lion which stood on the other.

"old Shylock."[6] Among other palaces pointed out particularly to our notice, was that in which Catherine of Cornaro lived, before she was made Queen of Cyprus & another inhabited for a long time by Lord Biron.[7] We examined a number of the churches, not so much because of their riches within, as for their being distinguished as the works of Paladio. The gallery of the Marquis Manfrini is the most celebrated & almost the only collection of paintings at Venice deserving of notice. The number are very numerous, but what pleased me the most were a Mary Magdalen & Saint Cecilia both by Carlo Dolci, two paintings the remembrance of which I shall never forget when I think of Venice.[8] The academy of the fine arts & where they are taught is only interesting to a stranger as containing an urn holding the heart of Canova, which he bequeathed to the city.[1] The "Bridge of sighs"

---

6. The Rialto was built with stone (1585–1592) to replace an earlier wooden structure. Shakespeare in *The Merchant of Venice* (1596?) made five scene-setting references to it or to its quarter.

7. Caterina Cornaro (1454–1510), a Venetian noble, was married by proxy to James II of Cyprus (r. 1460–1473). Widowed, she ruled Cyprus as a figurehead of the Venetian Republic until 1489. Threatened then by the Turks, she abdicated in favor of the Republic and spent the rest of her life in honorable retirement in or near Venice.

Byron took a three-year lease on the Palazzo Mocenigo, one of three adjoining residences overlooking the Grand Canal.

8. The gallery of the Marquis Girolamo Manfrini remained a private collection until 1856 when it was acquired by the Accademia. See n. 1, below. Carlo Dolci (1616–1686) painted at least two *St. Cecilias* and five *Magdalens*. None can be positively identified as part of the Manfrini collection in 1824; JCB may have seen copies or paintings mistakenly attributed to Dolce.

1. The Accademia di Belle Arte in 1807 moved into its present site, a Palla-

will recall to the mind of the stranger, those beautiful lines of Lord Biron, "I stood in Venice on the bridge of sighs, a prison & a palace on each hand" &c &c but from the position of it I doubt if mi Lordship actually stood upon it, but has only used a little poetic liscense.[2] The Arsenal is well worth visiting, but as far as naval affairs are concerned, a writer has well observed, that it is complete in every respect but for what all arsenals are built, stores & shipping. The halls are large & spacious & in one of them a fine statue of Canova representing fame crowning the late admiral Emo, the last of the heroes of Venice will amply repay the visitor.[3] Among the various curiosities shewn to strangers is the "luchetto" or lock of virginity, which Francis Carrara prince of Padua compelled his wife to wear during his absence. This mode of preserving your wifes chastity is indeed a whimsical one & is very good proof, he had not too much confidence in her

---

dian church built in 1552. Its holdings were then growing with works confiscated from churches and monasteries. Later in the century it added private collections such as the Contarini (1843), the Renier (1850), and the Manfrini (1856).

2. A flying bridge (ca. 1600) connected the New Prison with the Doge's Palace where suspects were hailed before the Inquisition of State. JCB quoted Byron's lines (*Childe Harold's Pilgrimage*, Canto IV, 1) evidently from memory, switching the words "prison" and "palace."

3. The Arsenal, a primitive example of mass production, founded in 1104, at its peak employed some 1,600 workers. JCB cites J. C. Eustace, *Classical Tour*, I, pp. 174 ff.

The memorial to Admiral Angelo Emo (1721–1792) was commissioned by the Republic in 1792 and completed in 1795 just before the extinction of Venetian naval power. It was later moved from the Arsenal to the Museum of Naval History.

Fidelity.[4] We remained only 5 days at Venice, which was ample time to see all its wonders, & a stranger not accustomed to the gondola very soon becomes tired of this dull mode of conveyance. The gondola is what we should call a light kind of skiff, but with a kind of cabin in the center, with windows & blinds. The cabins are elegantly fitted up & by shutting the blinds a party can be as retired as they please. The boat is managed by 2 boat men & those belonging to wealthy persons are in livery like English footmen. The prows are adorned with large polished plates of steel, but the tout ensemble has rather a funeral appearance, owing to the covering of the cabin with black cloth, adorned with tassels.[5] Previous to leaving we were rowed over to a neighbouring island, about a mile from the city, which has few or no inhabitants, but to which Lord Biron resorted almost every day, to take exercise & here he kept a number of fine horses.[6] His constant & only ride was over the fine hard sands upon the beach, which stretched along the Adriatic & where nothing intersepted the sight from the water & horizon—a lovely & romantic spot & well suited to the mind of that extraordinary man. The Mess. Heinzelman (Bankers) were our only acquaintances, & one of the partners is the owner of "the Hebe" by Canova, which we

4. The chastity belt forged especially for the wife of Francesco Carrara, one of a succession of Cararresi who dominated Padua in the fourteenth century.

5. JCB's description of a gondola should be compared to that by Byron in *Beppo: A Venetian Story* (1818), XIX.

6. The Lido, an island lying two miles to the southeast, divides the lagoon from the Adriatic. Byron imported four horses there, giving rise to the remark that in all Venice there were only eight horses, San Marco's four and Byron's.

saw.[7] Venice is a very fine place for those who love beautiful women & I believe no place in the world can surpass it in this respect, at least none that I have been in, have ever witnessed so many handsome females. To use the words of an American parson, "it is a gift lavished upon the multitudes."[1] But I believe the place cannot be noted for the chastity of the sex. The soft climate of Venice, the balmy breezes of the Adriatic all inspire to love & voluptuousness & last tho' not least, the poverty & pride of the great mass of the Venetians, lead the females to have recourse to a sale of their charms in order to recruit their finances. Thus Mi Lord Anglais who visits Venice with his pockets only moderately stocked with £ sterling, is not at all in want of the society of a fair lady to console him for the absence of those dear friends he has left behind in England.

Saturday March 27th. we bid adieu to Venice, well pleased with having visited this curious city & lamenting that this once proud & magnificent republic, celebrated alike for its arts & arms, as well as its commercial greatness, should be languishing & dying under the iron yoke of Austria.[2] The Gran Britagnia at Venice is an expensive hotel tho' the house is the most magificent Hotel I

---

7. The Heinzelmans, originally from Kaufbeuren in southern Germany, were, from the beginning of the eighteenth century, leaders of the German business circle and the Protestant community in Venice.

Canova executed four versions of *Hebe* in marble between 1795 and 1817. Only one, commissioned for a private collection in 1816–1817, remained in Italy. Probably JCB saw a working model cast in plaster.

1. A reference to Berrian, *Travels*, p. 307.

2. Venice surrendered to Napoleon in May 1797, was ceded to Austria in

have ever seen in Europe. 'Tis of marble & formerly a noblemans palace. We were afterwards at the Hotel de France—where we were well accommodated. We returned to Fusina by the same route where we again mounted our post chaise & having taken a last look at the wing'd lions marble pier[3] proceeded over the same road to Padua, here we stopped a few hours to view this ancient city. Its general appearance is too much like that of many other Italian towns—in a declining state, its population is about 40,000 & altho it formerly possessed woolen manufactures I could not learn that that or anything else flourished at present. For many ages the University was the glory of Padua, but this like everything else has declined, altho it still has a respectable number of students, say about 5 or 600.[4] The Church of Justinian is remarkable as being designed by Palladio, tho' not built by him, & is justly considered a very fine piece of architecture, its simplicity & plainness, free from such a load of ornaments with which most Catholic Churches are encumbered, is spoken of as one of its chief attractions—the exterior is yet unfinished.[5] The

October, and passed back and forth between French and Austrian control for the next seventeen years. By international agreement, it was incorporated into the Habsburg Empire in 1814, remaining under Austrian sovereignty until 1866. JCB's "iron yoke" echoes all the *bien-pensants* of his day.

3. A reference to Byron's *Childe Harold's Pilgrimage*, Canto IV, 1: "…many a subject land/look'd to the winged Lion's marble piles/Where Venice sat in state, throned in her hundred isles."

4. A medieval foundation, Padua's university once drew students from the entire Mediterranean world, including the Muslim. JCB cites figures from Eustace, *Classical Tour*, I, pp. 154–156.

5. The Church of St. Justina (1501–1532) impressed northern tourists with its

Town Hall of Padua contains a monument to Livy the historian who was a native of this city.[6] We arrived at Vicenza early in the evening 18 miles from Padua & stopped at the Hotel "Chapeau rouge"—a good house & not very dear. Vicenza is renowned particularly as being the birth place of Palladio, & the Olimpic Theatre will be viewed with admiration by every connoisseur in architecture, & especially as it bears a strong resemblance to the Ancient theatres of Herculaneum & Pompeii.[7] The town has a population of about 30,000 inhabitants, & is adorned with many superb palaces, the work of the immortal architect.

We left Vicenza early in the forenoon of the 28th (Sunday) & after a ride of 3¾ posts over a pleasant road entered Verona. We spent the remainder of the day here, & if our time would have admitted & the season further advanced, should have wished to have staid a longer time. Our first visit was to the Amphitheatre & altho it is an astonishing work in point of solidity & magnitude, yet after seeing the Coliseum at Rome, so much its superior in size, we did not view it with so much wonder as tho' we had come first to Verona. It is built of blocks of stone & can contain 22,000 people.[8] The name of Shakespeare is associated with that

---

simplicity. Joseph Addison (see p. 226, n. 1, below) considered it "the most luminous and disencumbered building" he had ever seen.

6. Padua's town hall (Il Salone or Palazzo della Raggione), begun in the twelfth century, boasted Europe's largest roof unsupported by columns. It had to be rebuilt in 1756. The monument to Livy (d. 17 A. D.) dated from the mid-sixteenth century.

7. Palladio's Olympic Theatre was built in the late 1580s for the Olympic Academy founded in Vicenza thirty years before.

8. Verona's amphitheater, with a capacity of 22,000, was the third largest in Italy.

Book Four: December 17, 1823, to March 31, 1824 | 223

of Verona. Every one will recollect with pleasure the play of the 2 gentleman & no stranger would visit this city without going to see the tomb of the lovely but unfortunate Juliet, which is immediately in the neighbourhood. We were shown the spot in the garden, where the hapless pair were buried, but the stone coffin which it is said contained their bodies, is taken up & kept in an adjoining house—the size of it is just large enough to hold two persons & I was very willing to believe that is was the identical coffin which once held Romio & his lovely Juliet.[9] Verona is situated upon the Adige, or rather the river divides the town. It contains 50,000 inhabitants & has a much more flourishing aspect than many other Italian towns. The silk trade is very considerable here, & we drank some excellent wine, made in the neighbourhood. Not much can be said of the beauty of Verona as a city, tho' there are some good streets & many large, elegantly built houses. From the garden of the Giusti family, are very extensive prospects, & in a clear day the eye can take in a large part of the vast plains of Lombardy, extending towards the Appennines. We visited this garden more perhaps because it is particularly mentioned by Addison, than on any other account.[1] The atten-

---

9. Shakespeare followed Italian and English sources in making Verona the setting of *The Two Gentlemen of Verona* and *Romeo and Juliet*, plays written in the early 1590s. Few visitors believed local pieties about the star-crossed lovers' tomb.

1. Gardens planted by Girardino Giusti in the mid-sixteenth century were notable for their cypresses and for a terrace with a view of distant Parma and Modena. Joseph Addison (1672–1719) in *Remarks on Several Parts of Italy etc.* showed little enthusiasm: "I saw the terrace-garden of Verona that travellers

tion of the world has been drawn to Verona more during the past year than for many ages before, as being the place fixed upon by the holy alliance, for the Congress of Sovereigns. The amphitheatre was fitted up for the occasion & some magnificent spectacles given in it by the Emperor of Austria.[2] Cornelius Nepos & Pliny the elder were born at Verona.[3]

March 29th. Left Verona for Mantua but owing to some mistake, took the great high road for Milan, which carried us two posts out of the way. About noon arrived at Mantua, more celebrated as the <u>reputed</u> birthplace of Virgil than for anything else. Virgil was however born at a little village called Andes or by some Pietole, not far distant (3 miles).[4] Mantua contains about 25,000 inhabitants, & is surrounded by a swamp or morass, formed by the overflowing of the Mincio, which empties into the Po. The

---

generally mention...." He thought most Italian gardens were inferior to the French and advocated "natural" as opposed to "formal" or "artificial" gardens. See *Miscellaneous Works of Joseph Addison,* A. C. Guthkelch, ed. (London, 1914) II, p. 43.

2. The Congress of Verona (October 1822) was the last of a series of meetings of European powers meant to plan joint action for the suppression of political unrest and the preservation of the peace negotiated by the Congress of Vienna in 1815. The issues in 1822 were: the Greek war of independence, the Spanish rebellion, and widespread agitation in Italy.

3. Cornelius Nepos (ca. 100–25 B. C.) and Pliny the Elder (ca. 23–79 A. D.), Roman historians, were born in Cisalpine Gaul. But Pavia and Como, respectively, had claims as valid as Verona's to be their places of birth.

4. Virgil was born ca. 70 B. C. at Andes (Pietole), a village some three Roman miles from Mantua.

Cathedal at Mantua is admired as being very much like the church of Santa Maria Maggiore at Rome.[5] We were shown to a small chapel beneath the Cathedral, where was a very rich Altar, adorned with some small pieces from Canova's chisel, & in the center of this altar, (which is kept locked by the priests) we were assured was some of the real blood of our Saviour. In the Town hall is the ancient bust in honor of the immortal poet. The history of it is, that it formed part of a statue of Virgil, but which during the barbarous ages was overturned & thrown into the lake.[6] It appeared to us that Mantua contained an unusual number of Jews. They have a Synagogue & live in a separate quarter of the city.[7] In the afternoon we continued our journey towards Parma. We had to cross the Po again some distance from Mantua, & after passing thro' a small corner of the Duke of Modena's dominions arrived at Guestalla the frontier town of the Archduchy of Maria Louisa.[8] We however did not stop but pursued our course to the

---

5. The Cathedral of Sts. Peter and Paul was a medieval structure with baroque additions. JCB follows J. C. Eustace (*Classical Tour*, I, pp. 226–227) in comparing its interior to that of St. Mary Major in Rome.

6. The bust of Virgil, venerated by Mantuans, was believed to be the severed head of a full-length statue that had been looted in the late fourteenth century. Restored in the late sixteenth century, it was looted by the French in 1797 and replaced with a plaster cast.

7. Mantua had attracted Jewish migrants long before the late fifteenth century when it became a haven for waves of refugees from Sicily and southern Italy. The ghetto was not set apart until 1610.

8. Marie-Louise (1791–1847), a German Habsburg princess, who married Napoleon in 1810 and bore his son in 1811, was awarded the Duchy of Parma and Guestalla by the Congress of Vienna in 1815. Her son, François (1811–

capital & arrived late at night in a drenching rain, distance from Mantua [*blank*] & from Verona [*blank*]. Our passports [*were demanded*?] to day 8 different times, but altho we passed from two separate powers to that of a third, we had no difficulty with our luggage, a small fee easily satisfying the custom house officers & guards.

March 30th # spent in Parma. The city with a portion of the surrounding country contains 40,000 inhabitants. It stands on a small river of the same name & is of very ancient origin. Since the downfall of Buonoparte, Parma has received no small celebrity in being assigned as the principality of his wife, who nominally reigns over this, in conjunction with Placentia & Guestalla, tho' in fact, they are under the dominion of Austria. It is a clean & a tolerably well built city, without any thing remarkable. The ramparts are shaded with trees & afford pleasant walks for the inhabitants. The court palace has nothing to distinguish it from any other large house, & unless a soldier mounted guard at the door was seen, it would never be taken by any one for a royal residence. There is however another palace with some pleasant gardins attached. It is not inhabited & is only worth visiting for a few fine frescos. The Museum or academy of arts contains a number of pictures by eminent artists & a good bust of the Archduchess by Canova.[9]

1832), titled "King of Rome" at birth, became "Duke of Reichstadt" in 1818.

9. Canova's bust of Marie-Louise, executed in 1821–1822, is now in the Palatine Library in the Palazzo della Pilotta in Parma.

We visited the interior of her palace and saw a few of the remains of her former greatness, the sumptious cradle, made for the king of Rome & presented by the city of Paris, & many rich & costly ornaments of her toilet, used by her when she kept her splendid court at the Tuilliries. We attended the Theatre in the evening & saw her majesty in the royal box with a few attendants.[1] The Austrian general, Count Nepirg placed to keep a watch over her by her father sat by her side; she was dressed in black (the court being in mourning for the Princess of Lucca) & her countenance had the marks of melancholy.[2] Scandal however, <u>does</u> say that Maria Louisa, like many other young, brisk widows has not been over faithful to the memory of her departed husband, but has consoled herself for his loss by admitting the Count to share her bed, & that two children are the fruit of this connection. For the sake of her son she ought to have had more respect to the memory of poor Nap—. But nature will prevail & the poet has truly said that "frailty thy name is woman."[3] Lord Biron in

1. The Farnese Theater, opened in 1628, was restored during the reign of Marie-Louise.

2. Adam Albrecht Neipperg (1775–1829) was appointed by the Habsburg imperial government to advise and escort Marie-Louise after her separation from Napoleon in 1814. She bore Neipperg two children before entering a morganatic marriage with him in 1821, four months after Napoleon's death. The marriage was well known but not publicly acknowledged until Neipperg's death in 1829. In 1834 she married Neipperg's successor, Count Charles de Bombelles.

   Lucca became a principality in 1805 and was bestowed on Napoleon's sister, Elisa. It was reconstituted a duchy in 1815 and awarded to Marie-Louise de Bourbon who died in 1824.

3. *Hamlet*, act 1, sc. 2, line 146.

his age of Bronze alluding to Maria Louisa, says "she rules the pastoral relm of cheese" for what is called the Parmisan Cheese is made here & in the neighbourhood.[4]

March 31st. Continued our journey & rolled along over the Via Emilia, to Placentia. This beautiful road is the work of Marcus Emilius Lepidus & was made 137 years before Christ. 'Tis kept in very good repair.[5] A ride of 5 posts brought us to Placentia We only stopped here an hour or two, to see the brazen equestrian statues of Alexander Farnese & his brother Ranuccio which ornament the public square. The former is very much admired.[6] Almost immediately after leaving Placentia, we crossed the Po again for the 3d time, & were soon after detained at the Austrian frontier to have our luggage examined. This was the first time since we had arrived in Italy that we had been required to open our trunks, & here the search was not at all strict. This ceremony over, we pushed on & passed the night at the town of Lodi 3 posts from Placentia.

_____

4. JCB refers to Byron's *The Age of Bronze* (1823), XVII: "What though she share no more and shared in vain / A sway surpassing that of Charlemagne / Which swept from Moscow to the southern seas! / Yet still she rules the pastoral realm of cheese...."

5. JCB's comments on the Roman road between Parma and Placentia (Piacenza) repeat those of Eustace, *Classical Tour*, I, p. 240.

6. Alexander Farnese, duke of Parma (1545–1592), was governor of the Low Countries under Philip II of Spain (1527–1598). Ranuccio I (1569–1622), his son and successor, commissioned equestrian statues of his father and of himself, executed (1612–1629) by Francesco Mochi (1580–1654). The former was much admired because both horse and rider were represented in violent motion.

#Sunday

[Editorial note: The fourth diary ends with the entry for March 31, 1824. It is followed by two notations, one in ink, one in pencil. The first lists the inns where JCB and his cousin were accommodated in Verona, Parma, and Lodi. The second records the dates and times of arrival at their destinations on the northern leg of their Italian tour from Bologna on March 20 to Lodi on March 31. The last note is: "1st of April entered Milan."]

Book Five

June 15 to August 20, 1824
ENGLAND, GERMANY, AND THE NETHERLANDS

#During the last night & also today, there was a good deal of rain & sometimes it came down merrily—but we are now getting into a county where we must expect wet weather.

LEFT LONDON on the 15th June 1824 intending to make a short tour into the Hanse Towns & return thro Holland.[1] The Coach left Aldgate Street at 1 PM, & at ½ past 7 I was set down at Colchester in the County of Essex. It was a delightful ride thro a perfectly level country, highly cultivated, & adorned with elegant seats & snug Boxes the comfortable retreats of many a London shopkeeper. We were drove at the rate of about 9 miles the hour.

Colchester is an ancient well built town & from the population which I saw in the Streets I should judge a large portion of them were Quakers. The "Cups Inn" is an extensive establishment & the first in the place, but I was not so "well" there, as at many others in the Kingdom. The following morning I mounted

---

1. "Hanse Towns" were German cities that formed the Hanseatic League, a commercial-military alliance which originated in the thirteenth century and dominated Baltic trade in the late Middle Ages. Since the League was never formally dissolved, Hamburg and Bremen continued to call themselves Hanseatic cities.

on top of the mail at 8 Oclk for Harwich. The Weather was very fine, & although we were fast approaching the seaside, the country exhibited nearly the same improvement & cultivation as before. We passed thro a number of neat little villages before reaching Harwich, which is situated quite upon a peninsula. No place that I had as yet visited in England appeared so dull & silent as this, not a cart, carriage or Gig was to be seen in the Streets & the population seemed to have entirely deserted it. It is the station for the packets to Holland & Germany & this with a few fish boats & small craft comprises its commerce.

After dining & the usual forms at the Custom House we embarked onboard the Lord Duncan packet for Cuxhaven. There were 4 other passengers besides myself on board, 2 Germans (both of whom had served in the late wars[2] & spoke English very well) one young fellow who had just returned from the West Indies as supercargo of a small Brig & the fourth a liberal, generous, open hearted John Bull, who had lately had a fortune of £15,000 left him by an old Uncle & who was going to Hamburg to join his brother in trade. The Packet put to sea about 4 Oclk. The wind tolerably favourable, but shortly after it came round directly ahead & blew a gale—raining very hard. We continued thro the night beating & pitching about in the North Sea. (all the passengers excepting myself sick a death[3] 'til the following day about 11 when seeing no prospect of a change, the captain thought best to put back & in a couple of hours we were again at Harwich. Such an

2. The wars with Napoleonic France which in 1813–1815 enlisted Britain and many German states as allies.

3. An obsolete phrase meaning "deathly ill."

unfortunate beginning rather discouraged me & if I could have got back my 5 guineas which I had paid for my passage or even ½ of it I should have returned to London; but they had got my money & said I might go or stay just as I liked. The time passed tediously at Harwich, until we again set sail Friday at 11 AM: with a pretty good wind & the following Monday at 6 in the morning were landed at Cuxhaven, without meeting any further adventures. Cuxhaven is situate not far from the mouth of the Elbe, on the right bank. It is a small neat Village, inhabited mostly by pilots, fishermen & persons attendant upon such occupations. There is a good Inn here (the Bath Hotel) & after breakfasting refreshing ourselves with a warm sea bath, & strolling about a little, we went aboard the regular packet boat at 2 P.M for Hamburg. The distance is [*blank*] German miles, or about [*blank*] English.[4] I was quite astonish to find the Elbe such a fine river, indeed it is a noble stream & is not less than a mile wide up to the city & in some parts much more. The Tide flows <u>strong</u> as far as Hamburg & even as far as Magdeburg tho, with much less force until within 10 or 12 miles to town both banks are perfectly level & an embankment appears to be necessary to prevent inundations—many small villages are scattered along the waters edge, which diversify the scene, & we saw a number of square rigged vessels laying at anchor. A few miles before the city are to be seen a great number of Elegant country seats belonging to the wealthy merchants of Hamburg.

At noon, on Tuesday 22d we had arrived & we landed at the "Bauernhaus" after a tedious journey of a week from London.

---

4. A German mile equaled between four and five English miles.

Took [*blank*] Hamburg is the largest of the Hanse Towns & the most commercial City in Germany. Owing to the late wars in Europe, its trade was very much wounded & altho at present it is reviving, 'tis far short of what it was formerly. Heavy contributions were levied upon it during its occupation by the French, & the merchants were plundered of much of their wealth by the rapacity of their invaders. The general appearance of Hamburg is very much like Dutch towns & a part of the city is intersected by canals for the more convenient transportation of merchandize, but the canals are not like those in Amsterdam with their borders planted with trees & generally speaking I dont think it as fine a city as the commercial capital of Holland. To the North of Hamburg is a delightful walk called the "Jung Fernsteig" or virgins walk. 'Tis upon the border of a large basin of water running from the Alster. 'Tis the most fashionable promenade & on a Sunday Evening is crowded with a large collection of fashionables. The ramparts & Boulevards have of late years been level'd & now form pleasant & shady retreats from the noise & bustle of the city.[5] Hamburg cannot bost of many objects of curiosity, to attract the attention of a Stranger. We looked in to the Museum, but there is nothing there worth noticing.[6] The Churches are all of brick, but within they are well finished supplied with large organs, especially the Church of Saint Nicholas which contains

---

5. Boulevards were once the top surfaces of ramparts, bulwarks, or earthworks which, when leveled, were made into broad, tree-lined thoroughfares.

6. JCB may be referring to the Hamburger Kunsthalle or to the Museum für Kunst und Gewerbe.

one of the finest Organs in Europe.[7] I visited the Orphan Asylum, an institution of which any city might be proud. It is upon a very extensive scale, & from what I saw & could learn respecting it, appears to be conducted upon correct principles.[8] But if the City itself is not very attractive, the environs are really delightful, & particularly upon the banks of the Elbe. Below Altona the seat of Mr Parish the great Merchant about 6 miles from Town is as pleasantly situated & has as commanding views as about any other I have ever witnessed in any Country. P. spends most of the year there & comes to town every morning & returns after business hours.[9] Mr. Gossler has a neat pretty Box only a short walk from one of the gates & upon the banks of the Alster.[1] In every direction are also numerous Tea gardens, for the public & which are thronged in pleasant weather upon a Sunday afternoon. There are not many public amusements in Hamburg, only one German Theater, which I attended & where I heard some good singing. In the Winter season however, I understand that the city is very gay with dancing, Assemblies, & concerts.

---

7. Hamburg's Nicolaikirche, begun in the early thirteenth century, was destroyed by fire in 1842.

8. The *Waisenhaus*, or orphanage, supported by both public and private funds, could accommodate 600 children.

9. Most likely one of the sons of John Parish (1742–1829), founder of a prosperous trading company who had migrated from his native Scotland to Hamburg at the age of fifteen. In 1793 George Washington appointed him the first United States consul in Hamburg. His sons inherited his business and property when he retired to England in 1814.

1. Johann Heinrich Gossler (b. 1775), a prominent merchant and member of the city's senatorial elite.

"The Salons" of Hamburg are one of the distinguishing features of the place. Every evening one or more are open & at 11 o'clk: are crowded with public girls, & men & strangers who are accustomed to frequent such places. The prostitutes are under the immediate direction of the police, & regularly examined twice a week by doctors (who signify on their "carte de santé" the condition of their health [J]. Most of the girls were handsome & many would pass for elegant, genteel women. From the very great number of fille de joie [sic] seen at the Salons a stranger is led to believe that fornication is one of the principle amusements of the Hamburgers.[2] After remaining in Hamburg a week & having visited every object worthy of attention & made myself well acquainted with the local situation of the place, I bid adieu to my friends & commenced my journey to Bremen.

Altona, a free town, but under the protection of the King of Denmark is situate upon the Elbe immediately below Hamburg, & only a short walk from the gate. It contains about 40,000 inhabitants, & is built altogether of brick in the Dutch Style.[3] I passed thro Altona frequently during my rides into the Country, but having no letters & not finding it contained any objects of curios-

---

2. Most German theaters, like those in England, depended on royal or princely patronage. Hamburg, because it was self-governing, well-to-do, and cosmopolitan, was the first German city to have a "national" theater (1765), able to break away from the French classical tradition that dominated court theaters.

"Salons," or brothels, and the conduct of "public women" first fell under civic control in 1807, during the French occupation.

3. Altona was a free city, as were Hamburg and Bremen, but was also a protectorate of Denmark. It passed under Prussian sovereignty in 1866 and was incorporated into Hamburg in 1937.

ity, I only stopped a few moments to view the Tomb of Klopstock the poet who is buried in the grave yard of one of the Churches. 'Tis a simple marble slab, with a short inscription in German.[4]

June 29th at 4 PM, I left Hamburg in the passage boat for Haarburg, & crossed the Elbe passing between a number of Islands which makes the river very narrow immediately opposite the City. It was past 6 before I was landed & at ½ past 7 started alone in a horse waggon for Bremen. This road is said to be by far the best of any in the north of Germany. It was began by Buonaparte & as the territory now belongs to the King of England it has been completed by the English & is kept in tolerable repair, yet in England 'twod be called a very bad road.[5] We jogged on at a slow pace thro' the night, sleeping a little myself & sometimes finding both horse & driver sleeping together. At Tostold, a miserable little village we stopped to bait our worn out horse, where I got some excellent coffee, which served to keep me awake during the remainder of the night. For I found it necessary to stand watch

---

4. Friedrich Gottlieb Klopstock (1724–1803), a poet who had a profound influence on the revival of German literature in the late eighteenth century, was buried in Ottensen, a suburb later absorbed by Altona. Some of his verses were set to music by Beethoven and Schubert.

5. Hanover, raised to the status of a kingdom in 1815, had been joined to Britain in a personal union in 1714 when its Elector George Louis inherited the English throne as George I. The line of succession passed through his mother who was a great-granddaughter of James I (r. 1603–1625). The personal union was dissolved at the death of William IV in 1837. The accession of Queen Victoria to the throne of Hanover was barred by Salic law which precluded females from inheritance.

myself, lest some accident should happen thro' the negligence of my German driver. I knew not a word of German, nor he of English or any other language, so it was all dumb show between us. At Rotenburg we stopped at a pretty good Inn, but the others on the road were such as I had often heard before described, but never met with. They were houses or rather barns of a huge size; the fire built in the middle of the stone floor, the cows & horses in one corner & the pigs in the other. The two other corners were divided off, by slight partitions where all the household turned in Together, & this mode of living I observed to be most generally the case among the B[*auer*]s thro, the part of Hannover & Germany I passed. Altogether there was very little to interest upon the route & I was very glad at 1 o'clk on Wednesday to be set down at the "Lindenhoff" in Bremen. Not expecting to remain more than a day or two here I only took a single letter to the Commercial house of Meyer & Company the principal of which Mr A[*illeg.*] was extremely polite & attentive to me by introducing me to many agreeable Gentlemen for of female society, I saw none, owing to the shortness of my stay & ignorance of the Language.[6]

Bremen is the second most commercial Town in Germany & is a free City, being governed nearly in a similar manner to Hamburg. Tho in some respects its institutions are more democratic, for the Senate composed of 24 members, instead of filling up its own vacancies, like the latter are obliged to select from 3

---

6. H. H. Meier and Company of Bremen, with a branch office in New York, did a brisk business with the United States, tobacco being one of its principal imports.

chosen by the burghers. The population is about 40,000 & including the few little villages in the neighborhood the whole population of this little republic amounts to something like 60,000. The situation of Bremen is favorable for commerce, situated upon the Weser & is by far the greatest Market for Tobacco of any upon the Continent. Bremen is in general a well built town, like Hamburg and mostly in the same style & the Ramparts laid out in the most elegant & tasteful manner, for as pleasant a promenade as any other of the kind I have met with in Europe. They extend quite round the principle part of the town which is upon the right bank of the Weser. The town is divided by the river & indeed a small part is upon an island formed by two of its branches. The Domo or Cathedral is a very large edefice built of brick & the inside exhibits some fine traces of Gothic architecture. But what is most singular respecting this church is its cellar, the air of which possesses the peculiar property of preserving dead bodies from putrifaction. I saw a number of bodies some of which have laid there 3 & 400 years. About 40 years since a dead body was placed there to see if the place still preserved its virtues, it was found that it did. The skin appears to dry upon the bones & altho it looks dark & wilted yet beating upon it, it sounds like a drum head. I believe there is but one other place in the world similar to this celar in Bremen & that is somewhere upon the Rhine.[7]

The Town Hall is a fine old building, but its cellar is the most attractive. It is a wine Establishment of very ancient origin

---

7. The cathedral, an eleventh-century, romanesque structure with thirteenth-century additions, had a *Bleikeller*, or lead vault, where bodies were preserved.

& entirely under the control of the Senate, being in fact a grand depot for Rheinish wines, of every quality. Here the purchaser can be certain of getting the pure juice of the grape, for the concern is managed by the Government who appoint superintendants, with fixed salaries & who can have no object in deception. As one of the most interesting object in Bremen I visited this famous cellar with some of my friends & we tasted a ½ bottle of the oldest 1624[,] 1632 & 1706 with other descriptions of later date. The 1624 has a strong aromatic flavor & altho perfectly sound, yet it was much too sour for my tast & I judge would only be relished by long drinkers of old Hoch.[8] The number of gallons of wine I understood to be 1,500,000 but I did not hear or have forgotten the number of pipes.[9] Leading out of the main Cellar are smaller appartments, containing the oldest & choicest wines. One is called the 12 Apostles, because it contains just 12 large casks, or Hogsheads & curious enough it is that the Judas cask has the best wine. Another cellar is called "the Rose," because a very large rose is painted on the ceiling & any thing said or done in this place is always considered "sub rosa". This cellar contains the oldest of all the wines. Until lately the <u>very</u> oldest were not allowed to be sold (such ages as I have before mentioned) without the especial permission of the Senate & then only allowance was granted to sick persons & upon the article of

---

8. The *Rathaus*, or town hall (1405–1412), with a Renaissance façade added in 1609–1612, housed a *Ratskeller* which stored and sold German wines. "Hock" (Hoch) was a common English word for German white wine, not to be confused with "hooch," an illegally distilled whiskey.

9. A "pipe" was a cask with a capacity of four barrels.

some physician. In the principle cellar some of the Hogsheads are of enormous size adorned with carved work & painted & gilded in curious manner, over some of them, sits Baccus, with old Silenus, enjoying themselves with the generous liquour.

While at Bremen I ordered a quantity of wine from this famous Establishment for my friends in Providence. The few days I spent in this City were passed very agreeably. The weather was pleasant & I had some good society. The 4th of July I dined a mile in the country, at a dinner given by Mr Delius (one of the first merchants in the place)[1] at which was present the few Americans who were in Bremen & some of the merchants engaged in the American trade. Some patriotic toasts were drunk & we had a good dinner. Returned early to town & at 10 in the Evening left Bremen for Amsterdam in company with Mr Lord a Gentleman from Portsmouth, N. H.[2] The road was very sandy & we proceeded at a very slow pace. The night was cold & rainy, but in the Morning it cleared up, & at $\frac{1}{2}$ past 5 we found ourselves at Oldenburg, the capital of the Dutchy of the same name. While breakfast was preparing we walked out to see the town. 'Tis a small & rather mean place, & by no means well built, & the only object that deserves the least notice is the palace of the Grand Duke. This even cannot boast of any architectural beauties. 'Tis a large 3 storied building, of a gray stone & gambled roof; with-

---

1. Probably Everhard Delius (1777–1866), member of a prosperous mercantile family. One of his uncles was in 1794 appointed first United States consul to Bremen.

2. Probably Samuel Lord (d. 1871).

out any garden or pleasure ground around it. We did not see the inside of the palace, but took a look into the Dukes stables, where he had a handsome stud of horses.[3]

From Oldenburg at 8 we took "extra post" as it is called to Leir. Posting is the best mode of travelling in Germany, & this owing to the badness of the roads is tedious enough. The German postillions I found the most accommodating & easiest satisfied of this description of people I have yet met with in Europe. I heard not the least grumbling from any of them. The road all the way to Leir is sandy & dreary & nothing agreeable presents itself to relieve the eye. At Lier we arrived at 6 PM. Being some what pressed for time we stopped only long enough to dine & change horses. Lier has the appearance of thriving town [?] for its size.[4] The houses have a general look of neatness & it contains 7,000 inhabitants.

Shortly after leaving Lier we crossed the river Ems, & proceeded rapidly (5 miles an hour) over a pretty good road 'til we reached Nieschamps. As it was nearly 11 we concluded to lay by the remainder of the night & a good supper & bed reinstated us after a tedious days journey.

---

3. JCB is referring to the palace of Duke Peter, also bishop of Lübeck, who in 1823 inherited Oldenburg from a mad cousin. Although Oldenburg had been upgraded to a grand-duchy during the Napoleonic wars, Peter refused the title of grand-duke.

"Gambeled" roof is an obsolete variant of "gambreled," a term describing a "gambrel-roof" or "hipped roof," because the roof's outline resembles the shape of a horse's gambrel or hind leg.

4. Leer was chartered as a city in 1823.

July 6th at ½ past 7 we took the "trak schuit"[5] for Gronningen. For a long distance I have before observed that this is not the most agreeable mode of travelling & so I found it upon this route. For most part of way the country presented nothing very pleasant or attractive, unless a constant succession of fertil medows, filled with horn cattle can be considered as such. Winschoten is the most considerable town upon the Canal, until within 6 miles of Groningen where are there a succession of small villages.

It was 6 in the Evening before we reached Gronningen & employed 2 or 3 hours before dark in taking a general survey of this fine town, for such it is described & such I should really pronounce it to be. Formerly it was a free town & had an extensive trade. This in latter times has much fallen off. The population is now 24,000. The marketplace is a large & fine square, containing the town house a stately elegant building & in one corner a church the loftiest edifice in Holland, the steepel of which has a considerable resemblance to that of the grand Cathedral in Antwerp.[6] We walked in the plantings a very pleasant promenade & took a cursory survey of the Botanical Gardens, attached to the Universtiy of Gronningen.[7]

---

5. A roofed, flat-bottomed, horse-drawn canal boat, sixty to eighty feet long, eight to ten feet wide. Traveling at the rate of three miles per hour, it provided cheap, quiet, tedious transportation through Dutch interior waterways.

6. The Groote Markt, one of the largest market squares in the Netherlands, was flanked by the Martinikerk, a church with a tower (1477) 430 feet tall.

7. The University of Groningen, founded in 1614, had botanical gardens to the north of the city which furnished promenades for the fashionable.

The following morning at 4 we departed in a four wheel'd vehicle with two horses for Lemmer upon the Zuyder Zee. During this days ride we passed thro' probably the worst part of Holland. No people but the Dutch could ever have brought to the present improved state so vile a part of Gods creation. For the greater part of the way it seemed to be but one continual marsh & a large proportion of that, nothing better than a peat bog. Large herds of cattle however covered most of the fields & the villages & houses of the peasantry along the road by their neatness & comfortable appearance, presented positive proof of the astonishing perseverance & industry of the Dutch. As we approached the Zuyder Zee, creation presented a still more dismal appearance & many parts of the country were literally overrun & intersected by arms of the sea. One would suppose that population would have at least deserted this region, but no, villages & hamlets were still seen scattered around, some of which, almost entirely surrounded by water, & which was restrained from overflowing the whole concern only by a slight embankment.

The people here seemed to be occupied mostly in preparing peat &c. which I should judge formed their most considerable branch of commerce. This was made by scooping up the mud & letting it dry after being smoothed & cut in pieces about twice the size of a Philadelphia brick.[8] Being situated so near Amsterdam I supposed the advanced price of this kind of firing makes it if not a profitable at least a living business.

---

8. The size of bricks made in the United States was not officially regulated as in Britain, but did not vary much from the English standard which in the early

Before entering Lemmer, we alighted from our carriage to examine the Dykes by which the Zuyder Zee is restrained from overflowing the country. 'Tis impossible to view these immense works, without thinking well of the Dutch & to wonder at the extraordinary exertions of a people who have reclaimed their country from the waters.

Lemmer where we arrived at 5 P.M. is a bustling little place, & is the most direct route by water to Amsterdam. We took passenger in one of the regular packet boats (a vessel of about 100 tons) at 8 in the Evening & owing to constant head winds did not arrive 'til 9 oclk: on Thursday 8th:

Friday call[ed] on the Messers Crommelins[9] & quite to my surprise found Mr I[ves] still at Amsterdam, where he had been for nearly 5 weeks attending to the business of the Ann & Hope. It was pleasant to find an old companion, tho we were together only for a short while. Dined to day at the house of the elder Mr. C. Their two young ladies were at home, but I saw very little difference in them from the last year at Brussels.

Saturday 10th, Mr I[ves] having made his arrangements to leave Amsterdam for Antwerp &c. &c. Mr. C[rommelin] & myself joined him to make a short excursion in the neighbourhood of

---

1800s was nine inches long, four and one-half inches wide, and three inches thick. In Philadelphia bricks used on the façade of a house were commonly longer than those used on the rear or side walls. That may be what JCB had in mind in this otherwise obscure reference.

9. A trading company, and Brown and Ives's principal correspondent in Amsterdam. See Introduction.

Utrecht. We left the City at noon & took the same route to Soes-dyke[1] I took the year before with Mr C. Every thing about the country had a similar appearance & the roads being good, we postted over the ground at a rapid rate. After strolling around the princes domain, viewing the palace & triumphal column we dined & passed the night there. The next morning before breakfasting we walked 3 or 4 miles in the woods & grounds of Soesdyke. We then drove to Zeist, & passed the remainder of the day in this charming little village.[2] It being Sunday there were a large concourse of well dressed people from Utrecht (some of whom sported elegant equipages) & lively villagers who like ourselves came to enjoy the pleasant & refreshing walks of this Moravian village.

Monday after making some further excursions in the immediate neighbourhood we reached Utrecht at an early hour. At 6 we sat down to a sumptious dinner & as it was the last repast we should take together, we uncorked a bottle of Burgundy & Mr. C. treated with one of Champaigne. This served to call forth the flow of soul.[3] The Evening passed agreeably & the following morning

---

1. Soestdijk, a seventeenth-century hunting palace, twelve miles south of Utrecht, was presented by the Estates General to Willem, Prince of Orange-Nassau (1792–1849), in recognition of his valor at Waterloo. It became a royal residence in 1840 when he became king.

2. A small Moravian colony settled by a Hussite sect expelled from central Europe in 1746.

3. JCB takes this phrase from Alexander Pope's _Satires and Epistles of Horace Imitated_, Satire 1, ll. 127–128, where the poet celebrates Henry St. John, viscount Bolingbroke: "There St. John mingles with my friendly bowl / The feast of reason and the flow of soul."

we all parted. Mr. C. at 5 by the Diligence & Mr. I. at 9 for Rotter-dam. I remained enjoying the fine walks of Utrecht 'til 1 P.M when I left by the Trak Schuit & reached Amsterdam at 9 in the Evening. Every part of the route during this excursion led thro' a highly fertil & cultivated country. Holland is generally, but very erroneously considered as altogether a grazing country. North Holland & the Friezelands may properly be considered in this light, for there I saw little else but widely extending field covered with numerous herds of cattle. But in the province of Utrecht the richest crops of Buckwheat & almost every kind of Grain were waving on every side as far as the eye could reach. I think I never saw such luxuriancy any where, if I except Flanders than I saw in this part of Holland—where was apparently but very little mead-ow ground.

Wednesday 14th I passed at Amsterdam, & Thursday at 4 PM took the dilligence for the Hague, passing thro' Haerlem, but having Leydan in sight. The Dutch I learn have very much improved in travelling within the last few years. The roads are very firm, being paved with brick & the dilligences roll over the ground with a great deal of rapidity. It was late before arriving when I took up my quarters at the Doelen Inn.

Friday 16th. The weather was delightful, & I enjoyed a prome-nade in the wood at the Hague.[4] Some parts of this City are really

---

4. The Hague Wood with its oaks, alders, and avenues of giant beeches, was considered one of the area's chief attractions.

as noble & magnificent as any thing I have seen in Europe, & what especially delights an Englishman is to see so much cleanliness, with all this grandeur. The same thing is often to be met with in other cites in France & Italy but not unfrequently the houses are so surrounded with "degredations" & other filth that one turns away with disgust. I did not look at any cabinets of pictures, or curiosities, having seen the same on my former tour. In the afternoon took the Trak Schuit for Rotterdam. This mode of travelling altho a novelty at first, soon becomes tedious to most people altho it seems well suited to the phlegmatic disposition of the Dutch. 'Tis a cheap mode of travelling & the porterage of luggage from one point to another costs more than the fare itself. On arriving at Rotterdam I found that I had received incorrect information respecting the sailling of the Steam boats for London, & that none went on Saturdays. Unwilling to spend 4 days here, for it seemed so much time lost, I engaged a carriage to be ready on the following morning to carry me to Helvoetsluys, where I should find the British packet for Harwich. Accordingly Saturday morning I was up at a little after 3 & the wind I saw was favourable. Taking a hasty cup of coffee, we sta[r]ted, but what with the delay in crossing the "Meuses,"[5] & these other ferries, & infamous roads, (the fellow driving me thro' swamps & cow yards to shorten the distance, as he called it), delays in changing horses & then having horses imposed upon us that were draft teams I arrived at

---

5. The Meuse (Maas) River divides into many branches before flowing into the North Sea.

Helvoetsluys just ½ an hour after the packet had sailled with a strong breeze.

After this disappointment, & the fatigue I had endured not to mention the heavy expense, my chagrin can better be immagined than described, but cursing my fate & damning the coachman (who understood not a word of English) was all to no purpose, so I was obliged to make the best of a bad bargain & consoled myself phylosophizing upon the evils of this life. All that part of Holland below Rotterdam seems to present but a miserable prospect for a man to live in & the soil is barren & marshy, & the luxuriant crops seen in other parts of Holland, were not here to be met with, from its—being so even & on a level with the sea, is exposed to continuous cold & uncomfortable winds. Yet the country is thickly settled on the route to Helvoetsluys & I passed thro' one or two populous towns. The costume of the women here as to their caps & ear rings was something quite different, from what I had before observed in any part of Holland. Helvoetsluys is small fortified town on the island of Voorn & one of the depots of the Dutch navy. The harbour is spacious & can contain a large fleet.[6] Nothing now remained for me to do but to get back again to Rotterdam & wait for the steam boat on Wednesday. By the advice of the Landlord, instead of returning over the same route, I drove across the Island a distance of 7 miles to Brill. In this direction the country presented a rather more favourable aspect, at any rate the road was a very good one paved with brick.

---

6. In addition to having a navy yard and arsenal, Helvoetsluys was an important harbor for East India traders.

Brill is a town of considerable importance, & contains rising 3000 inhabitants. It gave birth to the celebrated van Tromp & the vice admiral Di Witt.[7] At about 4 in the afternoon leaving my carriage at Brill I took the passenger boat for Rotterdam & the wind blowing strong was landed about 7—thus ended my day's excursion, which almost knocked me up in body & very much lightened my purse. My expenses were something like 25 gilders.

Sunday 18th July—A good nights rest very much relieved me from the fatigue of the following day. My late travelling companion Mr Lord was still in Rotterdam. In the forenoon we attended devine services, at the presbyterian & church of England chapels —both services were in the English language, & at each was a respectable congregation.[8] In most of the considerable Towns in Holland, religious protestant services are in English & French. Accordingly this makes it very convenient for the numerous English who are settled here. In the afternoon of the day, all was life & gaiety, as it always is on a Sunday afternoon all over this continent, & a fair which was going on just at this time out side of one of the gates, had collected together a large number of the

---

7. Admiral Maarten Harpertzoon Tromp (1597–1653) won victories over the Spanish (1639) and English (1652). Admiral Witte Corneliszoon De With (1599–1658) commanded Dutch naval operations off the coast of Brazil and in the East Indies.

8. The English Presbyterian Chapel was established by expatriates in the seventeenth century. The Church of England Chapel was built (1704–1708) by the duke of Marlborough and bore his coat of arms over the entrance. It was razed in 1913.

neighbouring peasantry, which mingling with the <u>bougoise</u> of Rotterdam, formed a curious group. Stalls & booths, were erected in great number. Fandangoes &c &c &c were in operation for the amusement of the multitude. The lads & lasses were all in high glee & seemed to enjoy themselves quite as much as they do in America when going to a conference meeting. What a contrast are these customs & manners, to the puritanical, psalm singing habits of America, &—especialy Connecticut. How different a mode of spending the Sunday?[9]

Monday & Tuesday I remained in Rotterdam. 'Tis purely a business place & particularly at this season of the year was very dull, & as I had no companion & no letters to assist in passing the time, was obliged to "retire within myself" as I have often been before.[1]

Wednesday 21st—returned to London by the Steam packet & arrived the following day at 1 P.M. after a pleasant passage. No particular incident occured worth relating—the passengers were prety numerous, & of almost all nations. Those with whom I was most intimate were an English post Captain[2] just returning from

---

9. "Conference meeting" was a New England term for an assembly engaging in prayer and moral exhortation. JCB's reference to Connecticut suggests that he was recalling his early adolescence when he attended a school in Hartford.

1. "Retire within thyself, and thou wilt discover how small a stock is there." (*Tecum habita, et noris quam sit tibi curta supellex.*) Aulus Persius Flaccus (34–62), *Satires*, iv, l. 52.

2. A naval officer holding a captain's commission for active duty as distinguished from one with the courtesy title of captain.

a tour in Italy, & a german who had travelled a good deal in Russia, both intelligent men & both took me to be an Englishman until I explained. After showing my flag, John Bull was not the less polite, complimented me upon the future greatness of my nation & thought the Americans "a damd fine set of fellows."

[*Four blank pages. One cut blank page.*]

There yet remaining some important parts of England which I had not visited & which I felt the curiosity to explore, & as it would not be convenient to comprehend this in my final tour to Liverpool, I determined to leave London with Mr I[*ves*] & to have the benefit of his company at least a part of the time.

We took seats upon the "Tally Ho" coach[3] for Cambridge & left town Monday Afternoon August 2d, at ½ past 2. The weather was remarkably fine, & the road one of the best I have travelled upon in England. For the first 20 miles it was perfectly level & we moved on at a rapid pace. The Country all the way was highly cultivated, & notwithstanding the outcry of some of the radicals (& which unfortunately is too much believed in my own country) of the poverty & wretchedness of Britain, we could see nothing but what indicated ease & plenty.[4] The road led over Stamford

---

3. A "tally ho coach" was a fast coach running between London and Birmingham, a service introduced in 1823. The name was later applied to other express coaches on other roads.

4. "Radicals" was a common term for political extremists after 1797 when Charles James Fox (1749–1806) called for "radical reform." Between 1815 and 1832 it was applied to writers and agitators such as William Cobbett (1762–

Hill; "Edmonton so gay" (as John Gilpin says)[5] Roysten & a number of other pleasant little villages & after 5½ hours ride we were set down at the Sun in Cambridge having come 51 miles in that time,—for such a distance the fastest driving I ever was witness of. In the Evening we promenaded the city. & viewed the venerable piles which gives it its celebrity & which seemed more awfully grand when seen by the faint light of an over shadowed moon.

Tuesday August 3d. Today our time was fully occupied in viewing the Lions of the University. But were sorry to find that we were as unfortunate as when at Oxford, for it was vacation time, & but few of the members of the Colleges were in town.[6] Perhaps however it was quite as well, for we neither of us had any letters of introduction & by properly applying the all efficient means viz the silver key we obtained admittance to every thing worth seeing. The Chapel at Kings College is the great boast of this University & well it might be for it is one of the wonders not merely in the science of Architecture, but of the world. It was commenced in the time of Henry the 8th, & I believed finished during that monarchs reign.[7] Its proportions within are as follows—

1835) and Henry "Orator" Hunt (1773–1835).

5. Edmonton was a popular resort for London day-trippers. The phrase is from "The Diverting History of John Gilpin" (1780), a poem by William Cowper: "Thus all through merry Islington/These gambols did he play/Until he came unto the Wash/Of Edmonton so gay."

6. Cambridge University's "Long Vacation" extended from a moveable date in June to Michaelmas Term that began on October 1 and ran to December 16.

7. JCB has conflated the reigns of Henry VI (r. 1422–1461; 1470–1471) and

[*blank*] Length [*space left for dimensions not given*] The roof supports 12 hugh stones of tons weight & this it is that always surprised & caused the admiration of all architects. The difficulty is as Sir C. Wren said "how to lay the first stone."[8] The Walls are covered with work carved upon the stones & the windows are of old painted Glass, representing scripture history. We mounted upon the roof & as the sun shone clear, we had a fine view of Cambridge & its environs. The Colleges of Cambridge are very numerous, but not so much so as at Oxford, yet there are some at Cambridge which I think surpass in magnificence any at the Sister University, Trinity College for example. Nothing at Oxford can I think compare with the inner court (or Neville Court) as it is called.[9] One side of this superb structure contains the Library, which we visited; the number of volumes is not large, but the hall itself must strike any one as being a remarkably fine room. The bust of Newton by Rubilliac & some others by the same master, are particularly admired.[1]

Henry VIII (r. 1509–1547). King's College chapel, with its great fan vaulting, was begun in 1446 and completed in 1515.

8. The line attributed to Christopher Wren (1632–1723) may be apocryphal.

9. Trinity College was founded by Henry VIII in 1546, largely endowed with funds taken from suppressed religious houses. Thomas Neville was master of the college from 1593 to 1615.

1. Trinity's library was designed by Wren.

Louis François Roubiliac (or Roubillac) born at Lyons, 1695, settled in London ca. 1720 and became England's most popular portrait sculptor. He did a series of portrait busts for Trinity College (1751–1757), including one of Sir Isaac Newton (1642–1727), who had been Lucasian Professor of Mathematics there.

There is at Cambridge a small collection of pictures & curiosities called "The Fitzwilliam Museum" as I presume it was a present from some of the family of that name.[2] Of the pictures a few are deserving of notice; being the productions of some of the most celebrated Italian masters. Carlo Dolce & Lianado di Vinci, a head of a Magdalen by the former, would at once be known by anyone who had ever before witnessed the productions of his pencil. The Botanical Garden belonging to the U— consists of 5 acres of ground, as neither of us have much tast in Botany, we spent but little time here. It contains a great variety of rare plants, among others I noticed the Tea plant & the mahogany tree, with a variety of the different American Aloes.[3] The City of Cambridge has nothing in general appearance at all attractive, the streets are narrow & houses mean. The small Cam runs in the rear of most of the Colleges & altho a very insignifikent stream to be called a river yet as the banks are green & well shaded by ancient trees it affords a fine promenade for the literary gents. I regretted that we did not visit this celebrated place under more auspicious circumstances. It would have been gratifying to have had letters to some of the members that we might have seen something more of the interiour or oeconomy of the University & put such questions as might naturally arise respecting its var-

2. Richard, viscount Fitzwilliam (1745-1816), bequeathed his art collection and library to the university in 1816. The neo-classical building designed to house his bequest was not begun until 1837 and has since been greatly enlarged.

3. In 1762 the university acquired property from the Austin Friars for use as a botanical garden. In 1831 a much more spacious garden was planted farther from the center of town.

ious establishments. As it was however, our only conductor was "Boots"[4] & from this dignified character we received such information as he was able to give, & which by the way was almost equal to nothing at all.

He said that at times the students were very riotous & made a great deal of noise in the town, & it is probable for the sake of keeping them in at night that the Colleges are all built in the form of a hollow square, which certainly seems better calculated for the purpose than as they are built with us. Mr I[ves] intending to proceed on his journey towards Norwich in the afternoon, I resolved on accompanying him as far as Newmarket. I had never yet visited this famous sporting place & felt hardly willing to be so near & not to see what sort of a place it was. We took the coach at about ½ past 3 & as the distance is only 13 miles from Cambridge we were there shortly after. The road offers nothing remarkable & just on entering the town we passed on the left hand side the race course. The Coach drove to the "White Hart Inn" & after ordering dinner we hastened to tread upon the race ground, celebrated from time out of mind for the resort of rogues & royalty, peers & pickpockets. As far as I am a judge, there could not well be a finer place for a horse race. The course is 4 miles & called a "straight on,"[5] & I am very sorry that I have never improved some opportunity of being present at a run. The village of New Mkt.

---

4. A hotel servant, usually a young man, who cleaned boots and shoes and performed other menial jobs.

5. The track was linear rather than circular or elliptical, and ran over some gentle slopes. Wagers were laid at the settling house.

itself is really nothing at all, one short street & a population of only about 12 or 15 hundred inhabitants is all it can boast, & I presume it depends upon the races alone for its support. The settling house, where the "<u>business</u>" is transacted was directly opposite to our Inn. At 9 oclk in the Evening I took leave of Mr. I. & mounted the Coach to return to Cambridge. We shall in all probability not meet again on this side of the ocean if we ever do on the other & with these not very cheering reflections upon parting with an old friend, I was drove on at a rapid rate, 'til within 6 miles of C—when one of the heaviest rains I almost ever remember came pouring down. This roused me from my reverie, for Faith it was more like a deluge than anything else & I will venture to say, it never rained harder at Noah's flood than it did that night. About ½ past 11 I arrived dripping & wet to the skin & found a good Bed quite as <u>comfortable</u> at [*least?*] as anything I had met with during the day.

Wednesday Augt., 4th. Notwithstanding the disagreeable circumstances of the last night, I was up at 6 this morning & at 7 took the coach for Woburn. There is no seat in England which I have always wished to see more than Woburn Abbey the proud domaine of the noble house of Russell, perhaps the allusion to it by Junius in his letter to the Duke of Bedford, has served more than any thing to create this desire.[6] The most considerable town we passed thro' was Bedford, & arrived at Woburn at 2 PM.

---

6. A Cistercian abbey, founded in 1145, granted in 1547 to the Tudor courtier Lord John Russell, who was created earl of Bedford in 1550. The fifth earl,

The Village itself is small & has nothing particular to boast of, but the park, grounds & Abbey itself I found to be well worth coming 50 miles to see. The park which I believe is one of the most extensive in England being 12 miles in circumference is bounded on one side by the village, but the house stands back, very far removed from the road, & being "embowered in ancient Oaks & Elms" cannot be seen until you have intered the gates & walked at least ¾ of a mile. From its name "Woburn Abbey" I expected something very different from what I found it. I had figured to myself an ancient monastery of the gothic order, with its moss grown towers & grey with age. I almost thought I should hear the bell toll for vespers, & see the pious hooded monks coming out of their cells to offer up their evening orisons. But it was no such thing, for it has all been modernized & was nothing more or less than a large house built in the form of a hollow square, the grand front of which exhibited some taste in Grecian Architecture.[1] The house is only shewn on Mondays (much to

who had served under Cromwell, was made duke of Bedford after the Revolution of 1688.

Junius was the pseudonym of a political writer, probably Sir Philip Francis (1740–1818), who between 1769 and 1771 published a series of "letters" in *The Public Advertiser*. His attack on John Russell, fourth duke of Bedford (1710–1771), especially his letter of September 19, 1769, was considered a masterpiece of character assassination. JCB recalls the peroration: "Whither shall this unhappy old man retire?.... If he returns to Wooburn [*sic*], scorn and mockery await him. He must create a solitude round his estate, if he would avoid the face of reproach and derision." *The Letters of Junius*, John Cannon, ed. (Oxford, 1978), p. 124.

1. Woburn's wings, built principally in the eighteenth century, enclosed a courtyard that may have been the cloister of the vanished monastery.

my disappointment) so I could only see the outside of the edifice, but I looked in vain for anything ancient. The Abbey which formerly did stand upon this very spot, is almost entirely demolished & I was told by those I met in the park, that there is scarcely any part of it now remaining. The out buildings to this grand establishment are not only numerous but magnificent, & the stables of the noble Duke in point of solidity & elegance rivals any thing in the state of R.Id. The whole park is agreeably diversifyed with hill & dale, & studded all over with venerable trees. Directly in front of the house is a large running stream of water, which adds much to the prospect, & the Deer seemed almost innumerable, on no estate, not even excepting Blenheim were they any way so numerous. As the Weather was very fine, I passed a number of hours in wandering about this fine estate & in refreshing myself under those old Oaks which have shaded many a noble Russell. I passed thro the farming Establishment, but this department is not now kept up with so much spirit as in the time of the late Duke, who as is well known—besides being a great Wig politician was a practical farmer.[2] In the show house I saw the paintings of the "South Down Sheep" & in the Barn yard pigs of the "Bedford breed" but as I am not such a judge of swine as I presume my Brother F[*rancis*]. to be, will not venture an opin-

---

2. Francis Russell, fifth duke of Bedford (1765–1802), a notable agronomist who founded an agricultural society and developed a three-hundred-acre model farm for experimental crops and soil research. JCB would have known about the experimental farming of Charles Frederick Herreshoff (1763–1829), a cousin-in-law, in Bristol, Rhode Island, on land inherited from JCB's great-uncle, John Brown. See Introduction and p. 260, n. 3, below.

ion as to their qualities.[3] Thus much however they certainly had not that presbyterian <u>look</u> about them, as many pigs have that I have seen in R.Id.

Altho <u>my</u> expectations were not altogether realized at Woburn Abbey, yet no one I think could see such a princely estate, without admiring its beauties or take leave of it without at least hoping that he might see it again.

At 6 oclk: I took a seat in the inside of the coach for London. It was my wish to have crossed the County to Oxford & so on to the West, but it would have been attended with delay & I determined on the whole to go first to town. The road led thro Saint Albans, but as night fell & rain soon came on I know nothing of the country. The distance was about 45 Miles, & it was ½ past 11 oclk: when I was put down at the Angel Inn, Angel Street, Saint Martin le grand, where I took my bed for the night.[4]

Augt. 5th. Being determined to pursue my original plan of going into Cornwall, & that without delay, I took a seat in the Coach for Exeter, which left London at 3 PM. This route was thro' Salisbury

---

3. "Brother Francis" is an evident reference to John Brown Francis (1791–1864) who became JCB's brother-in-law in 1822 when he married Anne Carter Brown. Francis had earlier inherited farmlands from his grandfather, including a large tract in upstate New York and was, at the time of his marriage, trying to save a small farm community established there by his uncle, C. F. Herreshoff.

4. Of the many "Angel Inns" in London, this one, dating from the seventeenth century, was distinguished for its reputation as a smugglers' drop. Built on piles over the Thames, it had a balcony and trap doors for the surreptitious loading or unloading of contraband.

but as I have spoken of this place before, having a year ago travelled the same road, shall not again mention it. We supped at a little place called Basing Stoke & passing thro' Dorchester, breakfasted at Bridgport 15 miles beyond.[5] As we advanced further westward, the Country became much more hilly, & many fine views of the Coast & County of Devon presented themselves. At 3 oclk: we arrived at Exeter, where I stopped for the night. During the last night & also today, there was a good deal of rain & sometimes it came down merrily—but we are now getting into a county where we must expect wet weather. Exeter is the largest city in the West of England & contains something like 20,000 inhabitants. As to situation it has nothing at all to recommend it, & altogether is a dirty & ill built town, being situate upon the brow of a steep hill, 'tis very difficult to enter it from the Westward, & there is but one street that is at all passable. The Gothic Cathedral is the most striking object in this place, & this is truly a venerable pile; built however in the same stile with all other similar edifices & I could not perceive that there was any thing peculiar to this.[6]

Just a little back of the town, there is a very pleasant walk, shaded by old trees, & the prospect from it would be fine, were it not for a huge jail & Bridewell staring us directly in the face, & which it must be confessed are not very agreeable objects for the

---

5. A misspelling for Bridport, Dorset.

6. JCB did not see, or chose not to see, the decorative and structural differences between the "decorated Gothic" of Exeter Cathedral, mainly built in the early fourteenth century, and the style of Salisbury Cathedral, mainly built in the early thirteenth century.

mind to dwell upon.[7] The river Ex runs near the town & I saw vessels of perhaps 150 tons laying at the wharfs. Having no letters to detain me at Exeter, I took the coach the following morning for Plymouth at 7. The only considerable towns we passed thro' were Newton Bushel & Totness, which latter place is said to have the best Cattle market in the Kingdom Smithfield in London only excepted. We were highly favoured in the weather, having a bright sun shine all the way. This of course added much to the fine views which offered themselves continually from the lofty hills of Devonshire. The County every where looked rich & well improved, & from present appearances the crops must be very abundant. At about 2 PM, I was set down at the Devonshire Hotel (one of the greatest establishments I know of in England) in Devon port.

What Strangers generally understand by "Plymouth" is in fact 4 seperate towns. The oldest tho' not the most populous is the Borough of Plymouth; Stonehouse; & Devonport, each a mile apart. The two former stand at the head of Plymouth Sound & the latter the most westward upon the river Tamir. Devonport is the old Plymouth Dock, as it was formerly called, but in the course of time it has out grown either of the others. & the inhabitants determining not any longer to be considered an appendage to Plymouth assumed a more dignifyed name than that of "Dock." The village of Stoke to the northward of them all also forms a part & the population of the 4 is about 70,000. It was owing to my

---

7. "Bridewell" was a generic term for a prison, taken from the name of a London palace built by Henry VIII. It was used later as a school for apprentices, and still later as a house of correction.

ignorance of these divisions that I did not stop at the Borough but was permitted to be drove over to Devonport.[1]

After dining I walked over to the old town to deliver a letter of introduction from Mr Price of London to his Uncle Mr Hingham a Quaker who received me very politely & whose family contributed much to render my stay while at Plymouth pleasant & agreeable.

Sunday—was an exceedingly dull & unpleasant day, it raining nearly all the time. In the morning I stepped in to a Church of the Established order & heard service read. A sermon was delivered but it was quite as dull & stupid as the weather without. At 1 oclk: I dined by invitation with Mr H. & for the first time since I have been in Europe sat down to such a "Sunday dinner" as I have always been accustomed to at home. Mr H. always has a "picked up dinner" on Sundays.[2] How different is this from the customs in Paris & London, where their "grand Dinners" are more frequently given on Sundays than on any other day—of the week. In the Afternoon after Tea, I went with the family to Quaker meeting. The number of Friends in Falmouth are not numerous & today owing to the rain but few were present. It was all a dumb show till towards the last, one of the old ladies who sat on the

---

1. The conurbation JCB referred to, commonly called "the three towns," consisted of Plymouth on the east, Devonport on the west, and Stonehouse between them. It came under one authority in 1914 and was raised to the status of city in 1928.

2. A "picked-up" or, more commonly, a "pick-up" dinner was a buffet or self-service meal usually consisting of cold leftovers. It allowed servants to observe the Sabbath.

high seat arose & gave us a short disertation. The burthen of her song was, "Little children love one another."

Monday Augt. 9th The weather to day was perfectly fine, & I improve it to visit the delightful seat of the Earl of Mount Edgcumbe which lays on the Northwestern bank of Plymouth sound. The house is nothing remarkable & is not shewn but the magnificent views from various parts of the cliff always attract the traveller & have often roused the poetic muse of the first genius' of the age. Garrick & the late Lord Lyttleton are among the number who have eulogized its beauties.[3] The views from the "White seat" & from Redding Point are extensive & beautiful, but cannot be called grand & indeed altho I was much pleased with them, yet there are many others that I should think much more deserving of the praises, that have been lavished upon Mt Edgcumbe, for example, the view from the Alemeda on the Rock of Gibralter, & many others in the neighbourhood of Naples.[4]

Tuesday, I employed the morning to examine the "Plymouth Brakewater." The weather was rather hazy but this was of no consequence. I dont know that it would be called out of the way to

---

3. The castellated manor at Mount Edgcumbe was built in the 1540s, destroyed by bombs in 1941, and rebuilt, 1958–1960. In July, 1771, the actor, David Garrick, who called it "the Paradise of the West," was a house guest there along with George, first baron Lyttleton (1707–1773), a politician and patron of literature.

4. The "White Seat" and Redding Point afforded sweeping views of the sea. JCB preferred the Alameda Garden overlooking the Strait of Gibraltar which he had frequented during his layover at Gibraltar in May and June, 1822.

pronounce this "the greatest work of modern times after the Simplon.["] Excepting Buonapartes great road nothing that I have met with in all my travels can be ranked with it, & altho the aqueduct built by Charles of Naples on the road to Caserta & the works of Catwyke in Holland are stupendous undertakings, yet in my opinion they are far inferiour to the Breakwater.[5] The object of this is to form a safe anchorage in Plymouth sound by breaking the force of the waves which roll in from the channel (hence its name). It is formed of high rocks at first thrown loosely into the sea, 'til upon a level with low water mark & above that they are laid with more form & order. The whole length of the work is 850 fathoms. Its base is about 70 yards broad & Top 10 & as it is now finishing is 10 ft. above low water mark. tho' before the whole is completed it is supposed it will be raised still higher. Some of the rocks weigh 10 & 11 tons & when the length, breadth, & depth of the work is considered & the immense quantity of stone it will require, one can form some idea of the undertaking. The stone is got out of Quarries many miles distant & the labour & expense of removing the same must of course be very great.[6] The first estimate of the cost of the Breakwater was 1,170,000 £

---

5. The Plymouth Breakwater, stretching some 1,700 yards into Plymouth Sound was begun in 1812 and completed in 1840. JCB's bases of comparison were such other engineering marvels as: Napoleon's road through Simplon Pass in the Leopontine Alps of southern Switzerland, built 1800–1806; the aqueduct at Caserta (see above, entry for February 5, 1824); and the drainage canal at Katwijk, built in 1807 through a swampy tidewater to open the mouth of the Rhine to navigation.

6. The Oreston Quarries, east of Plymouth, supplied limestone for the break-water which had a final cost of some £1,580,000.

sterling but this sum will fall far short of completing the object. Ages to come this celebrated work will probably be looked upon with as much astonishment & as much admiration as similar works of the Romans at the present day. From the Breakwater I was rowed over to the East side of the Sound, to view the great resoirvoir & which is connected to a small Pier running out into the water for the still greater preservation of ships at anchor within. The resoirvoir itself is about ¾ of a mile distant back among the hills, & contains 13,000 tons of water, which is led by pipes down to the abovementioned pier. Here a Fleet of almost any size can water in a very short space of time, & without almost any inconvenience.[7] Thus the English with all their improvements, are continually commencing some new work for the ornament & utility to their little Island, & in whatever part of the country one travels in, he sees Canals, roads, bridges & a hundred other things going on to benefit the country. This has been the case particularly since the peace which seems to have given a new impulse to internal improvement.

At 3 Oclk: to day I dined with Mr H[*ingham*] & after spending the Evening at his house in agreeable company returned to my lodgings in a heavy shower of rain.

Wednesday 11th August. Being disappointed by not going on to day to Falmouth as was my original intention, I called towards

---

7. A stone reservoir supplied the naval base with water from the Dartmoor watershed, north of Plymouth. JCB estimated its capacity at over three million gallons. The pier with its water pipes was 1,500 feet long.

noon upon my friends in Plymouth & with young Mr H[*ingham*] took a walk to view the Quarries, from whence the stone is taken to build the Breakwater. To see what a large space of ground has been covered by the stone that has already been taken away & yet how large a portion of the Break water remains unfinished, must strike any one as much as anything with the magnitude of the work. I will only observe that their Quarries are of marble, some of which when polished is very fine; but it is in such vast quantities around Plymouth, that it is held in no higher estimation than common stone—& the sidewalks of the town, are flag'd with it. Altho the weather today was thick in the morning yet it clear'd off fine & was pleasant the remainder of the day. I dined again with Mr H. & in the Evening took my leave of this amiable family. Altho quakers they are by no means austere in their manners. Mrs. H. would any where be called a genteel woman, & I was so much pleased with the modesty & softness of manner added to the beauty & good sense of the pretty little Quakeress her daughter, that I should have been very well pleased to have prolonged my stay in Plymouth. But the time was fast advancing for me to turn my face towards the Western Continent & I with reluctance took my leave of a place where I had passed my time so agreeably. There are many object[*s*] in & about Plymouth, well worthy the attention of a traveller, most of these I examined. The Navy yard, in "dock" I did not visit as it is only <u>inferior</u> to that at Portsmouth which I had previously seen.[1] For the mouth of the Tamar & far

---

1. JCB missed an opportunity to inspect the Royal Navy's new Victualling Yard at Plymouth which was nearing completion. It would cover fourteen

above it, is filled with ships of war of every size laid up in ordinary & military Hospitals & Barracks & prisons are to be met with at every turn for this is one of the great depots of the Royal Navy—& other purposes of war. Upon the fortifications & ramparts, the inhabitants have, pleasant walks & fine views. The Hoe upon the cliff near the Borough, is another of these charming promenades which I have every where met with & every where admired in Europe.[2]

Thursday at 7 in the morning I left Plymouth for Falmouth. We crossed the Ferry in a boat & took the coach on the opposite side of the Tamer. The distance between the two towns is about 60 miles, & for such a length there is scarcely any part of N[*orth*] England so hilly as this part of Cornwall. I believe we had to put on the drag[3] at least 20 times, & the coachmen in England priding themselves so much on being "good whips" are not in the habit of doing this when it can any ways be avoided.

We travelled thro today the best part of the Country. Yet I could perceive a sensible difference between this & other parts of the Island. As we proceeded west the soil had a more barren appearance, & scattered mounds of earth shew that we were

---

acres and include warehouses, bakeries, slaughterhouses, a brewery, and a cooperage. The Naval Hospital, dating from 1762, covered twenty-four acres and could accommodate 1,200 patients.

2. Plymouth Hoe, a high ridge forming the town's sea front, was considered one of the finest promenades in England. It gave lookouts their first view of the Spanish Armada in 1588.

3. A weight attached to a vehicle to slow its motion.

entering a mining county. Among other places we passed thro Grampound, which until lately was a borough town & sent 2 members to parliament but has lately been disfranchised.[4] It is a most miserable place, containing only a few thached houses built of mud. Truro is 12 miles from Falmouth. 'Tis the most considerable town in Cornwall. We only changed horses there. Penryn is the last town 3 miles distant. It was extremely difficult to get in or to get out of it, & from what I saw from the top of the coach, nothing can be said in its favour. At 5 PM we were safely set down in Falmouth. With the exception of a smart rain for about 10 minutes it was as fine a day for travelling as could be expected in this part of England. About sun set I took a walk to Pendennis Castle 4 miles from the town, from whence is a commanding prospect of the surrounding country and the British Channel.[5]

Friday 13th It rained hard nearly the whole day which discouraged me from quitting comfortable quarters to "expatiate" in the open fields. I called & delivered my letter to the messrs Foxe's who are Quakers. They gave me every information respecting visiting the Fag End & also furnished me with letters to enable me to see the ruins near Redruth if I wished.[6]

---

4. Persistent charges of venality and electoral corruption in Grampound led to a parliamentary investigation after the elections of 1818. The borough, which had sent two members to the House of Commons since 1553, was disenfranchised in 1821.

5. Pendennis Castle is a sixteenth-century tower guarding the approaches to Falmouth Harbor. Its fall in 1646 to parliamentary forces ended the Civil War in Cornwall.

6. G. E. and R. W. Fox and Company were prominent merchants and ship-

At sun set it cleared up & then I took a full survey of Falmouth. This place derives it[s] [*notice*] from being the station of the H.M. foreign packets. It has a population of about 6000 & from what I could learn has no trade of any consequence. Falmouth stands upon the West side of a fine bay, which has all the appearances of a beautiful Lake, particularly on entering the town.

Pendennis Castle stands in a very elevated situation on a point of land & commands the harbour. It is now only garrisoned by some dozen soldiers, yet it is a very comfortable sinecure for some body or other as it has a governor & Lieut. Governor.

Saturday at 10 left Falmouth for Penzance by the coach not being able to procure a Gig as I wished. We rode thro a very barren & uninteresting county & passed thro only one considerable town Haliston[7]—for most part of way the British channel was in sight & at about 4 miles to the East of Penzance the Island had become so narrow that both the British & Bristol channels were in full view—passing the village of Marazion[8] or jew Market (as it was formerly called) the rode ran along the shore a short distance from the foot of Saint Michaels Mount, on the top of which is an

---

ping agents in Falmouth. Robert Were Fox (1789–1877) served as United States consul. The "Fag End" was JCB's term for Land's End. The "ruins" near Redruth included the remains of a prehistoric arena with a capacity of 2,000.

7. The town of Helston had been known by various names, among them, Henliston, Helleston, and Haliston.

8. Reputedly the oldest town in Cornwall, settled by Phoenicians bent on mining tin. The nearby hamlet was called "Market Jew," probably a corruption of "Marchas dyow," which means "market south."

old castle.[9] Early in the afternoon we arrived at Penzance & just as I entered the Inn & enquired for a conveyance to the Lands End, a well dressed gentlemanly man stepped up to me & observed that as he was upon the same expedition he should like to have the pleasure of joining me. As I was quite alone I had no objection to his company & after a hasty repast, we stepped into a post chaise & were drove to the little village of Senan. The face of the country appeared more & more dessolate as we proceeded, few or no trees after the first mile or two from Penzance, the few fields that were under cultivation bore but thin crops & the others were covered with stones. From Senan we walked nearly a mile & half to the very Lands End, & "I hastened to set my foot on the last rock of this proud Isle."[1] Longships light is not far from the land, situate on a small rock, & as the weather was clear, we saw the Silly Islands plainly.[2] The whole of the coast around Lands End, is very rugged & the cliffs very high, accordingly very dangerous. Lands End is 300 miles from London, but ere I took a final leave of this Fag End of all things—I could not view with uncon-

---

9. A miniature copy of Mont St. Michel in Normandy, this rocky islet with its chapel tower rises 250 feet above sea level. It was connected with Marazion by a natural causeway passable at low tide.

1. A granite promontory, rising sixty feet from sea level, Land's End is the westernmost extremity of England. JCB inexactly quotes Benjamin Silliman (*Journal*, ii, p. 187): "[I] hastened to place my foot on the last cliffs of this proud island." He also echoes Silliman's home thoughts from abroad and his anxiety about recrossing the ocean.

2. The lighthouse was built in 1090 on the largest islet of a small archipelago known as the "Long-ships," one and one-quarter miles offshore. The Scilly Islands lay some twenty-eight miles southwest of Land's End.

cern the stormy ocean which lay before me & upon which I soon
expected to embark to return to my friends after a long absence.
Retracing our steps to the little village, we refreshed ourselves at
[*a*] little Inn on the sign of which was written the "last Inn in
England" & on the side towards the Lands End "the first Inn
in England." We returned to Penzance by a road heading along
the southern Coast, which afforded an opportunity to view the
"Laggan rock" supposed to be about 300 tons weigh & which
until very lately could be moved by the shoulder with ease, so
exactly was it poized. But an officer of his majesty's [*p—t—i—?*]
service, having nothing better to do went with a party of men &
threw it over. This wanton piece of mischief, is of course justly
reprobated & 'tis said measures are in train to try to replace it,
but I very much doubt if they will be able to do it. The rock is situated in a dangerous place to get at, for in case of a misstep it
would be certainly destructive yet I, like a foolish, fellow as I generally am, could not be easy 'til I had climbed up to it.[3] It became
quite dark as soon as we resumed our seats when a violent breeze
caught us & it was past nine before we reached Penzance where
I passed the night. Considering we were in such a watery region,
we were much favored in the weather today, for from every thing
that I hear, a day scarcely passes but what it rains more or less. I
remember as we entered the British Channel in the good ship

---

3. The Logan Rock (Loggan Stone) was a sixty-ton, irregular mass of granite
freely poised on a small stone knob. Slight pressure could rock it three inches.
The young naval officer who in 1824 used levers to overthrow it was ordered
to put it back in place, a week-long operation requiring naval equipment and
a crew and burdening him with life-long indebtedness.

G.H.,[4] more than 2 years ago, every 10 minutes we had sunshine & showers. The Sailors called it "the Devils piss-pot."

Sunday 15 Augt I was out early this morning to take a look at Penzance, but the clouds were very thick & a drissling rain—I however promenaded the town which is second in Cornwall. Tis situated to the West & over Mounts Bay is furnished with a commodious pier & a light-house upon it. After breakfast I took leave of my friend, who was polite enough to give me his card & invited me to come & see him when I get to London. His residence is at West end, & from our short acquantance, I think him to be an intelligent man. The rain "came faster & faster" but as I had ordered my Gig I did not let this prevent my operations. As I repassed Saint Michaels Mount I stopped a few moments to observe it more particularly, but the fog was so dense that it would have been useless to have ascended it. At high water this mount is an island, at its foot are a number of habitations & at the castle on the top the family of Sir John Saint Aubyn sometimes spend a few weeks "to enjoy the "Sea breezes" & I suppose the fogs & rains, which I think could no where be met with to greater advantage.[5] 4 miles I stopped at the neat little village of Cranbourn Hale to water my horse. The tavern keepers name was Knap, &

---

4. The *General Hamilton*, a Brown and Ives merchant ship, carrying JCB as its supercargo, ran aground in the English Channel off the coast of Normandy in July 1822, while en route to St. Petersburg. See Introduction.

5. Sir John St. Aubyn (1758–1839), an amateur geologist with a large family. His forebears had bought Michaels' Mount in the seventeenth century.

sure enough he knaped me well.[6] I had an insuperably vile lunch but wen he brot in his bill, I found he was one of those landlords who are determined to make hay while the sun shines. I drove into Redruth at 2 PM. At 3 oclk: I walked to "<u>the church</u>"[7] which is about a mile from the house. There was a one eye'd parson in the desk, but he was one of those lifeless inanimate number of the established church, everywhere to be met with, & excepting the old chick, there was hardly any one present to his dull sermon. 'Twas literally preaching to empty boxes. At ¼ before 6 I looked into the Baptist Chapel opposite to the place where I was. Here was a man holding forth exactly in the same strain as the same sect in America. There was a numerous & judging from their dress, a respectable congregation present, & the singing was quite as bad as we have it in Providence. After this was over, I went to the Methodist Chapel which was crowded to over-flowing, so that it was a long time before I could make my way into the house. I suppose there were people enough standing without the door to have filled it the second time. I will here remark that the number of dissenters in this county are very great particularly Methodists & Quakers but the miners who of course are a large class & generally an orderly, religious people, belong most wholly to the Methodists & Baptist congregation.

---

6. "Knap" was early nineteenth-century slang for "rob" or "steal."

7. JCB observes the English distinction between "church" (Church of England) and "chapel" (sects such as the Methodists or Baptists).

Monday 16th. Was up & breakfasted at an early hour, & then proceeded on horseback to the "great Poldice Mine" which lays about 4 miles from Redruth the road leading thro' the little village of Saint Day. Owing to losing my way, I was later on the spot than I expected to have been. The Messr[s] Foxes had given me a line to Captain Magor,[8] one of the overseers, from whom I received every attention, & facility in examining the concern. "The Poldice Mine" tho' not <u>the</u> largest, is one of the largest in Cornwall. 'Tis worked both for copper & tin, & 13–1400 persons men, women & children are employed. It has the largest Engine probably in the World, of 900 horse power.[9] The process for preparing the copper ore for market is very short & simple, merely to separate the ore from the rock—but it requires a much longer time for tin & the various washings &c. &c. which it is necessary to undergo before it is fit for market, makes it a more tedious & of course a less profitable business. At 12 oclk I prepared myself to descend into the shades below, but I confess I debated a long time before making up my mind. Having come into Cornwall more particularly to view the mining districts, I felt unwilling to go away without seeing something below the surface.

After stripping myself of all my own clothing I put on the miners dress, which consisted of a shirt & trousers of coarse blanketing, & over this a pair of old duck trousers & a coat very

---

8. "Captain" was the customary title given one who supervised mining operations. Silliman (*Journal*, II, p. 176) mentions meeting Mr. Magor, a manager of the mines.

9. The great steam engine at the Poldice mine was used for pumping.

much resembling a sailors monkey jacket. A clean white night cap was drawn over my head which was crowned by a hat much like a barbers bason, made thick & stiff, to protect the head from the rocks. An old pair of shoes were tied to my feet, thus equipped, carrying a lighted candle in my left hand which was stuck in a lump of clay & another hung to my button hole, I commenced the arduous task. My two guides were careful, & intelligent men, & directed me how to act, but in cases of this kind, everything relating to your own safety mostly depends on yourself. We descended more than 100 fathoms, or about 600 feet from the level of the Earth in a perpendicular direction. We explored various parts of the mine & saw the miners at work, some drilling & others picking out the ore with axes. The rock is so hard that it is necessary to blast or blow it, otherwise it would be impossible to make much progress. We heard frequent explosions which blow, & the clouds of smoke that found its vent thro' the various stratas we explored was almost suffocating. The miners notwithstanding the deplorable occupation as it seems to us in which they are engaged, appear to be in general a contented race of labourers. I conversed with them all & found them civil & obliging. As I had seen the whole oeconomy of mining at the depth above mentioned it would have been quite useless to have fatigued & worried myself in going any further. So I ascended forthwith by the same shaft at which I had descended. This opperation was vastly more fatiguing than the first—& long before I saw daylight I was completely exhausted, but there was no other alternative but to persevere 'til finally I reached the mouth of this almost infernal region in safety & thanked God, that he had preserved us thro' so many dangers.

Now it is finished I feel highly gratifyed that I indulged my curiosity. Tho' I am aware it would not be called a laudible [*impulse*], when it is necessary to run such risks to satisfy it. I am certain I would never attempt the like again, & would dissuade any friend from doing the same. Many parts of the mine was like an oven, & this added to my great exertions, kept me during the whole time in a high state of persperation, so that while undressing I found a few stiff glasses of <u>eau de vie</u> were very salutary in restoring exhausted nature. After having resumed my original dress & remunerated my guides, I bid adieu to my worthy friend Captain Magor, who had been so particularly attentive to me, & mounted my horse & returned to Redruth. The descent occupied nearly 4 hours, so that by this time it was quite late in the afternoon. After dining I felt too much fatigued to set out again, & went early to bed.

Tuesday Augt. 17. I yesterday brought away a few specimens of the Copper ore & this morning purchased a few others in Redruth.

As I found I could gain no further benefit by remaining longer in the mining districts, I took a Gig to Falmouth, altho it rained & the fog was so thick you could scarcely see your hand before you. The distance is [*blank*] miles & the road as hilly as any other part of Cornwall. Nothing presented itself worthy of notice. Breakfasting at Falmouth, I called about noon to pay my respects to the Gentlemen. to whom I had been introduced.

They were just going to leave town with their "families," & of course I could not expect any civilities, & as I had made myself acquainted with the local situation of Falmouth (which is all that can detain a stranger) determined to take the Royal mail at 2 PM for Exeter. As far as Truro it was the same road I had travelled coming from Plymouth passing the 4th time thro the disagreeable town of Penryn. I had no letters to Truro & so did not stop, for the town can be seen much better from the top of a coach, than walking thro' its streets. We were now upon the great Western road, & passed thro' the vile little Borough of Saint Michaels which is only a few mud cottages & sends two members to Parliament.[1] Bodmin was the next town of any importance containing about 2000 inhabitants. The country looked very dessolate & seemed to grow more so as we approached Launceston the frontier town of Cornwall. We supped here at 10. The wind blew fresh, & made it very uncomfortable travelling over the dreary downs. The sea was often in sight & there was no wood country or anything to protect us from the blasts. ½ an hour before reaching L[aunceston], by way of change, or for sake of variety—it began to rain & the floods fell in torrents. The coach was full inside so I was forced to sit & take it. From Launceston to Exeter we did not stop excepting to change horses, & as an example of the changeable climate of England, the rain and wind did not last more than ¾ of an hour. The moon shone out bright & it proved a most delightful evening for travelling. At ½ past 4 we were at

---

1. A "rotten borough" which was one of fifty-six that were disenfranchised in 1832.

Exeter [*blank*] miles from Falmouth. I was but little fatigued with my journey, & having no object in passing any longer time than I had already done in this place resolved to proceed immediately on to Bath, especially as the weather promised to be very fine. So at 6 I resumed my seat on top of the Royal mail. We were now in a very different country from that just passed thro', rich in itself & highly cultivated, indeed, the whole road from Exeter to Bath it is like riding thro' a garden. Taunton, Bridgwater, & Wells are the towns of the most importance on this route. At ¼ before 5 I was set down in this fashionable watering place. During all the time that I have been in England I never witnessed the climate quite so variable as today. One moment it would be mild & the sun out bright, & then in a few moments after, the sky would be clouded, & the winds & rain seemed as if they were trying which could beat the hardest. When these elements got to work I sheltered myself in the inside of the coach.

Thursday Augt. 19th. I spent in Bath to recruit a little after my laborious adventures in Cornwall & long journey from Falmouth —& the warm spring Baths conduced not a little to restore exhausted nature. At this season of the year Bath is always dull, & it was more particularly so to me as I had not acquaintances & no travelling companion. Withal the day was gloomy. I could see but little improvement in the place from the last year, & I believe that Bath is not generally considered to [*be*] so flourishing as many other Towns in the interiour of England. The celebrated Mr Beckford had commenced his projected improvements in the rear of Lansdown Cresent. From all that I have heard of this character, he must certainly be a most singular genius.[2] I having concluded not to extend my journey any further than Bath, shall return to town tomorrow.

Friday 20th Augt. Was off in the coach at ½ past 5 oclk: & arrived in London at 4 PM to dinner a distance of 108 miles—such is the rapidity of travelling in England. We breakfasted at Marlborough with an allowance of 20 minutes & passed thro' Newbury, Reading, Maidenhead & a number of other small towns. The road all the way was very delightful & studded with a great number of gentlemens seats & finely cultivated farms—the most considerable of which was that of the Earl of Aylesbury.[3] Near Newbury was fought the celebrated battle of that name in the time of Charles 1st[4] For miles after leaving Bath the Country was rather mountainous & the scenery picturesque but as we drew near the town, it became much more level.

---

2. After selling Fonthill in 1822, William Beckford retired to Lansdowne Terrace in Bath where he assembled his favorite books, paintings, and curios. See entry for August 27, 1823.

3. Charles, earl of Ailesbury (1773–1865), had a large estate at Tottenham Park. William Cobbett (*Rural Rides*, November 6, 1821) called it "extensive and uncommonly ugly" and complained that the earl "seems to have tacked park on to park, like so many outworks of a fortified city. I suppose here are 50 or 100 farms of former days swallowed up."

4. Two battles were fought at Newbury during the Civil War, one on September 20, 1643, the other on October 27, 1644.

[Editorial note: Three blank pages are followed by JCB's notes recording distances from Bremen to Oldenburg and successive stopping points en route to Amsterdam. Two more blank pages are followed by an entry noting JCB's arrival in Bremen and appending a list of inns and hotels where he visited on his tour of the West Country.]

From Bremen to Oldenburg— 25 Miles
" [*Oldenburg*] to Leer—27"
" [*Leer to*] Nieuweschans—15"
" [*Nieuweschans to*] Gronningen—45"
" [*Gronningen to*] Lemmer—60"
" [*Lemmer to*] Amsterdam—70"
 cross the Zuyderzee

[*Two blank pages.*]

Arrived in Bremen 30th June at 1 PM. having: left Hamburg the following day at 4 PM—

At Cambridge—"The Sun" a pretty good house & not dear.

"Newmarket"—"The White Hart" only dined here,—reasonable

Woburn—"Bedford Arms" passable for a Country Inn

Exeter—"New London Inn" a great Establishment & tolerable—

Plymouth, or rather Devonport, "Devenport Hotel" a great Establishment very good house, good attendance & very reasonable in charges—

Falmouth, "Pearce's Hotel" a very good house & very reasonable—

Penzance,—Hotel, kept by the brother of the Falmouth Pearce, but by no means so good a house.

Lands End—"Last Inn in England," partly a pot house, but tolerable for Fag End.

Redruth—Hotel" a very decent house—

Bath,. "York House" a noisy place, & most exorbitant, in charges —(avoid such an Inn.)

EPILOGUE

"Voyaging"

REMARKS BY J. CARTER BROWN
BROWN UNIVERSITY CONVOCATION
November 14, 1996

I FEEL particularly privileged to have been roped in by Vartan Gregorian, the most undisobeyable of University presidents, and asked to speak today on this festive occasion.

I hope you will forgive me if my viewpoint this afternoon is that of a member of a family, one that has had a deep interest in the Library that we celebrate today, as well as in other libraries in this town and in this University.

Underlying so many of the anniversary presentations of the past two months has been a common theme that goes to the heart of this Library's history and its relationship to the family that created it, and that is the concept of voyaging. Exploration, both geographical and intellectual, underlies its origins and its significance.

A grant from the National Endowment for the Humanities has made possible the archival ordering of the Brown family papers currently housed at the JCB Library, at the Rhode Island Historical Society, and at the family house at 357 Benefit Street, now the John Nicholas Brown Center for the Study of American Civilization, a recent gift to the University.

Some of this material yielded the landmark, two-volume study by the late professor James B. Hedges at Brown, but his work was cut short by his death, and much additional documentation will be made accessible to scholars as a result of the NEH grant, when the archive project reaches completion in June of 1997.

Voyaging. It begins with Chad Browne, who with his wife and his eight-year-old son John set out across the Atlantic in 1638 and went on to the experimental colony founded just two years before by Roger Williams.

The family's involvement with books and documents has been closely tied up with maritime voyaging from early on. We know from a description of 1719 in the flyleaf of a book of nautical problems that Chad Browne's descendent, the second James Brown, was learning how to go to sea in his early twenties. In 1750, John Carter Brown's grandfather, the first Nicholas Brown, of the famous surviving four brothers (Nicky, Josey, Johnny, and Mosey), inherited the pilot book of his elder brother James (the third of that name) "describing The West India Navigation, from Hudson's-Bay to the River Amazones." An inscription in the flyleaf records Captain James Brown's death while on a voyage, at "York in Virginy." He was 26.

As to intellectual voyaging through books, the JCB Library has family-owned books inscribed in 1740 and 1749. Nicholas (the first of four of that name, to make matters confusing), began buying books about the New World at auction as early as 1769, and as the JCB's first full-time librarian, George Parker Winship, records, since that date "there have been few years during which purchases were not made at book-auctions for the Brown family library, and scarcely one in which the library records do not show that some addition was made to the collection."

Meanwhile, this University's commitment to intellectual voyaging was a subject of continuing interest to a family that had donated the land and raised the funds for the College Edifice, and staged a lottery to build the first Baptist meeting house to double as "a place to hold Commencement in." One of the four brothers, Joseph, the architect of that great building, joined the University faculty as a professor of science, then called natural philosophy.

Joseph's elder brother, the first Nicholas, died in 1791. His son, Nicholas Brown II, was one of the fifteen members of the class of 1786, and a classmate of Benjamin Carter, the brother of Ann Carter, the girl Nicholas II married. Ann Carter Brown and her brother Benjamin were children of John Carter Brown's other grandfather, John Carter, who had studied printing with Benjamin Franklin in Philadelphia, and had come to Providence to take over from William Goddard the influential *Providence Gazette*. Benjamin, entering the College at the age of eleven, got early grounding in Latin and Greek, and went on to take a degree in what is now the University of Pennsylvania Medical School. He knew at a young age, in addition, French, German, and Dutch. When he first arrived in Canton on a family ship, he undertook to learn Chinese with the Jesuit author of a Chinese-Latin dictionary, now in the Brown University Library, inscribed admiringly by his nephew John Carter Brown. Benjamin went on to study Hebrew, Syriac, Persian, Hindustani, and Armenian. He made a succession of various voyages on the family ships (on one of which were discovered and accurately located some of the Fiji Islands; on another, he managed to visit the universities of Leiden and Utrecht). Subsequently he spent eleven years in

England at Cambridge and the hospitals of London, corresponding with the president of the Royal Society, Sir Joseph Banks, the botanist of Cook's voyages, Sir Ashley Cooper, and other intellectuals of the day.

It was handy to have a doctor as a brother-in-law when a new family ship was being dispatched to China. Nicholas Brown II's sister, Hope, had married the talented Thomas Poynton Ives (from whom the Goddards and Gammels, so loyal to this University, descend), and Nicholas and Thomas became partners in business, naming a new Providence-built ship the *Ann and Hope*, after their respective wives, Ann Carter Brown and Hope Brown Ives. The *Ann and Hope* probably took Dr. Carter along for good business reasons, to help keep down losses in the crew from disease. However, his journal reflects an intellectual curiosity about everything he saw.

His detailed observations at and near Botany Bay on the *Ann and Hope*'s maiden voyage in 1798–99 make fascinating reading (after one wades through rather monotonous days at sea), particularly the description of an all-day fight between two groups representing Botany Bay and Sydney. When they had thrown all their spears, one side would have their spears generously returned to them by the opposing side. Spears were dodged with notable alacrity, but would occasionally pierce through various parts of the participants' anatomies. "On this," he writes: "the women set up a dismal yell like the howlings of the infernal spirits, & beat their sides with great violence." The stoic heroism displayed was prodigious, and Dr. Carter is reminded of descriptions in Homer, which he quotes from the original Greek. At sunset there is a victory celebration, with no explanation attainable as to what was really going on. (Sounds like the gang warfare portrayed in the recent film "Romeo and Juliet" or was it to the Aboriginals more like a college football afternoon?)

The same Nicholas Brown II who was gambling on the risky China trade had been appointed a trustee of the College at age twenty-two, in 1791, the year his father died. He succeeded his uncle John as treasurer five years later, and would have been aware of the unsuccessful attempt to raise $6,000 in 1795, the year before he took office, despite the offering of a "naming opportunity" to a donor coming forward within a year.

His uncle John died in 1803, and had expressed a hope that the University would establish a professorship in English. Meanwhile, that year the trustees in some desperation re-offered the opportunity to name the College to anyone giving $5,000, which was the amount Nicholas II had donated that year to endow a professorship in English and Belles Lettres. The oral tradition in the family is that Nicholas II had asked that the University not change its name to his, but at their annual meeting in the fall of 1804, they named it for the family anyway. (The University archives furnish only the most minimal record of what actually transpired. They do contain a document that could offer one possible source of the confusion: an elegant letter from John Carter Brown turning down an honorary doctor of laws degree on the grounds that he was not sufficiently versed in jurisprudence; but the University conferred it on him anyway.)

In any case, adopting the family name turned out to be one of the wiliest fund-raising gambits this University ever made, in that Nicholas went on to increase his giving over his lifetime some thirty-two times, donating, among other gifts, Manning Hall for the college library, and a $10,000 book acquisition fund. (If before the days of tax deductions, an endowed chair might be considered to be the equivalent of two million present dollars, thirty-two times that would have made for a significant piece of philanthropy, even by the standards of Vartan Gregorian.)

From a library point of view, it is interesting also to note that this second Nicholas, together with other family members, were founders of the Providence Athenaeum in 1836, building on the collection of the Providence Library Company of 1753.

Nicholas II and Ann Carter Brown had three children, the eldest of whom was also called Nicholas, the third in succession. He graduated from Brown in the class of 1811, and was an avid book collector. Nicholas III's interest in voyaging found him largely in Europe. Many of his books were of American interest, and when he moved to Rome to become U.S. Consul, he sold his collection to his younger brother.

The year was 1846, and the brother was John Carter Brown, named in honor of his mother's distinguished father, from whom, one might surmise, he inherited an interest in the printed word.

This is the watershed date that we have chosen to commemorate this fall. It should be said that John Carter Brown, class of 1816, was fascinated by travel and history from his undergraduate days here, and his early book buying already showed an interest in books relating to New England. John Carter Brown bought his first rare book in his twelfth year.

His own unpublished diary of a voyage taken between the ages of 25 and 27 (1822–1824) has recently been transcribed as part of the family archives project, and its significance is currently under study by the brilliant Brown historian, Professor Donald Rohr. We know from his letters that he was sent by the family business on a merchant ship, the *General Hamilton*, to Gibraltar to buy Spanish dollars with tobacco, for trade in St. Petersburg, when the ship was wrecked on its way north. The young John Carter Brown found himself stranded on a beach south of Boulogne, France, without any papers clearing the ship for this unexpected stop. Taken over by French soldiers and housed in what he calls "a filthy hovel a few rods from the beach," they were charged with illegally importing silver and were ordered to surrender it. After protracted negotiations, appealing to the restored Bourbon Regime via the American minister to the court of Louis XVIII, Albert Gallatin, JCB was finally able to salvage the bullion after paying a healthy duty.

The commercial voyage soon changed to a cultural one, however, when he was granted permission by the family to remain in Europe for some R & R after the traumatic events of the summer. And so he spends the next five months in Paris, enjoying life with the banking family with whom he connected via the banker's wife, the former Martha Redwood of Newport, R.I.—another good library name. While in Paris, he went to the theater, the opera and ballet, and toured the cathedrals around Paris, and then began his diary as he crossed to England in March of 1823 and traveled to Scotland, Ireland, and Wales, returning to France, to the Rhône valley and then to Marseilles. From there he sailed to Naples and spent the winter and spring of 1824 in Italy, traveling through Rome and Florence to Venice, ending up that final summer in the ports of northern Germany and the west country of England. The diaries show that rather than spending time checking out business contacts, his passion was for the churches, historic houses and castles, art collections, and performing arts centers that would appeal to the traditional north European on the Grand Tour—a subject of much scholarly interest in recent years.

Touring was arduous in those days, but his interest in history shines through the diaries, as in his notation after visiting Glamis in Scotland (a name familiar from *Macbeth* and also its current occupant, the Countess of Strathmore who maintains a keen interest in American history):

> In the long hall are to be seen a great number of family portraits. I don't know how it is, but whenever I'm in one of these famous old establishments, I take more pleasure and satisfaction in viewing the portraits of a long line of illustrious ancestors than in any other paintings.

In the 1830s, John Carter Brown had become aware of the work of a Frenchman, Henri Ternaux, who had been collecting, and publishing a bibliography of Americana, and who had brought out a series of nineteen volumes of "Voyages, Relations, Mémoires" relative to the "découverte de l'Amérique." (It was still okay for a European to use "discovery" rather than "encounter.") In 1841 , JCB's father, Nicholas Brown, died, and his control over the family resources must have taken a quantum jump. By the end of 1846, JCB had bought not only his brother's library, but a large part of the Ternaux collection. With the help of the colorful Green Mountain Boy Vermonter, Henry Stevens, who stationed himself in London to scout for Americana for JCB and his arch-rival James Lenox, JCB began from that point on to focus his collecting interests specifically on books relating to the Western Hemisphere. He was prodigiously generous in lending his books to those who wished to pursue scholarly interests based on them, and 1846 has become the traditional starting date for the history of the John Carter Brown Library as a focused scholarly resource.

Another turning point came with another death: that of his elder brother, the third Nicholas Brown. Shortly thereafter JCB, at sixty-two, was married, for the first time, to a woman named Sophia Augusta Brown (no relation) of New Providence (Nassau) who was both interested in books and, at thirty-four, well able to have children.

No longer would the collection be housed in the upstairs hallway at 357 Benefit Street (later to carry the load of my mother's book collection, the Anne S. K. Brown Military Collection now at the John Hay). The leading New York architect, Richard Upjohn, was commissioned to build a modern, fireproof addition to the house to accommodate the library, which benefited greatly from the scholarly acumen of the polymath, John Russell Bartlett.

Although books flooded in on their own from alert dealers at home and abroad, voyaging did not cease as the couple brought up their young offspring. The unpublished diaries of their eldest son, John Nicholas Brown, and subsequently, of his wife, Natalie, and their son, John Nicholas Brown II, bear witness to the voyaging spirit that had become an ineluctable family tradition.

John Carter Brown died in 1874, leaving in his will funds for a new, state-of-the-art building for the University library, Robinson Hall. (In 1910 the University's library was moved to the John Hay Building, occupying land that had been given by the second Nicholas Brown for a president's house.) JCB bequeathed his library to his widow, maintaining its separate and private existence, albeit accessible to qualified researchers.

JCB had died on the 10th of June, and by mid-October of 1874, his widow bundled the three children—John Nicholas, thirteen; Harold, eleven; and seven-year-old Sophie (Noreen Drexel's and Eileen Slocum's grandmother)—to Europe, for a voyage of just under two years. Young John kept a succession of diaries, and luckily his handwriting is quite legible. Leaving from New York (where John visits the Metropolitan Museum on 14th Street), they travel to London and Paris, where John is taken to the Louvre, the Bibliothèque nationale (requesting the Mazarin Bible on vellum), and various churches. ("We went to the Madeleine. The church has no side chapels, but is extremely beautiful"). The winter was spent in Cannes, and visiting Nice, Monaco, Monte Carlo, Genoa, Bologna, and Milan. John's diary records in great detail what they saw at the Biblioteca Ambrosiana, including a unique Columbus letter in Spanish, a Virgil with notes by Petrarch, and letters and drawings by Leonardo and Galileo.

In the spring they go north, to Switzerland and then to Germany. He was excited to see the first Gutenberg Bible. In summer they swing through the Hague and Brussels, visiting the Royal Libraries in both cities, and return to Paris. ("In the morning I went with Mamma to the Ministry of the Interior to get the catalogue of Papa's Library.") From there it was back to Nice for the winter. John's diary reads: "We had school from 9:45 a.m. until about 12½: then M. Surleau, Harold and myself went to walk. We climbed up the mountains, returning at 1:30. We had dinner at two, and school from 3:30 to 5:30 p.m."

The second spring, 1876 (John Nicholas I is now 14), they proceed via Paris to England, visiting the Bodleian Library, where John admires Miles Coverdale's English Bible of 1535 and other historical documents, and visit the University library. On their return in September of 1876, they are met by John Russell Bartlett and Moses Brown Ives Goddard.

The family would spend a scant eighteen months in Rhode Island before voyaging once again, this time for a year and a half in Europe, beginning in April, 1878, John now aged sixteen and seventeen. The family visits churches and museums in England, including Canterbury Cathedral, and then to Paris, where he was disappointed in the Salon—too many nude women. (A few years later he was buying Monet and Pissarro, well in advance of French official taste. "I think," he is later to write his cousin, "that *old* books and *new* pictures are weaknesses of mine.")

They then tour France—Bordeaux, Carcassonne, Nîmes, Lyons, Voltaire's residence at Ferney, and on to Switzerland, Italy, and Austria. (On September 17, he saw the emperor, who was smoking a cigar. "He is not very good looking…. It struck me that he looked rather troubled, as well he may at the way affairs are going in Bosnia….") He saw the Imperial Treasury with Charlemagne's regalia (not knowing that six decades later, at the end of World War II, his son John Nicholas II would be returning it to that spot from a cave in Nuremberg). He saw the paintings of the princes of Liechtenstein (not knowing his grandson would be helping bring their Leonardo painting permanently to America), and from Trieste he went to Venice, where he was particularly impressed by the Byzantine art in St. Mark's (not knowing his son JNB would later be president of the Byzantine Institute, and his name inscribed in the treasure room of St. Mark's as a donor to the basilica's restoration). Then via Milan, Bologna, and Florence, he returns to France and England, for Cambridge, Oxford, Stratford, and Warwick Castle.

After his return to Providence, he is at Brown University, with summer trips out West to inspect family-owned properties or to summer camp in the Adirondacks.

A third European diary has him there for another year and a half in 1883 and 1884, aged twenty-two and twenty-three. In London he records visits to booksellers in quest of early Americana, and they proceed from France to Germany to Switzerland to Prague to Dresden, where the family resides while John proceeds to Berlin, where, as he writes his cousin and closest friend, Desmond Fitzgerald, he is residing in

> the bosom of a German family,—where at all hours of the day (*zu jeder tageszeit* [sic]) I endeavor to fire off correct sentences and sentiments in the Teutonic tongue.... My thoughts are constantly wandering across the mighty deep to the dear old home at 357 Benefit Street, where at this moment I should like to be.... I look with anxiety at the result of the November elections. Will not the next President be a Democrat?

The next summer, after more travels, including Copenhagen and Hamburg, they go to England, where he visits the Library of the Earl of Spencer, located at the childhood home of Princess Diana. He marvels at the 50,000 volumes, including "57 Caxtons" and lists in great bibliographic detail some of the treasures he is shown.

The last European diary we have is for the summer of 1887, where, at twenty-five, he writes to his cousin Desmond Fitzgerald from Paris:

> As usual I am after the old booksellers, and if you could have looked in on me for a half an hour this afternoon, you would have seen me in a dingy room, in a back courtyard, leading from a narrow street, jabbering French at the top of my voice about books to an old and not very clean party with long hair, said party being a great authority on early French typography.

The archives at the JNB Center reveal that John Nicholas Brown I's wife, Natalie, a Newport girl whom he meets in Paris where she is studying art, picks up the same pattern after her husband's untimely death in 1900, at age thirty-eight, ten weeks to the day after the birth of his only son (my father), John Nicholas Brown II. (Harold, who had come back from Europe to be at his brother's bedside, died one week later.) The cause of death is hard to pinpoint in those pre-antibiotic days, but it stemmed probably from an influenza he caught dedicating another library—the Providence Public Library—whose building he had made possible.

But the voyaging did not stop. When my father was just eight, his mother records a trip from the south of France through Pisa and Rome, taking young John to see the art in the Borgia Apartments, and elsewhere in the Vatican; visiting the Palazzo Doria Pamphili to see the Velasquez Innocent x [a painting that finally made it to this country for a visit to the National Gallery just this year]; and motoring out to Tivoli, and on to Orvieto, Perugia, Assisi, Siena, and Florence.

The following summer Natalie and son John are off on another European tour, sailing on the *Lusitania* to London, then Paris, Rheims, for the cathedral, Koburg, Mainz, Wiesbaden, Bad Homburg, Frankfurt, Darmstadt, Heidelberg, Baden-Baden, Strasbourg, and then Dijon, Avalon, Bourges, Tours, Amboise, ending up at her sister's château in Normandy, and back via Versailles and Paris—a motor trip of a little over two months and 6,000 kilometers. In 1914 they leave to spend the winter out West, visiting the Grand Canyon and California, returning via Yosemite, Salt Lake, and Colorado Springs. It seems to have been enough of a success that the next winter, they also went West, after spending Christmas in the backwoods of North Carolina with Natalie's sister Edith and JNB's uncle George Vanderbilt at Biltmore, roughing it in the largest house in America. From there, they travel through Louisiana to San Antonio, and via Tucson to Pasadena. And then, in the summer of 1919, they crossed Canada in a private railroad car and boarded the *Empress of Asia* for the 12-day passage to Yokohama and three months in Japan.

Here we have both the mother and the son's diaries, quite detailed. Travel was not easy there in those days, but their instructions to their guide was to show them "Japan off the beaten track," and the sheer exoticism of it, in addition to the beauty of the landscape, art, and architecture, they found overwhelming. They also experienced regulation, "handbags examined (firearms and tobacco tabooed)." JNB II writes,

> Japan is most fascinating—and absolutely different from anything I've ever seen before . . . nearly everyone wears a flowing kimono, men and women, very open in the front. Every woman from eight years upwards seems to have a baby attached to her back.

He was meticulous in recording the name of every artist and temple. Adjusting to rickshaw travel (and the "wide-eyed, open-mouthed curiosity" with which this six-foot-six Westerner is greeted at every turn), their favorite conveyance was sampan, down the Hodzu rapids, or at Uji, where they catch a fireworks competition. As dusk fell, JNB described

> a scene of the utmost enchantment, . . . every boat nearly had a lantern, and lanterns swung merrily all along the shore, sounds of strange music and merry laughter filled the air, interrupted now and then by the burst of a sky rocket, and the unfailing answering 'A-a-a-h-h-.' On the islands, men like ghosts, some with lighted punk, others with lanterns ran hither and thither, arranging the great set pieces, by far the most marvelous I have ever seen. There were ten great displays in all. Perhaps the finest, though it was hard to judge, was an immense representation of a waterfall, stretching some 400 feet the whole length of the island and not only showering down into the swiftly flowing water a mass of gold-dust, but sending up into the air a wealth of bombs and rockets. The bridge across the river was lit up in a long-standing blaze that represented the Great Wall of China, and after it died away Chinese characters burning blue, red, and white, appeared meaning, so Nishi explained, 'Uji, August 1, fireworks.' To me it meant everything weird and old and magical. . . .

Three years later, after JNB has graduated from Harvard and begins his graduate study of Spanish Romanesque sculpture *in situ* in Spain, his mother joins him for a Nile River cruise in the beginning of 1923 . Her entry for Wednesday, January 24:

Luxor Valley of the Kings. We started off in our felucca about 9:15 rowed by four sailors to the Western Bank of the Nile, where two carriages awaited us. They and the two pair of horses had been taken across the river earlier in a sailing felucca, two donkeys for our servants and two more for the men who carried huge baskets with provisions for our lunch. And two huge dromedaries with armed policemen on them completed our caravan. The horses had difficulty in pulling us through.... After an hour we reached the narrow gorge which the kings of Egypt had chosen for their burial place. We were glad to leave the shabby, rickety carriage with their ill-matched horses...which had to be helped over difficult places by the runner who ran along beside the carriage for the purpose of pushing it uphill. A small crowd was collected about an opening in the ground and we naturally joined them.... There before us was a short flight of steps leading to a massive doorway, and beyond was darkness and the tomb of Tutankhamen. On a stone above and to the left of the door has been (roughly) carved the coronet and initials of Lord Carnarvon, the head of this particular expedition, the director being Howard Carter....

We waited, hardly daring to hope that any of the treasures would be brought out today. The sun baked down relentlessly upon our heads, and every once in a while we had to seek relief in the shadows of an adjoining tomb of Ramses VI. When there seemed to be a stir among the expectant crowd, I hastened with my camera all set and there slowly, reverently, the excavators and their Nubian assistants brought forth from the tomb of their King Tutankhamen a full-sized couch of gilded wood and carved. It was partly concealed by its wrappings of cotton-wool, but as it was set down and the coverings changed we had a chance to see it....

This thrill was hardly over, when there was another murmur of anticipation and we all once more crowded about the opening—there was a sight to satisfy the most eager. Emerging from the dark doorway was Mr. Carter and three others carrying a huge but attenuated figure of the cow sacred to the goddess Horthor with the sun disk between its horns and its tail curled over its back, its feet close together. As it advanced, the cow had almost a startled look, as though it realized that it had been aroused from its vigil in the outer chamber of the tomb of the king, a vigil which had lasted 3,500 years, and here in this 20th century it was to see the light of day.

Professor Breasted told us in Cairo that the treasures were beyond description beautiful, far ahead of any he had found. He had worked there for days deciphering the seals and cartouche, before they were removed from the door. The cow was the last thing taken out that day and it being 1:00 we were glad to partake of the excellent and well-served luncheon, which Mahmud had provided, and set out in the entrance of Tomb 10, King Amenmeses. It was very hot and very dusty. I never thought of having a picnic lunch in the tomb of the king.

The greatest of the twentieth-century voyages must have been the one in the summer of 1929, when my father chartered the *Iolanda*, a yacht which at 310 feet was five feet longer than J. P. Morgan's *Corsair* and comfortably staffed with fifty-five in the crew. On the day Mrs. Brown notes the *Corsair* had come into

Athens Harbor, she also records that she had visited the museum again, but "John of course was absorbed every day with his studies." Having talked Harvard into offering a concentration on the influence of Classical culture on the Middle Ages (I always envied the way he could read Latin and Greek off the page as if it had been written in English), he had returned to Harvard for further graduate work, and on this cruise was pursuing not only Classical but Byzantine monuments. Visiting the monasteries of Mount Athos in the company of Thomas Whittemore, who had arranged for Charles R. Crane to send the monks a barge full of necessities, they were received on the analogy of Christ's entry into Jerusalem, with palm fronds strewn in the streets and all church bells ringing. At the end of that summer JNB cabled back to his office at 50 South Main Street, Providence, to sell off everything and retrench into Government bonds. This was weeks in advance of "Black Friday," 1929. But the office disobeyed, figuring the boss would be pleased when he found out how much they were going to make for him by gambling on cornering rye.

So he returned to Providence with a family fortune in shambles.

His last diary, of a sailing cruise in the West Indies—where so many of his ancestors had voyaged for trade—is extraordinarily detailed. He writes,

> returning home euphoric, then came the awful *sight* of all our mail and all Anne's book offerings all over the bedroom floor. It has been a wonderful vacation, and I am most grateful for all the privileges I have had.

FINIS.

A year later, at 79, on the first night of a Chesapeake Bay cruise on his beloved yawl, *Malagueña*, with his wife and one crew, not far from where Captain James Brown had died aboard his sloop, John Nicholas Brown was stricken fatally by a heart attack.

Although his grandfather, John Carter Brown, was born in the eighteenth century, the second JNB could have been with us today, if he had lived to ninety-six, not so impossible in this day of age inflation. How happy he would have been to be here for the celebration of the 150th anniversary of the library, the key to whose present building he had handed over to the then-president of Brown at age four and on whose Committee of Management he served virtually all his adult life.

His voyage is ended. But this Library, this great international scholarly resource, which has so well served and been served by the distinguished and creative people whom the university honors this afternoon, looks to a voyage into the future of ever increasing brightness and report.

This book was designed and
set in type by Gilbert Design Associates
in Providence, Rhode Island.

It was printed by Meridian Printing
and bound by Acme Bookbinding.

The type is Bulmer
based on William Martin's types
for the Shakespeare Press,
London, c. 1790.

1,250 copies for
The John Carter Brown Library

MMV